Frommer's®

Napa & Sonoma day BY day™

2nd Edition

by Avital Binshtock

Wiley Publishing, Inc.

WELLINGTON
SMOTHERS
Chateau St. Jean
KUNDE
LANDMARK

CALISTOGA

Contents

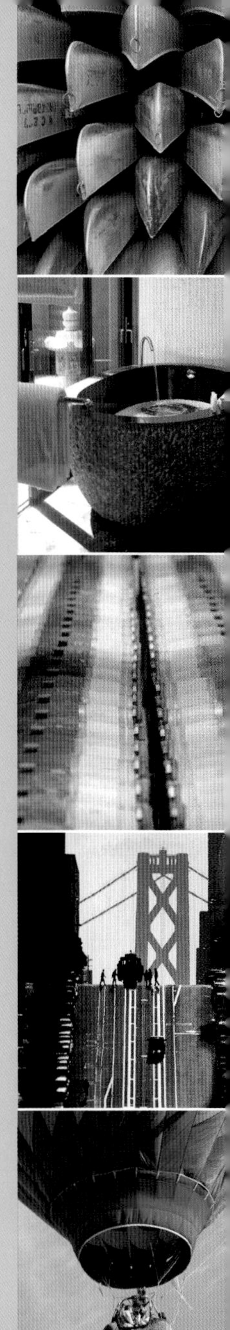

Published by:

Wiley Publishing, Inc.

111 River St.
Hoboken, NJ 07030-5774

ISBN: 978-0-470-50379-9

Editor: Stephen Bassman
Production Editor: Katie Robinson
Photo Editor: Richard Fox
Cartographer: Andrew Murphy
Production by Wiley Indianapolis Composition Services

For information on our other products and services or to obtain technical support, please contact our Customer Care Department within the U.S. at 877/762-2974, outside the U.S. at 317/572-3993 or fax 317/572-4002.

Wiley also publishes its books in a variety of electronic formats. Some content that appears in print may not be available in electronic formats.

Manufactured in China

5 4 3 2 1

A Note from the Editorial Director

Organizing your time. That's what this guide is all about.

Other guides give you long lists of things to see and do and then expect you to fit the pieces together. The Day by Day guides are different. These guides tell you the best of everything, and then they show you how to see it in the smartest, most time-efficient way. Our authors have designed detailed itineraries organized by time, neighborhood, or special interest. And each tour comes with a bulleted map that takes you from stop to stop.

Hoping to taste the latest Cabernet straight from the barrel at a family-owned boutique winery, learn about the winemaking process on a vineyard tour, or visit the *Peanuts* gang with your kids at the Charles Schulz Museum? Planning a walk through downtown Sonoma, or dinner and a bottle where you can rub shoulders with winemakers and other Napa and Sonoma locals? Whatever your interest or schedule, the Day by Days give you the smartest routes to follow. Not only do we take you to the top attractions, hotels, and restaurants, but we also help you access those special moments that locals get to experience—those "finds" that turn tourists into travelers.

The Day by Days are also your top choice if you're looking for one complete guide for all your travel needs. The best hotels and restaurants for every budget, the greatest shopping values, the wildest nightlife—it's all here.

Why should you trust our judgment? Because our authors personally visit each place they write about. They're an independent lot who say what they think and would never include places they wouldn't recommend to their best friends. They're also open to suggestions from readers. If you'd like to contact them, please send your comments our way at feedback@frommers.com, and we'll pass them on.

Enjoy your Day by Day guide—the most helpful travel companion you can buy. And have the trip of a lifetime.

Warm regards,

Kelly Regan

Kelly Regan, Editorial Director
Frommer's Travel Guides

About the Author

Avital Binshtock is *Sierra* magazine's lifestyle editor and a regular contributor to the *Los Angeles Times* Travel section, Frommers.com, and *The Huffington Post*. She lives, works, and trains for marathons in San Francisco. Read her blog and subscribe to get daily green-living tips at www.sierra club.org/greenlife. A California native to the core, Avital was educated at UCLA and Stanford University.

Acknowledgments

Special thanks to Stephen Bassman for his adroit and caring guidance in producing this edition, and to Tania Khadder, whose editorial assistance was essential. Appreciation, too, goes to Bob Sipchen, Steve Hawk, Catharine Hamm, David Lytle, and Jason Clampet for their ongoing support and partnership. This book is for my ever-supportive family, including Tim, Arie, Ruth, Eyal, Leor, and Sheindel.

An Additional Note

Please be advised that travel information is subject to change at any time—and this is especially true of prices. We therefore suggest that you write or call ahead for confirmation when making your travel plans. The authors, editors, and publisher cannot be held responsible for the experiences of readers while traveling. Your safety is important to us, however, so we encourage you to stay alert and be aware of your surroundings.

Star Ratings, Icons & Abbreviations

Every hotel, restaurant, and attraction listing in this guide has been ranked for quality, value, service, amenities, and special features using a **star-rating system.** Hotels, restaurants, attractions, shopping, and nightlife are rated on a scale of zero stars (recommended) to three stars (exceptional). In addition to the star-rating system, we also use a **kids icon** to point out the best bets for families. Within each tour, we recommend cafes, bars, or restaurants where you can take a break. Each of these stops appears in a shaded box marked with a coffee-cup-shaped bullet.

The following **abbreviations** are used for credit cards:

AE	American Express	**DISC**	Discover	**V**	Visa
DC	Diners Club	**MC**	MasterCard		

Travel Resources at Frommers.com

Frommer's travel resources don't end with this guide. Frommer's website, **www.frommers.com**, has travel information on more than 4,000 destinations. We update features regularly, giving you access to the most current trip-planning information and the best airfare, lodging, and car-rental bargains. You can also listen to podcasts, connect with other Frommers.com members through our active-reader forums, share your travel photos, read blogs from guidebook editors and fellow travelers, and much more.

A Note on Prices

In the "Take a Break" and "Best Bets" sections of this book, we have used a system of dollar signs to show a range of costs for 1 night in a hotel (the price of a double-occupancy room) or the cost of an entree at a restaurant. Use the following table to decipher the dollar signs:

Cost	Hotels	Restaurants
$	under $100	under $10
$$	$100–$200	$10–$20
$$$	$200–$300	$20–$30
$$$$	$300–$400	$30–$40
$$$$$	over $400	over $40

How to Contact Us

In researching this book, we discovered many wonderful places—hotels, restaurants, shops, and more. We're sure you'll find others. Please tell us about them, so we can share the information with your fellow travelers in upcoming editions. If you were disappointed with a recommendation, we'd love to know that, too. Please write to:

Frommer's Napa & Sonoma Day by Day, 2nd Edition
Wiley Publishing, Inc. • 111 River St. • Hoboken, NJ 07030-5774

18 Favorite **Moments**

Favorite **Moments**

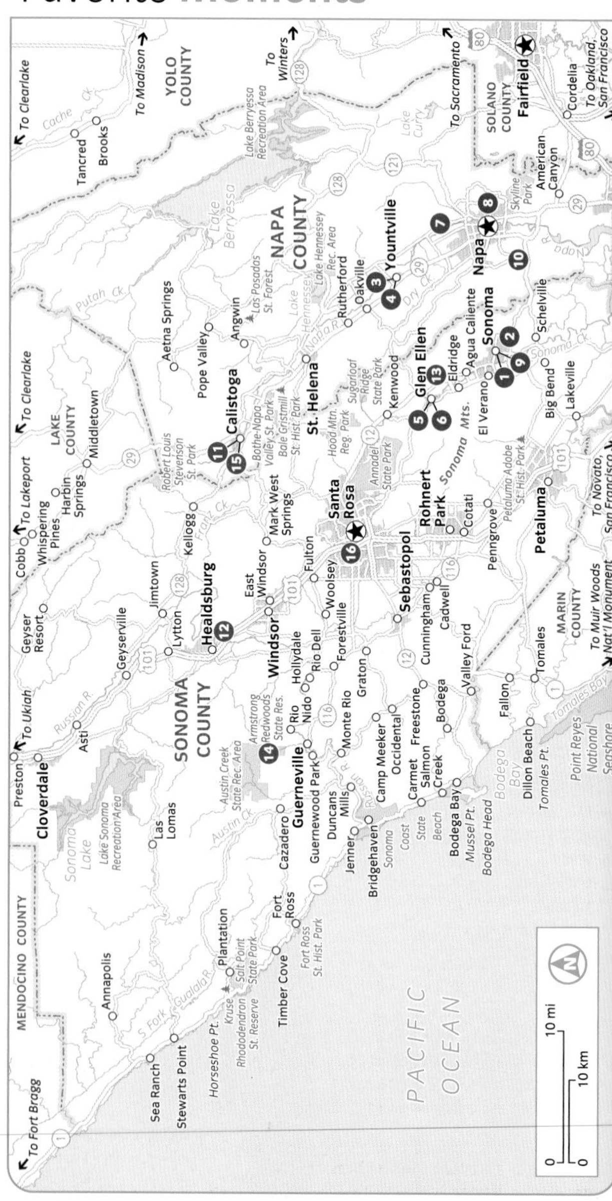

Previous page: Mustard plants act as a "cover crop" to benefit the soil.

Visiting a Farmer's Market is a fun way to embrace the local culture.

❶ **Reliving the Bear Flag Revolt and other significant parts of California history** while wandering Sonoma's historic town square. Seeing Mission San Francisco Solano, General Vallejo's home, and the Sonoma Barracks brings it all to life. *See p 49.*

❷ **Attempting a romantic tandem bike tour of Sonoma's charming wineries,** then enjoying an intimate lunch for two at Gundlach Bunschu's hillside picnic grounds. *See p 108.*

❸ **Savoring the perfectly crafted small dishes** off the tasting menu at one of Yountville's renowned restaurants, such as Thomas Keller's French Laundry (p 97), hailed by Anthony Bourdain as the best restaurant in America.

❹ **Trying to identify the 35 vintners** in the John Michael Keating painting on display at the Napa Valley Museum's permanent exhibit, *California Wine: The Science of an Art.* (Did you spot Robert Mondavi, Joseph Phelps, or Louis P. Martini?) *See p 52.*

❺ **Riding the tractor tram at Benziger Family Winery** through pastoral hills while learning about biodynamic wines and winemaking. Your tour ("the most comprehensive tour in the wine industry," according to *Wine Spectator*) winds through estate vineyards and into caves, and ends with a memorable tasting. *See p 136.*

❻ **Gasping at the beauty of spring wildflowers** bursting forth from Audubon Canyon Ranch's well-guarded Bouverie Preserve in Glen Ellen—don't be surprised if you spot a wild egret or a bobcat.

❼ **Enjoying an al fresco meal** on the grounds of a Silverado Trail winery.

❽ **Losing yourself in a foodie reverie** at the Culinary Institute of America's expansive campus store, Spice Islands Marketplace. *See p 33.*

❾ **Embracing local culture, flavor, and music** at one of wine country's many farmers' markets. You can find one nearly every day of the week; the most popular is the Sonoma Plaza Friday Farmer's Market. *See p 20.*

❿ **Getting current on modern and regional art**—while enjoying a breath of fresh air—at Napa's 217-acre (87-hectare) di Rosa Preserve,

Calistoga has its own Old Faithful.

The best way to grasp the scope of Napa and Sonoma is to float above its vineyards in awe.

local artists' works are on display throughout fauna-rich meadows. *See p 55.*

⓫ **Jumping back in (anticipated) surprise** at the eruption of Calistoga's famous Old Faithful Geyser. Sure, it happens every half-hour, but when was the last time you've seen water this hot shoot 60 feet (18m) into the air? *See p 38.*

⓬ **Kayaking or canoeing down the Russian River** on a lazy afternoon, looking for the perfect bank on which to savor your gourmet picnic. *See p 114.*

⓭ **Feeling the exhilaration as you drive** an open stretch of country highway like scenic Route 12; few windshield views surpass those that frame countless rows of grapevines fanning by.

⓮ **Relishing a contemplative moment** amidst the millennium-old trees at the Armstrong Redwoods State Reserve. *See p 111.*

⓯ **Immersing your body in mineral hot springs** or a soothing mud bath at one of Calistoga's therapeutic spas. Dr. Wilkinson's Hot Springs Resort in Calistoga is one of the best. *See p 120.*

⓰ **Chuckling at the antics of Lucy, Snoopy, and the rest of the Peanuts gang** during a stroll through Santa Rosa's whimsical Charles M. Schulz Museum, which honors the cartoonist's prolific contribution to American culture. *See p 37.*

⓱ **Floating aloft** in a spectacularly colored hot-air balloon, serenely surveying miles of vineyards. *See p 18.*

⓲ **Lingering over a bustling tasting-room counter,** quietly realizing you've just found the wine you'd like to use to toast your child's, or grandchild's, wedding. ●

The Peanuts gang makes an appearance in Santa Rosa.

1 Strategies for Seeing Napa & Sonoma

Napa & Sonoma

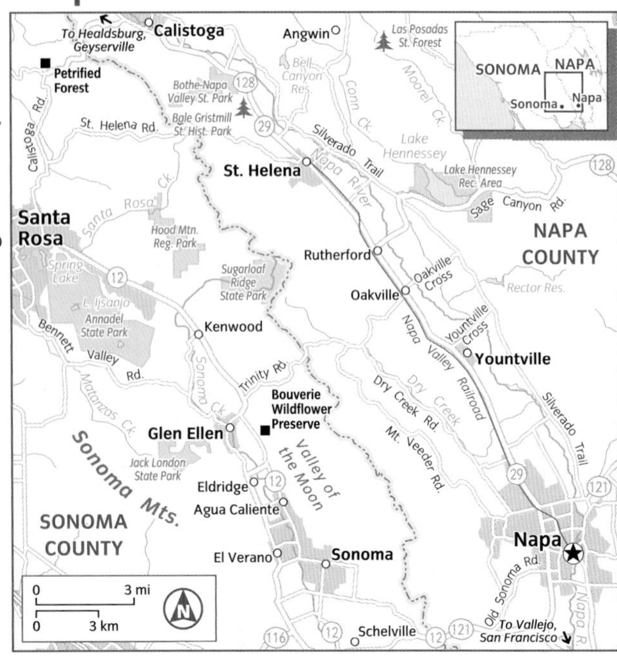

Napa and Sonoma have so much to see and do, and you won't have enough time to do it all—it's easy to get overwhelmed by all there is to experience. My advice is to have an itinerary and to decide what type of vacation you want before you arrive. Use this book to chart your course and choose the special-interest tours that appeal most to you.

Rule #1: Decide which county to focus on: Napa, Sonoma, or equal amounts of both. Once you know that, determine which parts of each valley seem to beckon (perusing this book's "Charming Towns" chapter, p 71, will help). Know that Napa Valley dwarfs Sonoma Valley in population, number of wineries, and sheer traffic. It's the more commercial region, boasting big names (Mondavi, Beringer, Krug), more spas, and a generally superior selection of restaurants and hotels. Sonoma, however, is catching up quickly, and many people prefer its brand of under-doggedness. It's lower-key, less snobby, and more backcountry—kind of like a Napa for insiders. Small, family-owned wineries are its mainstay; tastings are less expensive (sometimes free), and winemakers themselves are often in the

Previous page: A Sonoma winery directory points the way.

tasting room pouring your flight. Choose Napa if you want an active touring schedule, and Sonoma for a restful, leisurely vacation.

Rule #2: Don't drink and drive —and don't speed, either.
Those tiny tastes add up. There are plenty of taxi and limo companies that will be more than happy to chauffeur you if you have too much to drink. Otherwise, designate a driver.

Rule #3: Visit wineries early in the day, if possible.
Most tasting rooms open around 10am and, even on the busiest weekends, remain empty in the morning, leaving staff free to discuss their products. If you come after noon, the tasting room may be packed (especially if it's high season), and many will be waiting in line just to get a sample, much less the employees' prolonged attention.

Rule #4: To avoid the masses altogether, visit during off-season (Nov–May) or midweek.
The region's optimum time, "crush" (the late Aug through mid-Oct grape harvest), coincides with peak tourist season. However, if you can only get here on a high-season weekend, there are still ways to avoid the cattle drive: Opt for smaller, family-run wineries over the big boys. Even those along the Silverado Trail, which parallels Highway 29, receive significantly less traffic; locals use it as their main thoroughfare during high season. Another option is to stay in Sonoma. Though it, too, suffers from congestion, Sonoma gets less packed than Napa.

Note that most wineries are closed on major holidays, and many have restricted off-season hours, so call ahead if there's one you don't want to miss.

Rule #5: Be conscious of tasting fees.
Visitors didn't used to have to pay for sampling, but when Napa became a booming destination, wineries began collecting. To their credit, it wasn't so much to make a profit as to discourage visitors who, shall we say, preferred quantity over quality. Nowadays, the Napa norm is to charge about $2 to $8 per flight (though it's much higher at certain places), which is often refundable toward a purchase and sometimes includes a souvenir glass. Sonoma's wineries are less likely to charge for tasting.

Rule #6: Buying wine at the winery doesn't mean you're saving money.
In fact, you'll probably end up spending more at a winery than you would at stores that buy cases in bulk. Exceptions to this strategy are wineries that offer big discounts on cases and those that only sell their wines in the tasting room (that is, they have no distribution). Tip: If you're able to ship your wine directly from the winery, you'll avoid having to pay sales tax.

A field of mustard seeds in Napa Valley.

Remember: A visit to Wine country means you can (and should) drink champagne before noon. This is wine country—kick back and relax.

Rule #7: Don't let your wine cook in the back of your car, or you'll be unpleasantly surprised at its new flavor.

Buy a cooler and a couple of ice packs, place them in your car's trunk, and Voilà!—you own a portable wine cellar.

Wine shipping is an alternative to lugging around all that vino you bought, but it can be confusing, since it's limited by regulations that vary by state. Complicating the matter, shipping rules also differ from winery to winery. It's a good idea to check the current legal situation as it pertains to your home state before buying. Ask wineries and, if necessary, independent shipping companies about their wine-transporting policies.

Rule #8: Keep a light attitude.

If you don't yet know everything about wine and it seems that everyone around you does (to an almost silly degree), don't fall prey to the sometimes-snobby attitude of those who deem themselves worthier than thou simply because they're better versed in what's essentially only a beverage. Wine country is about relaxing, having fun, learning, and taking in the spectacular scenery—not feeling intimidated. If you encounter a superior attitude pouring your taste, move on.

Rule #9: Make time to veer away from the wineries to explore the region's natural splendor.

You can hike through a redwood forest, kayak the Russian River, stroll along the rocky Pacific coastline in Bodega Bay, and so much more. See "18 Favorite Moments" (p 1) and chapter 5, "The Great Outdoors," for ideas.

Rule #10: Get to know the wine and the winery. Talk. Listen. Learn.

When at a winery, take the time to really get to know not only the wines but also the company's story: its history, its vineyards, and its employees. Most staffers are quite willing to regale you with tales; if you want more, take a tour. You can drink California wine just about anywhere, but only by visiting a tasting room or touring a winery can you gain true appreciation for the painstaking and artistic processes that go into each bottle. ●

All roads lead to another fantastic winery.

2 The Best Full-Day Tours of Napa & Sonoma

The Best of Napa in One Day

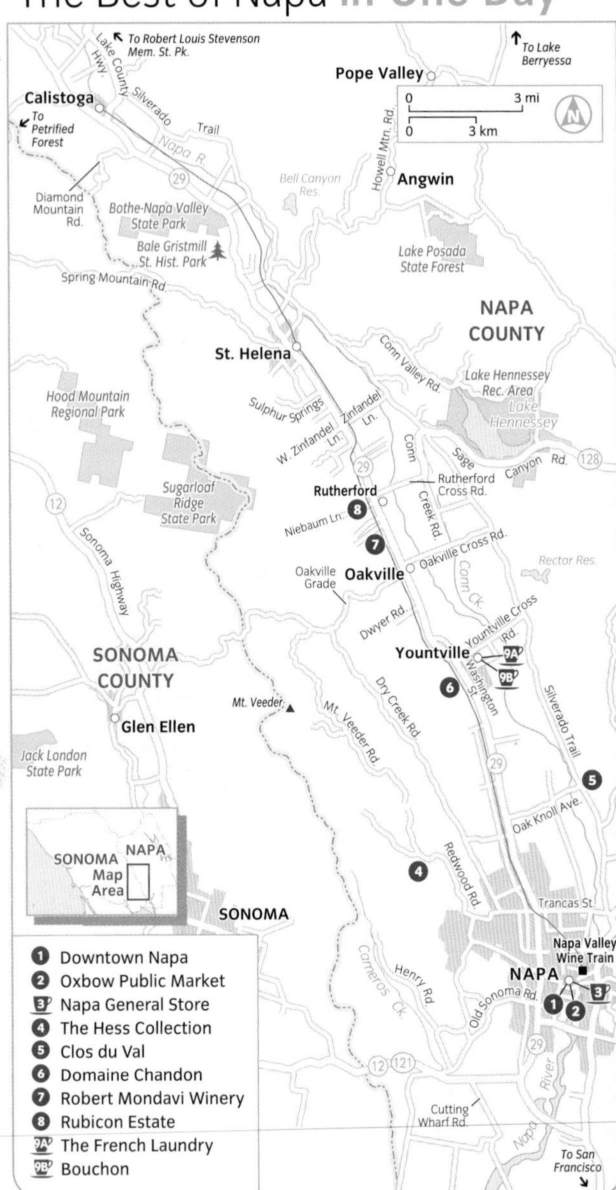
To Robert Louis Stevenson Mem. St. Pk.
To Lake Berryessa
Pope Valley
Lake County Hwy.
Silverado Trail
Calistoga
To Petrified Forest
Napa R.
Diamond Mountain Rd.
Bothe-Napa Valley State Park
Bale Gristmill St. Hist. Park
Spring Mountain Rd.
Bell Canyon Res.
Howell Mtn. Rd.
Angwin
Lake Posada State Forest
NAPA COUNTY
St. Helena
Conn Valley Rd.
Lake Hennessey Rec. Area
Lake Hennessey
Hood Mountain Regional Park
Sulphur Springs
W. Zinfandel Ln.
Zinfandel Ln.
Conn Creek Rd.
Sage Canyon Rd.
Rutherford Cross Rd.
Rutherford
Niebaum Ln.
Sugarloaf Ridge State Park
Sonoma Highway
Oakville Cross Rd.
Rector Res.
Oakville Grade
Oakville
Conn Ck.
Dwyer Rd.
Yountville Cross Rd.
Yountville
Washington St.
SONOMA COUNTY
Mt. Veeder
Mt. Veeder Rd.
Dry Creek Rd.
Silverado Trail
Glen Ellen
Jack London State Park
Oak Knoll Ave.
Redwood Rd.
SONOMA NAPA Map Area
SONOMA
Trancas St.
Napa Valley Wine Train
NAPA
Carneros Ck.
Henry Rd.
Old Sonoma Rd.
River
Napa
Cutting Wharf Rd.
To San Francisco
0 3 mi
0 3 km
1 Downtown Napa
2 Oxbow Public Market
3 Napa General Store
4 The Hess Collection
5 Clos du Val
6 Domaine Chandon
7 Robert Mondavi Winery
8 Rubicon Estate
9A The French Laundry
9B Bouchon

Previous page: Vineyard rows in Napa.

All you have is a day to make the most of Napa? That's a tall order because the valley is so rich with delightful towns, wineries, sights, and activities, but it can be done—and done well. This full-day itinerary, manageable in a day by car, introduces you to the region's fundamental character. At the end of the day, rest assured that you've truly experienced the essence of Napa. But remember, drinking-and-driving rules still apply, so designate a driver, don't swallow the wine, or limit your intake and eat heartily.

START: **1st & Main sts. Tour distance: About 36 miles (68km).**

You are officially here!

❶ ★★ **Downtown Napa.** Not long ago, the actual town of Napa would never have been listed in a "best of Napa Valley" tour—but times have changed and the town's recent redevelopment merits it a spot right at the top. Hit Napa Town Center to get a feel for everyday life here, as well as the striking Italianate-style Opera House. Pick up a picnic lunch at one of the town's upscale markets. *Napa Valley Conference & Visitors Bureau, 1310 Napa Town Center, Napa. ☎ 707/226-7459. www.napavalley.org. Mon–Sat 9am–5pm; Sun 11am–5pm.*

❷ ★ **Oxbow Public Market.** A foodie's dream destination that lets you discover the best of the region all under one roof. As you walk through the marketplace, you'll pass vendors selling artisanal cheeses, exotic spices, bottles from microwineries, and a plethora of other gourmet goodies. Free parking is available. *600 First St, Napa, CA. ☎ 707/963-1345. www.oxbowpublicmarket.com. Open Mon–Sat, 10am–6pm, Sun, 10am–5pm (closed Thanksgiving, Christmas, and New Years Day).*

❸ ★ **Napa General Store.** End your downtown Napa visit at the Historic Napa Mill to pick up a box lunch ($15); choose from a variety of fresh sandwiches and salads that come with a house-baked cookie and utensils. ***Note:*** Box lunches must be ordered a day in advance. If you didn't pre-order, get something to go from the market's cafe (sandwiches, salads, pan-Asian specialties, and hand-tossed pizzas) or sit down and eat here—a cozy option if the weather's unsavory. *540 Main St., Napa. ☎ 707/259-0762. $$.*

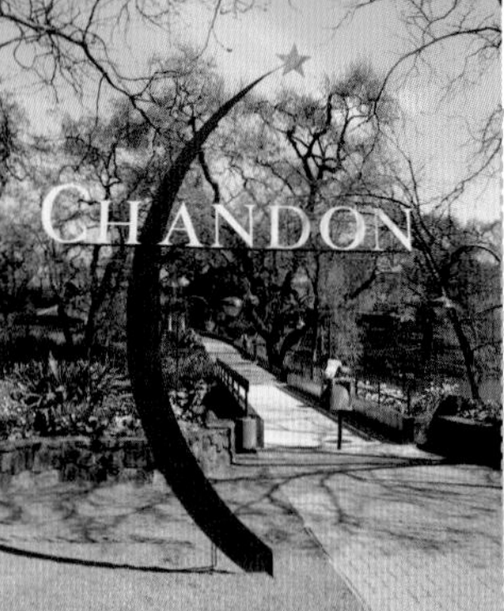

Stop off for a refreshing glass of sparkling wine at Domaine Chandon.

Take Hwy. 29 north and exit at Trancas St. Turn left on Redwood Rd., a four-lane road that narrows into a two-lane road. Turn left at the Hess Collection's sign.

4 ★★★ The Hess Collection. The beautiful drive up provides a good example of the pristine scenery that characterizes much of Northern California. The winery itself includes art galleries, a garden that fully blooms in summer, and an impressive stone-walled tasting room in the original 1903 winery that features a maple bar, barrel-lined walls, and the true highlight: a full selection of Hess's current releases, including superb cabernet sauvignon and chardonnay. *4411 Redwood Rd., Napa. ☎ 877/707-4377.* *See p 149.*

Wind back down Redwood Rd. and stay straight onto Trancas St., then turn left on Silverado Trail.

5 ★ Clos du Val. You can't say you've done Napa's best without having seen at least one small, exclusive winery in the Stags Leap District along the scenic Silverado Trail. Marked with both French and American flags to affirm that this estate is French-owned, Clos du Val's tasting room is behind ivy-covered walls. In it, try Ariadne, the winery's proprietary blend of sauvignon blanc and Sémillon. Ask tasting room staff for a tour of the demonstration vineyard, where you can learn about trellising techniques and how to identify different kinds of grapes. After trying the wines, settle into Clos du Val's beautiful olive grove and break out the food you bought earlier for a picnic lunch. *5330 Silverado Trail, Napa. ☎ 707/259-2200.* *See p 141.*

Head southeast on Silverado Trail and turn right at Oak Knoll Ave., then left on Big Ranch Rd. Turn right to get back onto Oak Knoll Ave., and right again to get on Hwy. 29 N. Exit toward Yountville and turn left on California Dr. and head up the long, vineyard-flanked driveway.

6 ★ Domaine Chandon. Cross a small footbridge over a life-filled pond (keep an eye out for egrets) and past some interestingly placed sculptures (including a faux mushroom field) to enter the educational visitor center, complete with a 28-seat large-screen theater, a wall made entirely of bottles, and interactive exhibits. Domaine Chandon specializes in "sparkling wine"—technically, it can't be called champagne because it's not produced in that proprietary French province. But since this winery is owned by the venerable French company Moët et Chandon, what you get is pretty similar. The knowledgeable staff explains the nuances of effervescent wine. *1 California Dr. (at Hwy. 29), Yountville. ☎ 707/944-2280.* *See p 144.*

Take California Dr. northeast to merge onto Hwy. 29.

7 ★★ Robert Mondavi Winery. This mission-style winery gives the valley's most varied and comprehensive tours. Given today's time constraint, however, opt for the basic tour or simply visit the art gallery before or after tasting in the Appellation Room, an outdoor tasting area that's open in summer. If it's winter, taste in the upscale ToKalon Room. *7801 St. Helena Hwy. (Hwy. 29), Oakville.* ☎ *707/226-1395. See p 155.*

Keep following Hwy. 29 northwest.

8 ★★★ **Rubicon Estate.** Sometimes better known by its former name Niebaum-Coppola (and even its historic name before that, Inglenook Vineyards), Rubicon is film director Francis Ford Coppola's ivy-draped 1880s stone winery that exudes momentous grandeur. Inside, it's an impressive retail center promoting Coppola's products and, more subtly, his movies. The Centennial Museum chronicles the winemaking estate's rich history, as well as Coppola's filmmaking—on display are Academy Awards and memorabilia from *The Godfather* and *Bram Stoker's Dracula.* Sample estate-grown blends, cabernet franc, and merlot—all made from organic grapes, but note the caveat: a $25 admission fee. For the price, you'll get a tour and a five-wine tasting flight. *1991 St. Helena Hwy., Rutherford.* ☎ *707/968-1100. See p 156.*

In 2006, Francis Ford Coppola changed the name of his winery from Niebaum Coppola to Rubicon Estate.

9A ★★★ **The French Laundry.** If you want the *best* of Napa dining, there's only one place to go: a very, very famous little restaurant called The French Laundry. Chef Thomas Keller's intricate preparations, often finished tableside, are presented with uncommon artistry. But when the check arrives, close your eyes and reassure yourself that this was a once-in-a-lifetime experience. Reservations are required and should be made at least 2 months in advance. *6640 Washington St., Yountville.* ☎ *707/944-2380. See p 97.*

If you've still got next month's rent to pay, dine at humbler **9B** ★★ **Bouchon.** You'll still be eating Keller's inspired creations, but in toned-down bistro environs that are far more friendly than frou-frou. *6534 Washington St.* ☎ *707/944-8037. $$$. See p 96.*

The late Robert Mondavi in the barrel room.

The Best of Sonoma in One Day

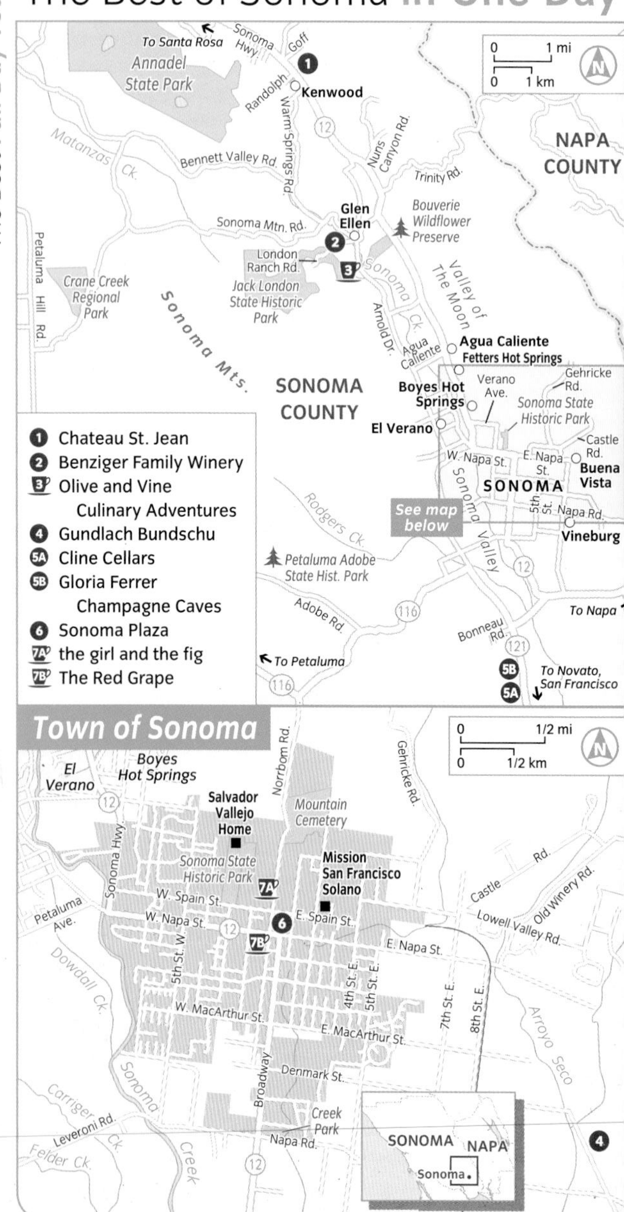

Sonoma Valley is a bit like a younger sibling to Napa Valley; it's made up of the same kind of magic, but one gets the sense that it tries hard to match Napa's renown. The struggle to measure up has certainly paid off, to the degree that many visitors profess that Sonoma has actually surpassed Napa in charm—and wine. This 1-day overview gives you a sense of the wineries, allows you to experience the small-town feel, and takes you along breathtakingly bucolic stretches of highway. START: **Chateau St. Jean, 8555 Sonoma Hwy. (Hwy. 12), Kenwood. Trip Length: 26 miles (42km).**

1 ★★ **Chateau St. Jean.** Notable for its grand buildings and expansive grounds, Chateau St. Jean is, in California, a pioneer in vineyard designation—the procedure of making wine from, and naming it for, a single vineyard. A private drive takes you to a well-manicured picnic lawn overlooking meticulously maintained vineyards. In the large tasting room, where there are plenty of housewares for sale, sample Chateau St. Jean's wide array of wines, including chardonnay, cabernet sauvignon, Johannesburg Riesling, and gewürztraminer. "Sideways" notwithstanding, merlot is the winery's bestseller. *8555 Sonoma Hwy. (Hwy. 12), Kenwood.* ☎ *707/833-4134. See p 140.*

Continue southeast on Hwy. 12, turn right onto Arnold Dr., then make a slight right onto London Ranch Rd.

2 ★★ kids **Benziger Family Winery.** This is a true family winery. At any given time, two generations of Benzigers may be present, and they make you feel like part of the clan. The pastoral property presents an excellent 45-minute tractor-tram tour ($15), which winds through the estate vineyards while providing a thorough explanation of why it's a certified biodynamic winery, and what that means. The tram stops often so that visitors can see exhibits and walk into aromatic aging caves, and the tour ends with an informative tasting. ***Tip:*** Tram tickets—a hot item in summer—are available on a first-come, first-served basis, so if the next tram ride is full, taste wines in the tasting

Striking structures define Chateau St. Jean.

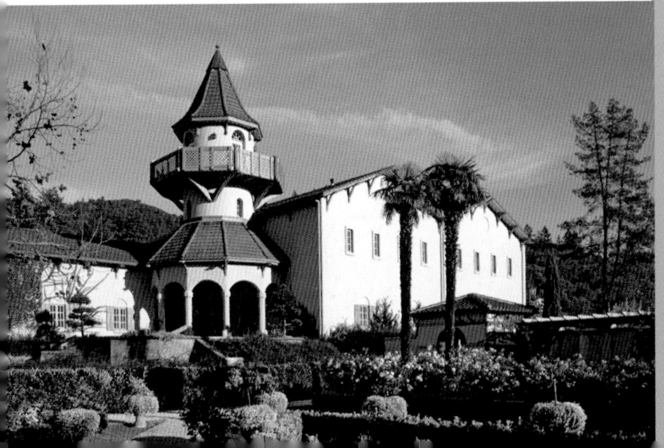

room first and take the tour after. *1883 London Ranch Rd., Glen Ellen.* ☎ *888/490-2739.* *See p 136.*

From Benziger, take London Ranch Rd. northeast (toward Chauvet Rd.), then turn right onto Arnold Dr., where you'll find the quaint Jack London Village complex, and in it:

3 ★ Olive and Vine Culinary Adventures. Grab a tasty box lunch at this Glen Ellen cafe and catering company whose food emphasizes fresh, local ingredients. Focaccia or ciabatta sandwiches come with salad, fruit, and a homemade cookie. Carry out your meal and save it for the outdoor picnic grounds at the next stop. ☎ *707/996-9150. $$. In case the weather's inclement, the cafe has a few indoor tables.*

From Jack London Village, take Arnold Dr. south (toward Holt), then turn left onto Leveroni Rd. Two miles (3.2km) after Leveroni becomes Napa Rd., make a left onto Denmark St. You'll almost immediately see:

4 ★★ Gundlach Bundschu. If it looks like the people working here are enjoying themselves, that's because they are. Gundlach Bundschu is the quintessential Sonoma winery—nonchalant in appearance but obsessed with wine. Members of this winemaking family are known for their mischievousness: They've pulled stunts like holding up Napa's Wine Train (p 67) on horseback and serving Sonoma wines to their "captives." The small, often crowded tasting room plays rock music as carefree—but attentive—staffers happily pour chardonnay, pinot noir, merlot, cabernet, and others. Now in its sixth generation, this is California's oldest continually family-owned and -operated winery. Unfold your lunch feast here; GB's picnic area is perched on the side of a small hill, giving it a sensational view of the Sonoma countryside. Work up an appetite by taking a short hike to the top of the knoll. *2000 Denmark St., Sonoma.* ☎ *707/938-5277.* *See p 148.*

Choose between visiting Gloria Ferrer or Cline, which are almost adjacent. Travel less than 2 miles (3.2km) north on Hwy. 121 and pull into either:

5A ★ kids Cline Cellars. If you're more interested in California history and tasting an array of unique wines, opt for this family-owned winery with a small, friendly tasting room and an intimate museum that showcases dollhouse-sized dioramas of all 21 California missions. *24737 Carneros Hwy. (Calif. 121), Sonoma.* ☎ *707/940-4000.* *See p 140.*

OR:

5B Gloria Ferrer Champagne Caves. If you've had it up to here with chardonnays and pinots—or are simply a big fan of champagne—choose Gloria Ferrer, which specializes in sparkling wine (pictured). It's a bit overrated as a tourist attraction—to see the eponymous caves, you merely stand at a railing and flip on a light switch, then wonder to yourself, "That's *it*?" But the bubbly's good, so come expecting just that, and you won't be disappointed. Also note that the tasting room only offers wine by the glass (not flights), so it's not the best choice if you want to try a variety. *23555 Carneros Hwy. (Calif. 121), Sonoma.* ☎ *707/996-7256. www.gloriaferrer.com. Daily 10am–5pm. Guided underground cave tours (free) daily noon, 2 & 4pm. Tastings $2–$10. Map p 147.*

A winemaker tops off barrels in Sonoma Valley.

Continue northwest on Hwy. 121/ Carneros Hwy./Arnold Dr., then turn right onto W. Watmaugh Rd. After about a mile (1.6km), turn left onto Broadway and stay on it until it ends on Napa St. Turn left or right and look for parking:

6 ★★★ kids Sonoma Plaza. The 8-acre (3.25 hectare) site of the 1846 Bear Flag Revolt is the pulse point of the entire county, and it hums with history and local culture. Despite the tense confrontation it commemorates, the plaza (California's oldest) couldn't be more relaxing; its parklike atmosphere promotes cheeriness, while well-preserved historic monuments—like the fascinating Mission San Francisco de Solano, City Hall, General Vallejo's home, and old army barracks—add mystique. You'll be hard-pressed not to leave the plaza lugging shopping bags, since the boutiques, bakeries, tasting rooms, and galleries are nearly irresistible. If your evening stroll is on a Tuesday in spring or summer, you'll catch the wonderful farmers' market and its accompanying music shows. (For more on farmers' markets, see p 20.) *Sonoma Valley Visitors Bureau, 453 1st St. E.* ☎ *707/996-1090. www.sonomavalley.com. Daily 9am–6pm in winter; until 7pm in summer. For more about Sonoma.*

7A ★★ the girl and the fig. For dinner, go with this local favorite right on the plaza. From its refusal to use uppercase letters to its insistence on using figs in many of its recipes, this warmly decorated eatery serving inventive nouveau French cuisine makes sure to defy convention, which works greatly to its benefit. Sit outside if the weather's pleasant, and save room for dessert. *110 W. Spain St. (in the Sonoma Hotel), Sonoma.* ☎ *707/938-3634. www.thegirlandthefig.com. $$. See p 81.*

If you're in the mood for great pizza, try **7B ★ kids The Red Grape,** a casual, artsy space a half-block from the plaza. Its unconventional selection of crispy thin-crust pies made with fresh local ingredients in woodstone ovens gratifies even the snobbiest of pizza connoisseurs. *529 1st St. W., Sonoma.* ☎ *707/996-4103. www.theredgrape.com. $$.*

The Best of Napa & Sonoma in Three Days—Day 3

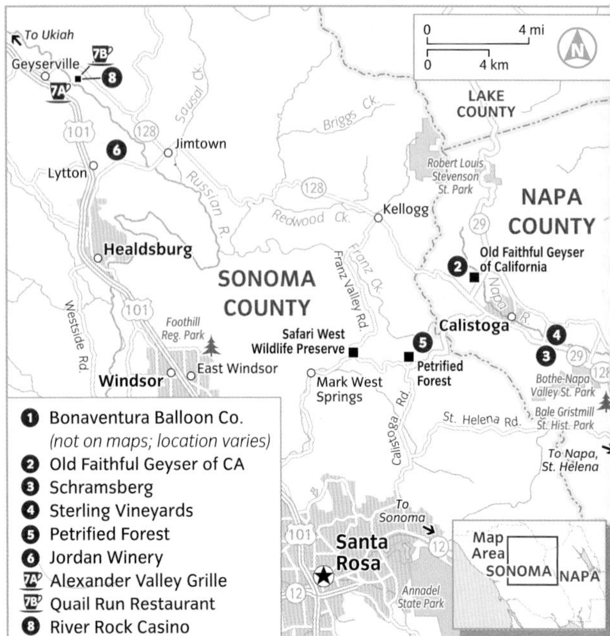

Follow the previous two itineraries for your first couple of days. On the third day, this full-day up-valley Napa and Sonoma tour shows you the natural lay of the land from above (think balloons and aerial trams), below (from whence the geyser spews), and through. ***Tip:*** Plan ahead—advance reservations are required for ballooning and Jordan Winery. Ballooning requires rising around 5 or 6am. START: **Your hotel. Distance: 50 miles (81km); not including transport to, from, and during the hot-air balloon ride, or the drive from your hotel to Old Faithful).**

1 ★★★ **kids Bonaventura Balloon Co.** If you've been in wine country this long, you've undoubtedly seen the colorful hot-air balloons floating above the vineyards. Sure, it means getting up at an ungodly hour—but once aloft, you'll know what true sanctity means. Bonaventura's (the name means "good adventure") expert pilot maneuvers the balloon into the clouds, creating a sublime experience. A full champagne breakfast is served upon landing. Reservations are required and should be made as far in advance as possible. ☎ *800/ FLY-NAPA. www.bonaventura balloons.com. About $225 per*

The vineyards of Schramsberg are high up on the west side of Napa Valley.

person, including transportation. See p 65. Another good company providing rides is ★★★ kids **Adventures Aloft**. ☎ *707/944-4408. www.nvaloft.com. $225 per person, including transportation to/from your hotel to the launch site. See p 64.*

Ballooning Tip

When the valley's foggy, companies drive passengers outside the valley to launch. Though they can't guarantee the flight path until hours before liftoff, they should refund your money if you decide not to partake.

Bonaventura will deliver you back to your hotel. From there, drive to

2 ★ kids **Old Faithful Geyser of California.** At this natural wonder (it's one of only three "old faithful" geysers in the world) surrounded by pleasant kitsch, you can dependably see 60-foot-high (18m) eruptions every 40 minutes. If you want, buy treats at the snack bar to munch on between spews. Or linger at the gift shop, where you can watch a video about California, get a penny stamped to remind you of your visit, or buy California-themed mugs, key chains, and wine glasses. *1299 Tubbs Lane, Calistoga.* ☎ *707/942-6463. See p 38.*

Take Tubbs Lane southwest and turn left on Foothill Blvd./Hwy. 128. Turn right on Peterson Dr., then right on Schramsberg Rd.

3 ★★ **Schramsberg.** This 200-acre (80-hectare) estate has a wonderful old-world feel—in his heyday, Robert Louis Stevenson was a regular. Schramsberg is the label presidents serve when toasting dignitaries from around the globe, and there's plenty of historic memorabilia in the front room to prove it. But the real mystique begins when you enter the 2½-mile (4km) aging caves (reputedly North America's longest), hand-carved by Chinese laborers in the 1800s. The free, comprehensive tour ends in a charming tasting room where you sit around a big table and sample varied selections of bubbly. *1400 Schramsberg Rd., Calistoga.* ☎ *707/942-2414. See p 157.*

Head northeast on Schramsberg Rd. to turn left on Peterson Dr. Turn left on Hwy. 29/128, then right on Dunaweal Lane.

4 ★★ kids **Sterling Vineyards.** An aerial tram brings you to this dazzlingly white Mediterranean-style winery, perched atop a 300-foot-high (90m) rocky hill. On the way up, marvel at breathtaking views spanning Napa Valley's vineyards. When you land, follow the multimedia self-guided tour (one of wine country's most thorough) detailing the wine-making process. This winery

Local Farmers' Markets

Wine country is alive and colorful with free farmers' markets from Tuesday through Saturday. Here's when to go where:

TUESDAY: The **Napa Downtown Farmers' Market** happens from 7:30am to noon in the Napa Valley Wine Train's parking lot. In addition to fresh, locally grown fruits and vegetables, baked goods, and coffee, there's live entertainment and representatives from nonprofit groups. *1275 McKinstry Street. May–Oct.* The **Sonoma Valley Farmers' Market** happens from 5:30pm to dusk; there's produce, food samples, flowers, crafts, nonprofit booths, and live music. *Depot Park.* ☎ *707/538-7023. Apr–Oct.*

WEDNESDAY: The energy-filled **Guerneville Farmers' Market** takes place on the town square from 4 to 7pm. ☎ *707/865-4171. May–Oct.* **Yountville's Farmers' Market** brings purveyors of organic produce, entertainment, wine tastings, and chef demonstrations from 4:30pm to dusk. *Vintage 1870 parking lot, Washington St.* ☎ *707/257-8481. June–Sept.* **Santa Rosa** holds two Wednesday farmers' markets: one operates year-round in the Veterans Building's east parking lot (at Maple St. and Hwy. 12) from 8:30am to noon (☎ 707/522-8629), and another downtown (May–Aug 5:30–8pm; 4th St. between B and D; ☎ 707/524-2123).

THURSDAY: **Santa Rosa's Downtown Market** happens again from 5 to 8:30pm. *May–Sept. See above for details.* At **Napa's Chef's Market,** farmers join musicians, artists, winemakers, brewers, and chefs to create a festive Thursday-night event from 5 to 9pm. *1290 Napa Town Center (at 1st St.).* ☎ *707/257-0322. May–July.*

FRIDAY: **St. Helena's Farmers' Market** at Crane Park (on Crane St., off Hwy. 29) showcases fresh produce, flowers, baked goods, live entertainment, and arts and crafts from 7:30am to noon. ☎ *707/486-2662. May–Oct.* At **Sonoma Valley Friday Farmers' Market** you might see some of the valley's most prominent chefs eyeing the goods. It's open 9am to noon. *Depot Park (at 1st St. W.).* ☎ *707/538-7023.*

SATURDAY: **Calistoga Farmers' Market** happens at Old Gliderport from 8:30am to noon. *1546 Lincoln Ave.* ☎ *707/942-0808.* Santa Rosa holds another market in the Veterans Building's east parking lot. *See above for details.* In Healdsburg from 9am to noon, the town's excellent, sometimes crowded, farmers' market happens a block west of the Plaza (at North and Vine sts.). ☎ *707/431-1956. May–Nov.* The same Napa Downtown Farmers' Market also happens on Saturday from 8am to noon. *See above for details.*

produces more than 500,000 cases per year (read: huge producer) and admission includes a sit-down tasting. *1111 Dunaweal Lane, Calistoga.* ☎ *707/942-3300. See p 158.*

Go south on Dunaweal Lane to turn right on Hwy. 29/128. Turn left on Petrified Forest Rd.

5 ★★ kids **Petrified Forest.** Volcanic ash blanketed this area after Mount St. Helena erupted more than 3 million years ago. As a result, the redwoods in this mile-long (1.6km) forest have turned to rock through the slow infiltration of silica and other minerals. If you look closely, you'll also see petrified seashells, clams, and other marine life, indicating that water covered this area before the redwood forest grew. Take the quarter-mile (.4km) walking trail to see a collection of petrified logs, the Pit Tree (a preserved pine in a 15-ft./4.5m-deep pit), a statue of Petrified Charlie (Charles Evans, this land's first owner), and other trees-turned-to-stone with names like The Giant (a redwood) and The Queen, which has an oak growing out of it. *4100 Petrified Forest Rd.* ☎ *707/942-6667. See p 37.*

Take Petrified Forest Rd. west and turn right on Porter Creek Rd./Mark West Springs Rd. Merge onto Hwy. 101 N, exit on Lytton Springs Rd. and turn right, then left on Lytton Station Rd., then left on Alexander Valley Rd.

6 ★★ **Jordan Winery.** With ivy-covered buildings reminiscent of an18th-century French château and hilltop views of Alexander Valley, Geyser Peak, and Mount St. Helena, Jordan Winery is a must-see in the Healdsburg area. Formal French gardens and a variety of trees (picnic tables are set under a massive, stately oak) add to the experience. Tours of the winemaking facilities happen every day except Sunday and conclude with tastes of cab and chardonnay. Reservations required. *1474 Alexander Valley Rd., Healdsburg.* ☎ *800/654-1213. See p 150.*

7A ★★ **Alexander Valley Grille/ Moving On Café.** Have dinner at Francis Coppola's winery's restaurant, formerly Chateau Souverain's Alexander Valley Grille. The menu lists pizzas, salads, seasonal soups, small platters, and a gourmet buffet. *400 Souverain Rd., Geyserville.* ☎ *707/433-3141. $$.* For a more casual meal, dine at **7B** **Quail Run Restaurant at the River Rock Casino.** It has a full 24-hour-a-day menu, plus a pretty typical casino buffet during more limited hours. *3250 Hwy. 128, Geyserville.* ☎ *707/857-2777. $$.*

Head east on Alexander Valley Rd. and turn left on Hwy. 128.

8 ★ **River Rock Casino.** Open 24 hours a day, 365 days a year, this bungalow-style casino owned by the Dry Creek Band of Pomo Indians has more than 1,600 slot machines, a variety of card tables, and frequent live entertainment. Try your luck, but if it runs out, gain perspective on the outside deck overlooking the magnificent hills surrounding Alexander Valley. *3250 Hwy. 128, Geyserville.* ☎ *707/857-2777.*

A vine grows on a wall at Jordan Winery.

The Best of Napa & Sonoma in Five Days—Days 4 & 5

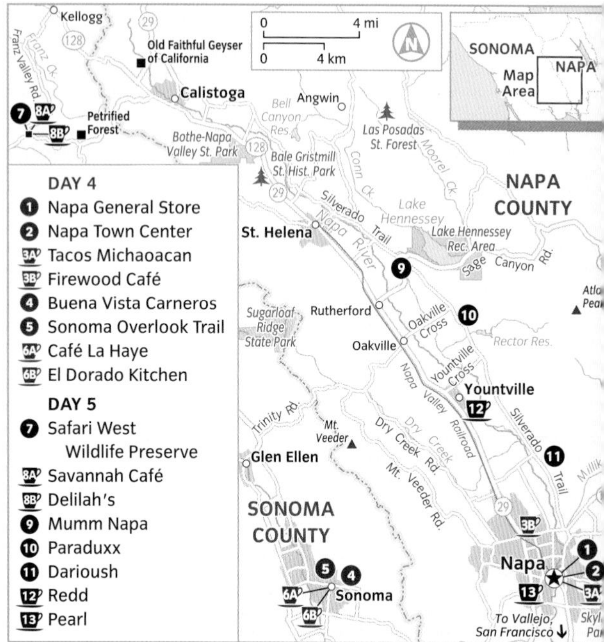

After conducting your first 3 days as outlined on the preceding pages, Days 4 and 5 will serve to solidify your sense of the region, as well as expose you to both valleys' more distinctive attractions. It's helpful if you spend the night of Day 4 in Sonoma; consider even staying overnight at Safari West, the starting point of Day 5. (See p 127 for lodging details.) **DAY 4 START: Napa Town Center, 1st & Main St., Napa. Distance: About 50 miles (80km). DAY 5 START: Safari West Wildlife Preserve, 3115 Porter Creek Rd., Santa Rosa. Distance: About 32 miles (52 km).**

DAY 4

1 ★★★ Napa General Store. Start your day with a satisfying breakfast at the Historic Napa Mill. Try the store's homemade granola or chocolate beignets. Eat outside to enjoy views of the Napa River, or inside to cozy up near the fireplace. While you're there, shop for handcrafted oils, soaps and decanters, all made by local artisans. *$$ 540 Main St., Napa. ☎ 707/259-0762. $$.*

2 ★ Napa Town Center. Head to this retail complex to grab a caramel apple at Rocky Mountain Chocolate Factory or gelato at

Christopher's Fine Foods, and stroll past shops including the 50,000-sq.-ft./4,645-sq.-m McCaulou's Department Store, known for its selection of affordable clothes for the whole family. All the retailers are housed in historic buildings and connected by a pedestrian street. Look for the two huge oak trees that serve as town landmarks. Here you'll also find the overachieving **Napa Valley Conference and Visitors Bureau** (☎ 707/226-7459; www.napavalley.org; Mon–Sat 9am–5pm, Sun 11am–5pm). Stop in for local information, money-saving coupons, and pamphlets outlining self-guided walking tours of the town's historic buildings. *1290 Napa Town Center.* ☎ *707/255-9375. 1310 Napa Town Center.*

3A **Tacos Michoacan.** Grab a bite at what used to be a well-known Napa taco truck but has graduated into a sit-down restaurant. *721 Lincoln Ave.* ☎ *707/256-0820. $$.* Feel like pizza instead? Try the casual, family-friendly 2I **Firewood Café** *3824 Bel Aire Plaza.* ☎ *707/224-9660 or www.firewoodcafe.com. $$.*

Your scenic 25-minute drive from Napa Valley to Sonoma Valley starts westward on 1st St., then merges onto Hwy. 29 S. Turn right onto Hwy. 12/121, then make a slight right onto Napa Rd. Turn right on 8th St. E., then right again on E. Napa St., then make a quick left on Old Winery Rd.

4 ★★★ **Buena Vista Carneros.** America's oldest continuously operating winery was founded in 1857 and is worth a visit for its historical relevance. A restored stone press houses the tasting room; in it, try what the estate calls the "Carneros Quartet": its pinot noir, chardonnay, merlot, and cabernet sauvignon—all crafted by artisan methods. *18000 Old Winery Rd., Sonoma.* ☎ *800/926-8504.* *See p 137.*

Start your day al fresco at the Napa General Store.

Take Old Winery Rd. southwest, then turn right on E. Napa St. Turn right on 1st St. E. Just beyond the Veterans Memorial Building is a small lot adjacent to the Mountain Cemetery entrance. Park, then look for the trailhead sign.

5 ★ **Sonoma Overlook Trail.** Take in sweeping afternoon views from this well-maintained trail, an easy 2-mile-plus (3.2km) loop accented by interpretive signage, seasonal wildflowers, and manzanita trees. Not long ago, this hillside was doomed to be developed as a resort, but locals worked with The Sonoma Ecology Center to preserve the scenic area. See if you can see San Pablo Bay and San Francisco's skyline; both should be visible on a clear day. Heartier tourists seeking a workout can experience this as a jog instead of a hike. If you're walking, though, allow about 2 hours. ☎ *707/996-0712. www.sonomaecologycenter.org.*

Contemplate the black and white stripes of a zebra at Safari West Wildlife Preserve.

6A ★★ **Café La Haye.** You'll have worked up an appetite, so dine at this petite restaurant offering seasonal cuisine. *140 E. Napa St., Sonoma.* ☎ *707/935-5994. $$.* 6B ★★ **El Dorado Kitchen,** a Mediterranean-inspired bistro, is a bit more upscale. *405 1st St. W., Sonoma.* ☎ *707/996-3030. $$$.* *See p 81.*

DAY 5

7 ★★ **Safari West Wildlife Preserve.** Depending on the season, tours at this 400-acre (160-hectare) home to more than 400 exotic animals—think zebras, giraffes, and gazelles—start at 9am or 10am. Though the organization's primary mission is wildlife preservation and breeding endangered species, it incorporates a strong belief that education and in-person contact with animals raises awareness about threatening issues that face them. During the preserve's daily Classic Safari Adventures, knowledgeable guides drive you around the surprisingly savannah-like environs in open-air vehicles from which you can see wildebeest, oryx, and ostrich, among many other species, freely roaming. You'll want to take lots of pictures in the open-air aviary, and of all the lemurs and buffalo within view. If you or your travel companion is into zoology, you can pay extra ($225 for two people; $50 for each additional adult) for a behind-the-scenes tour and chat with the keepers. Advance reservations are essential for all tours, which are about 3 hours long. *3115 Porter Creek Rd., Santa Rosa.* ☎ *707/579-2551 or 800/616-2695. www.safariwest.com. Apr–Oct 28 tours daily at 9am, 1 & 4pm; Oct 29–Mar tours daily at 10am & 2pm. Safari Tours $68, children 3–12 $28.*

8A ★ **Savannah Café.** Power up before leaving Safari West at its on-site sit-down restaurant. ☎ *800/616-2695. $$$.* Reservations are required; if you haven't made them, and it's summer, grab a bite from 8B **Delilah's,** Safari West's deli, where you can get sandwiches, salads, sides, and wines. ☎ *800/616-2695. $.*

Experience beautiful Silverado Trail. Drive about a half-hour to cross valleys again: Going east on Porter Creek, turn left on Petrified Forest Rd., then right on Hwy. 28. Turn left on Deer Park Rd., then right on Silverado Trail. Once on the Silverado Trail, this portion of the tour can be done either by bicycle or by car.

9 ★★ **Mumm Napa.** This winery in a big redwood barn looks almost humble at first glance. Once through the door, however, you'll understand that Mumm means big business. Just beyond the extensive gift shop is the tasting room, serving all manner of sparkling wines. Appreciate vineyard and mountain

views on the open patio, and don't miss the permanent Ansel Adams collection, a timeless staple amidst the winery's ever-changing photography exhibits. ***8445 Silverado Trail, Rutherford.*** ☎ ***800/686-6272.*** *See p 153.*

⑩ ★ **Paraduxx.** Rows of vineyards fan by as you travel farther south on Silverado Trail to reach this airy, chic tasting room. Try flavorful reds served in stemless crystal glasses alongside small plates of spiced almonds. ***7257 Silverado Trail, Yountville.*** ☎ ***707/945-0890.*** *See p 154.*

⑪ ★★ **Darioush.** Even farther south on Silverado Trail is this winery with dazzling, Persian-themed architecture. Wines worth trying include shiraz, merlot, cabernet sauvignon, viognier, and chardonnay, all served with pistachios. Opt for the appointment-only private tasting with cheese pairing ($35), and you'll get tastes of local artisan cheeses with your wine, plus a tour of the stunning facilities. ***4240 Silverado Trail, Napa.*** ☎ ***707/257-2345.*** *See p 143.*

Embrace California cuisine at Redd.

12 ★★ **Redd.** For an impeccable dinner, go to Chef Richard Reddington's global-inspired Yountville restaurant. His seasonal California creations include signature dishes like butternut-squash ravioli with ragout. ***6480 Washington St. Yountville.*** ☎ ***707/944-2222. $$$.*** *See p 97.* A more casual option is Napa's 13 ★ **Pearl,** a treasure of a restaurant with big, creatively fashioned entrees. ***1339 Pearl St., Napa.*** ☎ ***707/224-9161. $$.*** *See p 77.*

Hit the patio at Mumm Napa.

The Best of Napa & Sonoma in One Week—Days 6 & 7

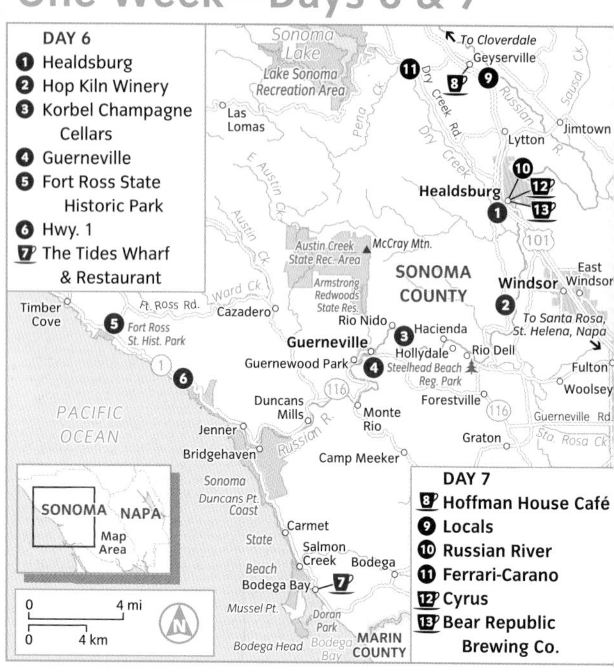

If you've followed these daily tours until now, you've gotten a good sense for lower Sonoma. An extra 2 days gives you the luxury of being able to fully explore northeastern Sonoma, which you got a peek of at the end of Day 3. This itinerary expands on the 5-day tour to include posh Healdsburg, charming Guerneville, and the resplendent scenery that typifies much of California (frankly, it would be a crime to be this close to the Pacific and ignore the rocky coast edging the famed California Hwy. 1). You'll also gain more knowledge of state history at Fort Ross and taste wines from the Dry Creek and Russian River Valley appellations. ***Tip:*** If you're staying in the area for a week or more, consider renting a vacation home instead of staying at a hotel. Consult chapter 6 for ideas, or check sites like www.beautiful-places.com and www.riverhomes.com. **DAY 6 START: Plaza St. & Healdsburg Ave., Healdsburg. Distance: About 62 miles (100km). DAY 7 START: Hoffman House Café, 21712 Geyserville Ave., Geyserville. Distance: About 21 miles (34km) not including river kayaking and shuttle.**

DAY 6

1 ★★★ Healdsburg. This up-and-coming town gets much of the credit for putting northern Sonoma on the tourist map. Until recently, it didn't even produce a blip on travelers' radar, but it's now a huge draw for those seeking true refinement in Sonoma. You'll find a plethora of tasting rooms (a few of the best are **La Crema, Chateau Felice, Cellar 360,** and **Gallo Family Vineyards**), excellent restaurants, fancy hotels, unique shops and galleries—and a modest small-town vibe. You can learn about the town's history at the **Healdsburg Museum** (p 88). Before leaving, patronize **Powell's Sweet Shoppe** and **Flying Goat Coffee.** *See p 86 for a detailed walking tour.*

You'll never forget the first time you stepped into a barrel room and inhaled.

Head south on Healdsburg Ave. to turn right on Mill St. Stay straight to go onto Westside Rd.

2 ★★ Hop Kiln Winery. Get your first taste of the Russian River Valley appellation at this California Historical Landmark. As its commemorative plaque says, this 1905 structure "represents the finest existing example of its type, consisting of three stone kilns for drying hops, a wooden cooler, and a two-story press for bailing hops for shipment." Indeed, this is a superb example of a stone hop kiln. In the rustic tasting room, sample zinfandel, chardonnay, and gewürztraminer—for free. Also on site: a duck pond and the Old Fig Garden, both perfect for picnics. *6050 Westside Rd., Healdsburg.* ☎ *707/433-6491. See p 150.*

Head southwest on Westside Rd. When you get to River Rd., make a slight right.

3 ★★ Korbel Champagne Cellars. Korbel, too, is within the Russian River Valley appellation, but it's been specializing in bubbly since 1882. The winery's colorful rose garden and free tastings make for a

Hop Kiln Winery's distinct architecture is a must-see.

Korbel's is often flanked by colorful ivy.

delightful visit. If you're getting hungry for lunch, a tasty sandwich from the gourmet deli will fill you up. *13250 River Rd., Guerneville. ☎ 707/824-7000. See p 152.*

Take the beautiful short drive southwest on River Rd., which becomes Main St.

4 ★★ **Guerneville.** This off-the-beaten-path village is perfect for a walking tour (p 92), and the town's predominantly gay and lesbian population is friendly, progressive, and proud.

Drive toward the ocean by heading southwest on Main St. (Hwy. 116) and making a slight right onto Hwy. 1.

5 ★★ kids **Fort Ross State Historic Park.** What's now a historic park was the Russians' southernmost settlement in their attempt to colonize North America. See the Call Ranch House and its gardens, the Russian Cemetery, and Fort Ross's natural wonders. *19005 Hwy. 1, Jenner. ☎ 707/847-3286. www.parks.ca.gov. Park grounds open daily a half-hour before sunrise & close a half-hour after sunset. Historical buildings, the visitor center & the bookstore open daily 10am–4:30pm. Parking $6. See p 114.*

6 **Hwy. 1.** Yes, this 21-mile (34km) drive is spectacular enough to merit its own bullet point on this tour—especially during sunset. You'll pass Goat Rock Beach, the Russian River headwaters, the seaside towns of Jenner and Bridge Haven, and a natural cutout called Duncan Cove. End in the resort town of Bodega Bay for a dinner overlooking the water. (See p 113 in chapter 5 for a more detailed description of this drive.)

7 ★ kids **The Tides Wharf & Restaurant.** All 150 seats at the Inn at the Tides's restaurant afford at least a decent view of the bay. Surroundings look familiar? You're perceptive: This dining room was the backdrop for scenes in one of Alfred Hitchcock's classic thrillers, *The Birds.* Menu options include seafood, pasta, and house-made desserts. *800 Hwy. 1, Bodega Bay. ☎ 707/875-3652. $$.*

DAY 7

8 ★★ **Hoffman House Café.** Buy a boxed lunch (about $10) from this family-owned restaurant specializing in California-style gourmet lunches and have a hot breakfast in this homey dining room, replete with a brick fireplace and stained-glass windows. *21712 Geyserville Ave. (at Geyserville Inn), Geyserville. ☎ 707/857-3264. $$.*

Take Geyserville Ave. southeast.

9 **Locals.** Taste Russian River–produced wines at this small, modern tasting room, which stocks more than 60 wines from about 10 tiny wineries. The educational—and free—tasting experience lines up varietal flights, which means you get to taste, say, five merlots or six sauvignon blancs (served in Riedel crystal), to determine how different producers interpret the same type of wine. Buy a bottle of your favorite to go with the lunch you bought at Hoffman House. ***21023 Geyserville Ave., Geyserville.*** ☎ ***707/857-4900. www.tastelocalwines.com. Wed–Mon 11am–6pm (Tues by appointment).***

Follow Geyserville Ave. southeast and get on Hwy. 101 S. Exit on Westside Rd. and turn left on Westside Rd. Stay straight to go onto Mill St., then turn right on Healdsburg Ave. Across the street from the state beach entrance (before the bridge) is the:

10 ★★★ kids **Russian River.** Rent a canoe or kayak from an excellent company called River's Edge (you can also buy box lunches directly from them if you didn't opt for the Hoffman House lunch, above) and float 15 miles (24km) from the Alexander Valley campground to River's Edge Beach in Healdsburg. Watch as the biome becomes wooded, and keep an eye out for swimming holes, vineyards, and a good riverbank on which to enjoy your food and wine. The beach at Rio Lindo, 11 miles (18km) down, is a good option, but part of the fun is choosing a spot and making it your own. To experience the river at a leisurely pace, allow about 5 to 6 hours. Guided trips are available upon request. Reservations recommended. See chapter 5 (p 114) for more details. ***13840 Healdsburg Ave., Healdsburg.*** ☎ ***800/345-0869. www.riversedgekayakandcanoe.com. Canoes & double kayaks $65 for full day; single kayaks $35 for half day. Rentals include paddles, life vests & shuttle rides.***

Head south on Healdsburg Ave. and get on Hwy. 101 N. Exit on Dry Creek Rd. and turn left on Dry Creek Rd. Turn left on Yoakim Bridge Rd. and right on Dry Creek Rd.

11 ★★ **Ferrari-Carano.** One of Sonoma's more beautiful wineries has an Italian château–style hospitality center. A highlight here, aside from tasting the chardonnay and other varietals, is walking through the wonderland of colorful flowers

Goat Rock Beach is one of the Sonoma coast's spectacular beaches.

Ferrari-Carano is known for its pristine grounds and landscaping.

in the formal garden. Ponds, waterfalls, and walkways make your visit all the more magical. ***8761 Dry Creek Rd., Healdsburg.*** ☎ ***800/831-0381.*** *See p 145.*

12 ★★★ **Cyrus.** The most upscale restaurant in Healdsburg—and all of Sonoma, for that matter—is talked about as though it's this county's French Laundry. In the unreservedly classy Les Mars Hotel, dinners here are prix-fixe, but you can mix and match courses. Reservations recommended. ***29 North St.*** ☎ ***707/433-3311. $$$$$.*** A more laid-back Healdsburg option is **13** ★ kids **Bear Republic Brewing Co.** This high-energy American brewery with kitschy-but-fun decor is a great place for trying house-made beer and a greasy (in a good way) appetizer, burger, or pasta. ***345 Healdsburg Ave.*** ☎ ***707/433-2337. $$.***

How to Wine-Taste Like a Pro

Stopping at tasting rooms to sample the goods, known as wine *tasting,* ranks as one of wine country's top rituals. It provides pleasure and a chance to learn why the wines of Sonoma and Napa rank high among the wines of the world.

Precautionary notes would say "taste moderately," for there are some 200 tasting rooms, and wine's virtues take time to notice. Because we're all on a very pleasant learning curve, you can discover wine at many levels. If you should encounter a winery staffer with "attitude" (unfortunately, it happens), don't buy any of *that* wine. Instead, move on to your next stop.

The time-honored techniques for tasting wine involve three steps: a good look, a good smell, and a good sip. You'll learn most quickly if you compare wines, ideally side by side. Almost any comparison will reveal features you might not discern by tasting one wine at a time. Think of it as the wines talking to each other ("I'm smoother than you are," "I'm more puckery than all of you"). By listening to these little conversations, you can discover just how you want your wines to be. Tasting rooms have their own rituals, usually offering a series of wines. When it seems appropriate, and when the tasting room is not too busy, ask your host if you can do some comparisons.

—*John Thoreen*

3 The Best Special-Interest Tours

Wine Country for Foodies

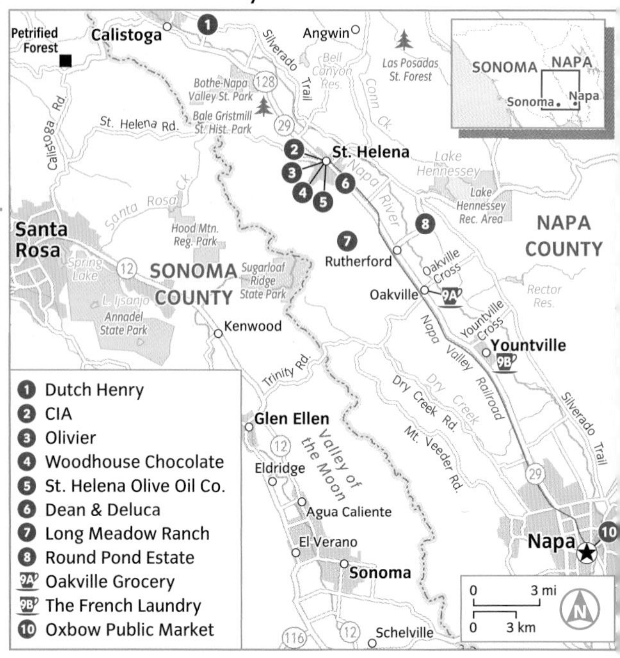

If you're a foodie, Napa's your ultimate vacation destination. Oodles of specialty food stores, farms, ranches, and culinary institutes will pique your interest. To whet your appetite further, there's a farmers' market virtually every day of the week (p 20). The endless food-and-wine pairings—mixed in with a smattering of some of the world's best restaurants and chefs—are the icing on the cake. START: **In Calistoga, at Dutch Henry. Distance: About 30 miles (48km), doable in a full day.**

1 ★ **Dutch Henry.** This small family-owned winery produces around 5,000 cases of wine annually and even fewer cases of its highly acclaimed olive oil, which is so distinctive that it has its own tasting notes. However, the expertly blended oil of Italian, Spanish, and Mexican olives, at $42 per bottle, isn't cheap, although you can taste it for free. Reservations recommended. *4310 Silverado Trail, Calistoga. ☎ 707/942-5771. www.dutchhenry.com. Wine tasting $10 for 5 wines, refundable with purchase. Olive oil tasting is free. Daily 10am–5pm.*

Head east on Silverado Trail. Turn right on Larkmead Lane. Turn left on Hwy. 29.

Previous page: In Napa, a table under a tree is a picnic waiting to happen.

❷ ★★★ **The Culinary Institute of America.** America's heavyweight of food education. The West Coast arm of the New York institution (CIA, to insiders) is an imposing stone château to which wannabe executive chefs flock to sharpen their skills. Not an enrolled student? No worries: CIA has lots of attractions for day visitors, including chef cooking demos, historical displays of ancient food-producing tools, and an extensive marketplace with all kinds of specialty ingredients, cooking tools, unique utensils, and more cookbooks than you could get through in a long lifetime. *2555 Hwy. 29, St. Helena. ☎ 707/967-2320. www.ciachef.org. Chef cooking demos $15; Greystone Restaurant entrees $18–$40. Daily 10am–6pm.*

Keep heading south on Hwy. 29. When it becomes St. Helena's Main St., park.

❸ ★★★ **Olivier.** Sample, sample, sample at this French-inspired purveyor of epicurean delights. Big copper olive oil dispensers line the walls, so try mixing your own—or shop for beautiful kitchenware from Provence. *1375 Main St. ☎ 707/967-8777.* *See p 83.*

❹ ★★ **Woodhouse Chocolate.** The gourmet handmade confections here cost a pretty penny, but to a true palate, they're worth the price. Try the fan-shaped Thai ginger tidbit or the brown-butter ganache ($1.85 each). *1367 Main St. ☎ 800/966-3468. www.woodhousechocolate.com. 10:30am–5:30pm.*

Chocoholics beware—Woodhouse will make you break out the emergency credit card.

Buy yourself a new kitchen toy at CIA's California outlet.

❺ ★★ **St. Helena Olive Oil Co.** True foodies will relish the many olive oils, vinegars, honeys, compotes, flavored salts, tapenades, syrups, and sauces available to try here. *1351 Main St. ☎ 707/968-926. www.sholiveoil.com. Daily 10am–5pm.*

Head a bit farther south on Hwy. 29.

❻ ★★ **Dean & Deluca.** California's only D&D outlet stocks fresh local produce, cheeses, and a fantastic array of international food products and gifts, not to mention 1,400 California wines. There's an espresso bar, too, if you need a pick-me-up after all of today's noshing. *607 St. Helena Hwy. (Hwy. 29), St. Helena. ☎ 707/967-9980. www.deandeluca.com. Daily 7am–8pm.*

Keep heading south on Hwy. 29, then turn right on Whitehall Lane.

❼ ★★ **Long Meadow Ranch.** This innovative organic farming operation is a winery known for its reds—but it's also an environmentally responsible ranch known for

Get a hands-on demonstration of the olive-oil-making process at Round Pond.

supplying the valley's best restaurants with extra-virgin olive oil, eggs, and heirloom fruits and vegetables. Make a reservation (they're required) for the $35 wine and olive oil tour, which happens only on Saturdays and includes seeing the frantoio (olive mill), the valley's oldest olive orchards (planted in the 1870s), and gorgeous views. You'll taste current wine and olive oil releases, too. The $150 "Experience the Excellence" tour includes a hike and an estate-farmed picnic lunch. ***1775 Whitehall Lane, St. Helena. ☎ 707/963-4555. www.longmeadowranch.com. By appointment only.***

Head northeast on Whitehall Lane, then turn right onto Hwy. 29. Turn left on Rutherford Rd.

8 ★★ Round Pond Estate. If it's not Saturday or you don't want to pay for Long Meadow's more expensive tour, make an appointment at Round Pond, which also makes artisan olive oil and premium red wine. During tours, guests see olive orchards and learn about harvesting techniques, growing olive trees, and oil-extraction processes. After, taste the Italian and Spanish olive oil varieties paired with estate-grown vegetables while an expert discusses the oils' many culinary uses. Reservations required. ***886 Rutherford Rd., Rutherford. ☎ 877/963-9364. www.roundpond.com. Tours ($25) by appointment only.***

9A ★★ Oakville Grocery. If you didn't already picnic at Long Meadow, Napa's two true foodie options for lunch are on opposite ends of the fanciness scale. Oakville Grocery is a casual, crowded little store selling gourmet foodstuffs (much of it locally made and available for sampling) and sporting a nice wine selection in the back. Buy ready-made sandwiches and entrees, and at the espresso bar, coffee drinks to go. If you're lucky, you'll spot Martha Stewart, a regular here, shopping for flavored salts. ***7856 St. Helena Hwy. (Hwy. 29), Oakville. ☎ 707/944-8802. $.***

The second option? You guessed it: **9B ★★★ The French Laundry,** a culinary experience every gourmand should have (p 97). ***Reservations required.*** Even if you can't get in, wander through Thomas

Keller's herb garden across the street from the restaurant. *6640 Washington St.* ☎ *707/944-2380. $$$$$.*

ORGANIC three twins ice cream™

From Round Pond Estate, go north on Rutherford Rd./Hwy. 128, which becomes the Silverado Trail. Turn left on Trancas St., then right back onto the Silverado Trail. Turn right on 1st St.

⑩ **Oxbow Public Market.** Finish the day by sampling the best in local wines and artisanal foods. A veritable farmers' market that's open daily, Oxbow sits in the heart of downtown Napa. Dessert sounding good right about now? Go for one of the spiced ice creams at Three Twins Ice Cream. *610 1st St.* ☎ *707/963-1345. www.oxbowpublicmarket.com.*

A Foodie Tour of Sonoma

If you're a foodie in Sonoma, here's your must-do list: Spend as much time as possible on **Sonoma County Farm Trails,** a network of local sustainable farms that encourages visitors to come and not only buy, but also have memorable experiences like picking berries, touring apiaries, taking hayrides, and petting farm animals. Visit the website to order a free map and guide. ☎ *707/837-8896 or 800/207-9464. www.farmtrails.org.* Try **El Dorado Kitchen's** seasonal menu. Chef Ryan Fancher was trained by Thomas Keller, who taught him to use French techniques while showcasing wine country's regional products. He takes familiar classics, like grilled cheese, and gives them a modern twist. Best of all? The prices are entirely reasonable. *405 1st St. W., Sonoma.* ☎ *707/996-3030 or 800/289-3030. See p 81.* If you're a fan of Italian, try **Della Santina's,** a family-owned trattoria just off Sonoma's town square. Its Northern Italian food has been a Sonoma staple for 16 years and is a local favorite. *133 E. Napa St., Sonoma.* ☎ *707/935-0576.* Visit **The Olive Press,** an exceptional Pieralisi olive-oil-pressing facility dedicated to making extra-virgin California oils, which are sold alongside culinary delights like tapenades, specialty crackers, and distinctive balsamic vinegars. *14301 Arnold Dr., Glen Ellen.* ☎ *800/965-4839. See p 100.* To satisfy a sweet tooth, visit the **Chocolate Cow,** tucked into a Sonoma Town Square alleyway. Choose from a variety of fudges and chocolates, or on a hot day, try a refreshing treat of ice cream topped with shaved ice ($6). *452 1st St E Ste F.* ☎ *707/935-3564. Open daily 11am–6pm (weekends until 9pm).*

Wine Country with Kids

DAY 1

1. Charles M. Schulz Museum
2A. The Cantina
2B. Fresh Choice
3. Petrified Forest
4. Old Faithful Geyser of California
5. Sterling Vineyards
6A. Checkers
6B. Pacifico

DAY 2

7. Train Town
8. Benziger Family Winery
9. St. Supéry Winery
10. Napa Firefighters Museum
11. Seguin Moreau Napa Cooperage
12. Downtown Joe's
13. Taqueria Rosita
14. Ben & Jerry's

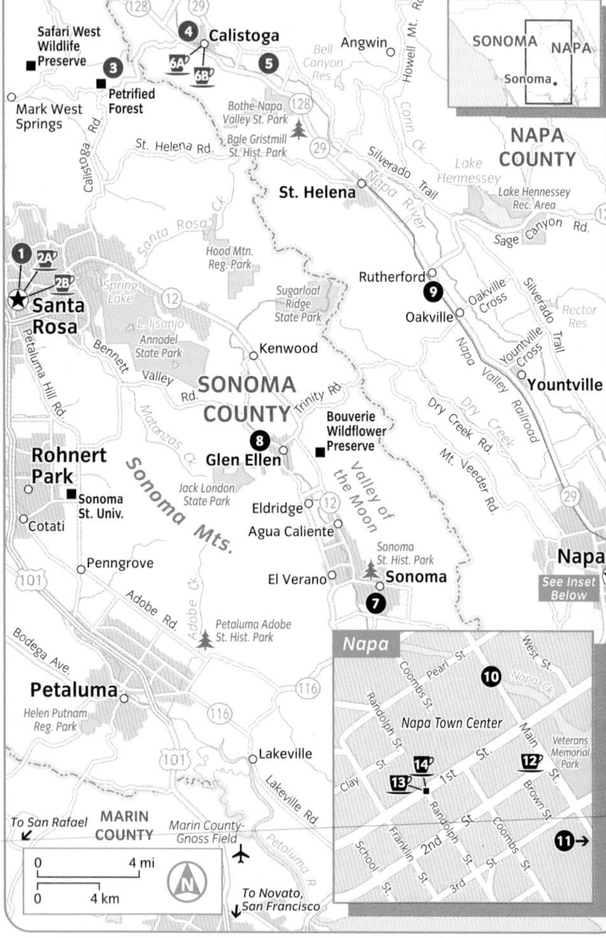

True, Napa and Sonoma are no Orlando or San Diego, but that doesn't mean there isn't lots to do for families wanting to spend quality time together. Some local attractions were in fact designed with kids in mind. Others, while not specifically aimed at entertaining children, can definitely accommodate kids while educating, even perhaps enthralling, them. ***Tip:*** Flip through this book for other attractions with the **kids** symbol. START: **Charles M. Schultz Museum. Time: 2 full days. Distance: About 20 miles (32km) on Day 1; 40 miles (64km) on Day 2.**

DAY 1

1 ★★ Charles M. Schulz Museum. Charlie Brown is practically Santa Rosa's logo: Charles "Sparky" Schulz lived here most of his adult life. In his honor, town residents opened this museum in 2002, less than 2 years after he died. An introductory video, narrated by Schulz's wife, Jean, reveals the local rituals that were a part of the cartoonist's daily life, including his involvement with the **Redwood Empire Ice Arena** adjacent to the museum. Exhibits include a faithful re-creation of Schulz's studio (with his original drawing board, books, and photos); the "Morphing Snoopy Sculpture," an immense artwork portraying Snoopy's many personas; and a mural that, at first glance, looks like that ubiquitous image of Lucy holding the football for Charlie Brown. Look closer, however, and you'll see that the image is actually made of 3,588 comic images printed on small ceramic tiles. You can buy just about any "Peanuts"-themed product you can think up in the massive gift shop. Outside, a Snoopy-shaped contemplative labyrinth adds dimension. *2301 Hardies Lane. ☎ 707/579-4452. www.schulzmuseum.org. Admission $8, $5 seniors & kids. Sept 1–May 25 Mon & Wed–Fri 11am–5pm (Sat–Sun opens at 10am); May 25–Sept 7 daily 11am–5pm (Sat–Sun opens at 10am).*

You're the greatest, Charlie Brown.

2A kids The Cantina, a big, festive Mexican restaurant, is particularly child-friendly. *500 4th St. ☎ 707/523-3663.* Also worth a visit is **2B kids Fresh Choice,** a healthy buffet-style restaurant where you can fill up for less than $10. *1018 Santa Rosa Plaza (at 4th St.). ☎ 707/525-0912.*

From Hardies Lane, turn left on W. Steele Lane, left on Guerneville Rd., then left on Hwy. 101 N. Exit at River Rd. and turn right on Mark Springs Rd. (it turns to the right and becomes Porter Creek Rd.). Turn left at Petrified Forest Rd.

3 ★★ Petrified Forest. Kids can find interesting petrified specimens at this 3.4-million-year-old grove. Volcanic ash blanketed this area after the same eruptions that caused Mount St. Helena to burst forth. The giant redwoods here have since turned to stone through slow infiltration of silicates and other minerals.

Stone logs fascinate—and perplex—both children and adults.

Take your kids on the quarter-mile (.4km) walking trail and tell them to keep an eye out for the park's many marine fossils. There's also an interesting museum, as well as a discovery shop and picnic grounds. *4100 Petrified Forest Rd., Calistoga. ☎ 707/942-6667. www.petrifiedforest.org. Adults $7, $6 seniors 60+, $6 kids 12–17, $3 kids 6–11, free for kids younger than 6. Daily 9am–7pm (5pm in winter).*

Head northeast on Petrified Forest Rd. for nearly 4 miles (6.4km), then turn left on Foothill Blvd./Hwy. 128. Turn right on Tubbs Lane.

4 ★ Old Faithful Geyser of California. One of the world's three "old faithful" geysers is named for its dependable eruptions every 40 minutes, spewing 350°F (177°C) water as high as 60 feet (18m). Kids will be delighted during the 3-minute performance. While waiting, they can peruse educational exhibits about seismic activity and California history in the exhibit hall, which also houses a gift shop and snack bar. The site is also home to fainting goats, which look like regular goats until they're slightly startled; then they stiffen up and fall over. *1299 Tubbs Lane, Calistoga. ☎ 707/942-6463. www.oldfaithfulgeyser.com. Admission $8, $7 seniors 60+, $3 kids 6–12, free for kids younger than 6. Daily 9am–6pm (5pm in winter).*

From Tubbs Lane, turn right onto Hwy. 29, then left on Silverado Trail. Turn right on Dunaweal Lane.

5 ★★ Sterling Vineyards. Now that your kids have developed a thorough affinity for the area, take them along for wine tasting. What's that? You can't do wineries with children? Think again. At Sterling, kids will love the aerial gondola that brings you to the winery. The $10 kids' admission fee includes a goodie bag (adults are $20, kids under 4 are free), and young ones might enjoy seeing the artifacts and videos along the multimedia self-guided tour. Parents will certainly enjoy tasting four wines in the panoramic tasting room. *1111 Dunaweal Lane, Calistoga. ☎ 707/942-3300. See p 158.*

Go south on Dunaweal Lane to turn right on Hwy. 29/128. Turn left on Petrified Forest Rd.

6A Checkers. Kids will love the pizza and calzones at this cheerful restaurant. *1414 Lincoln Ave. ☎ 707/942-9300. $$. See p 106.* They'll also enjoy the Mexican fare at colorful **6B ★ Pacifico.** *1237 Lincoln Ave. ☎ 707/942-4400. $$. See p 106.*

DAY 2

7 ★ Train Town. It may not be all bells and whistles for adults, but that's exactly what Train Town is for tots. In this mini-amusement park, the theme is locomotion—as in train rides along a scale railroad around the wooded property, over bridges, and past doting parents. Other attractions include a petting zoo, a Ferris wheel, and a carousel. *20264 Broadway, Sonoma. ☎ 707/938-3912. www.traintown.com. Tickets $4.75 (book of 8 tickets $10). Daily 10am–5pm.*

Take Broadway south to turn left on Leveroni Rd., then right on Arnold Dr. Turn left on London Ranch Rd.

❽ ★★ **Benziger Family Winery.** At this family-owned winery, the 45-minute tractor-drawn tram tour will entertain kids and educate them about the agricultural processes that make wine. Tours are first-come, first- served, so if it's high season, come in the morning to buy tickets for later. *1883 London Ranch Rd., Glen Ellen. ☎ 888/490-2739.* *See p 136.*

Go northeast on London Ranch Rd. and turn left on Arnold Dr. Turn left on Sonoma Hwy./Hwy. 12, then right on Trinity Rd., which becomes Dry Creek Rd. Stay straight onto Oakville Grade Rd., then turn left on Hwy. 29.

❾ **St. Supéry Winery.** The emphasis here is on education. During the self-guided tour, kids wander through a demonstration vineyard and learn about growing techniques. Inside, they'll gravitate toward coloring books and SmellaVision, an interactive display that sprays out smells of different grape varieties to teach how to identify different wine ingredients. *8440 Hwy. 29, Rutherford. ☎ 800/942-0809.* *See p 157.*

Take Hwy. 29 south and make a slight right on Solano Ave., then right onto W. Lincoln Ave. Turn right on Main St.

❿ ★ **Napa Firefighters Museum.** Kids' never-failing fascination for all things fireman-related will be stoked at this small museum, which exhibits antiquated as well as modern firefighting equipment, including a hand pumper from 1859, engines from the early 20th century, a 1904 horse-drawn steamer, plus uniforms and badges from all over the world. Little ones will particularly enjoy the collection of toy fire trucks and the two huge stuffed Dalmatian dogs. Older kids will take more pleasure in the model firehouse and the 1913 Model T Ford. *1201 Main St., Napa. ☎ 707/259-0609. Free admission. Open Wed–Sun 11am–4pm.*

⓫ ★ **Seguin Moreau Napa Cooperage.** If the Firefighters Museum is closed (Mon–Tues), take the kids to this facility, which offers a free tour that involves watching coopers make French-style wine-aging barrels using wood, fire, and water. *151 Camino Dorado, Napa. ☎ 707/252-3408. www.seguinmoreaunapa.com. Tours Mon–Fri 9, 11:30am & 1pm.*

12 ★ **Downtown Joe's.** A short walk from the Firefighters Museum is this family-friendly (and pet-friendly) American grill and brewery. *902 Main St., Napa. ☎ 707/258-2337. $$.* If the fam's in the mood for Mexican, popular 13 ★ **Taqueria Rosita** is inexpensive, yet maintains a Napa feel. *1214 Main St., Napa. ☎ 707/253-9208. $.* Afterward, stop at 14 **Ben & Jerry**'s for a big scoop of the Vermont-based company's latest flavor, whatever it may be. *1299 Napa Town Center, Napa. ☎ 707/253-0484. $.*

A tram ride AND a wine tasting? Only at Benziger.

The Big Splurge, Napa Style

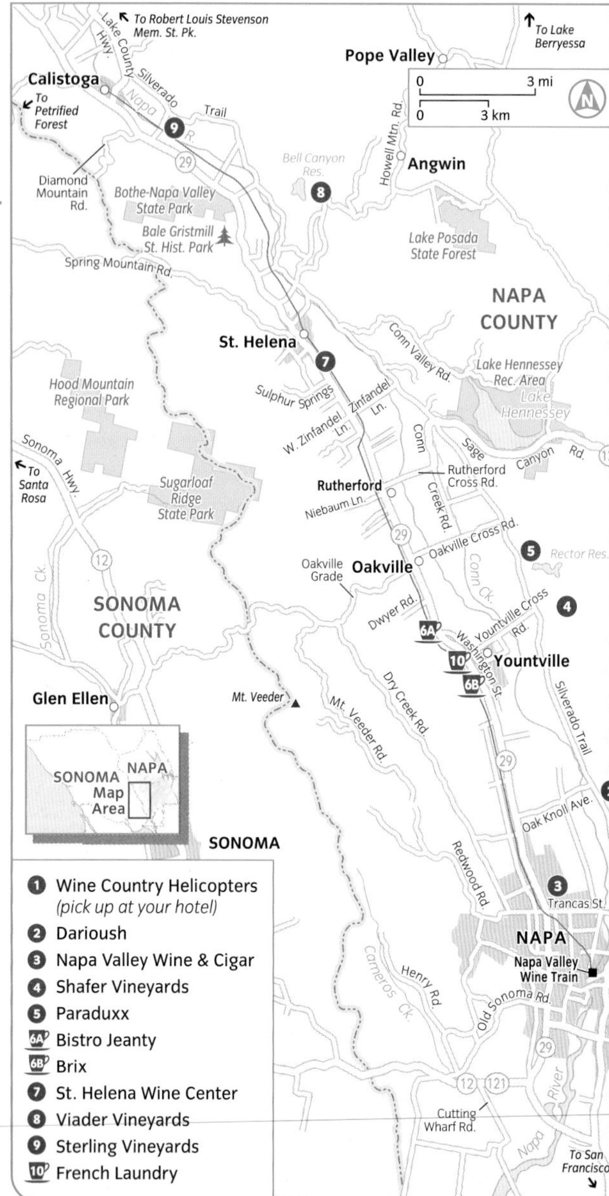

1. Wine Country Helicopters *(pick up at your hotel)*
2. Darioush
3. Napa Valley Wine & Cigar
4. Shafer Vineyards
5. Paraduxx
6A. Bistro Jeanty
6B. Brix
7. St. Helena Wine Center
8. Viader Vineyards
9. Sterling Vineyards
10. French Laundry

Napa can be the ultimate luxury vacation for those who have money and don't mind spending it. Because of its ever-present wine and food culture, as well as its physical beauty, this part of the world draws the world's most knowledgeable wine and food connoisseurs. This tour highlights just some of the exclusivity available in Napa. ***Note:*** This itinerary doesn't work on a whim; it requires advance planning to secure reservations, so read through to determine what needs to be done in advance. However, concierges at some of the area's luxury hotels would be happy to make the arrangements for you, provided you've already decided to stay in their hotel. **START: A helicopter. Distance: About 56 miles (90km), not including the helicopter ride. Doable in a full day.**

1 ★★★ Wine Country Helicopters. Start your day with an early-morning helicopter tour, one of the best ways to get an exclusive viewpoint of this stunning geographic area. WHC is a reputable company providing private, customized sightseeing flights that can include anything from private reserve tastings at usually inaccessible wineries to breakfast on the Russian River to an aerial tour of San Francisco. As the company's website puts it, "We are limited only by our collective imaginations and your credit card limit!" *2030 Airport Rd., Napa. ☎ 707/226-8470. www.winecountryhelicopters.com. Private Reserves Wine Tasting Tour $3,600; Russian River picnic $2,600; San Francisco tour $1,100. Tours accommodate 1–4 people. Arrange for the helicopter to pick you up near your lodging and drop you off at your next stop.*

Get an aerial view of Napa and Sonoma from a helicopter.

2 ★★ Darioush. Arrange for the helicopter to leave you at this opulent Persian-inspired winery, which offers several signature ways to visit. The most comprehensive is called the Private Tasting with Cheese Pairing Experience ($50). In addition to a private tour of the visitor center and amphitheatre, a personal host leads you to the classy six-seat Barrel Chai (say "shay") Private Tasting Room, where Darioush's finest wines are expertly paired with local cheeses. *Daily at 2pm; reservations required. 4240 Silverado Trail, Napa. ☎ 707/257-2345.* *See p 143.*

Limo Service

Arrange in advance for **★★ Antique Tours Limousine Service** *(☎ 707/226-9227; www.antiquetours.net),*

Pick up a fancy cigar to enjoy with your big wine splurge.

which operates an impeccable fleet of restored 1940s Packard convertibles and hard-top limousines ($120 per hour on weekdays and Sun, $130 per hour on Sat; 5-hr. minimum), to pick you up from Darioush.

3 Napa Valley Wine & Cigar. Tell your driver to take you to this in-the-know shop, where you can pick out a full-flavored cigar to go with whichever luxury wine you choose. Options range from the $300 Two Worlds Napa Valley/ Barossa Valley Red, which blends California and Australia grapes to very limited quantities of cult wines like the $725 Shafer 2001 Stags Leap District Hillside Select Cabernet Sauvignon. This is a great place to discover high-end, low-profile table wines, as well as vintage ports like a **1961** ***Warre's Colheita.*** As for cigars, brands like ***Montecristo*** and ***Arturo Fuente*** are available. If you're buying many stogies, splurge on a beautiful humidor. ***3780 Bel Aire Plaza, Napa.*** ☎ ***888/842-9463. www.napavalleywineandcigar.com. Sun–Fri 11am–6pm; Sat 11am–7pm.***

The French Laundry is the ultimate place to splurge.

4 ★ Shafer Vineyards. Next, have your driver take you to this upscale winery, where your visit ($45) includes a sit-down tasting of six wines, including the signature Hillside Select ($215 per bottle), and a short tour of the winery's cellar, barrel room, and cave. Reservations are required; you'd be well advised to set your appointment 4 to 6 weeks in advance, since Shafer hosts fewer than 20 guests per day. ***6154 Silverado Trail, Napa.*** ☎ ***707/ 944-2877.*** ***See p 158.***

5 ★★ Paraduxx. Be one of the first to enjoy Duckhorn Wine Co.'s modern new sit-down tasting room, where vintages and limited-production wines are served in stemless Riedel crystal. Appointment required. *7257 Silverado Trail, Yountville.* ☎ *707/945-0890.* *See p 154.*

6A ★★ **Bistro Jeanty.** Order an array of exquisite French appetizers before savoring your main course from this proficient kitchen. *6510 Washington St.* ☎ *707/944-0103. $$$.* Or visit 6B ★★ **Brix,** where food pairs well with wine in an elegant dining room. *7377 St. Helena Hwy.* ☎ *707/944-2749. $$$$.* Also see p 96 for other Yountville dining options.

7 **St. Helena Wine Center.** If your heart's set on taking home a bottle of elusive, expensive Screaming Eagle, you'll need to come to this well-stocked store, which also sells collectibles like the voluptuous $450 2001 Bryant Family Cabernet Sauvignon. *1321 Main St.* ☎ *707/963-1313. www.shwc.com. Daily 10am–5pm (6pm in summer).*

8 ★★ **Viader Vineyards.** Make your next stop at this gorgeous estate, where you can try and buy an exclusive, difficult-to-find blend called "V" ($100 per bottle). ***Make reservations*** 3 to 4 weeks ahead. *1120 Deer Park Rd., St. Helena.* ☎ *707/963-3816.* *See p 160.*

9 ★★ **Sterling Vineyards.** If you didn't get a chance to make a reservation at Viader, head for Sterling. Aside from getting the valley's best sunset view from the aerial tram that takes you into the winery, you'll experience a multimedia self-guided tour that'll let you get to know the entire winemaking process at your own pace. *1111 Dunaweal Lane, Calistoga.* ☎ *707/942-3300.* *See p 158.*

10 ★★★ **French Laundry.** It's indisputable how to end your day: with dinner at what's often called the world's best restaurant. ***Make reservations*** as soon as you know you're coming to Napa; the waiting list is always months long—and be sure you're willing to pay for this truly one-of-a-kind dining experience: Dinner for two—without wine—costs an average $480. *6640 Washington St.* ☎ *707/944-2380. $$$$$.* *See p 97.*

Driving along a scenic highway never gets dull.

Wine Country for First-Timers

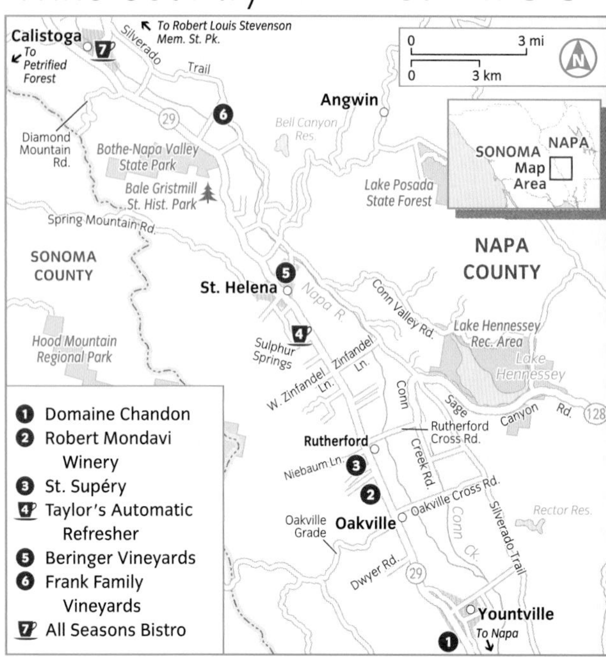

A Napa novice? Not to worry: Highway 29 will show you the way. Following the path outlined below will up your wine-knowledge quotient and ensure that you leave wine country closer to "connoisseur" than ever before. Plus, you'll be able to go home assured that you've really gotten a sense for Napa Valley and its wineries. START: **Domaine Chandon, 1 California Dr. (at Hwy. 29), Yountville. Distance: About 17 miles (27km), doable in a full day.**

1 ★ Domaine Chandon. The comprehensive tour walks you through the entire bubbly-making process, from the cellars to the riddling room and bottling line. You'll also learn about the winery's history, including how the French champagne house Moët et Chandon founded it in 1973. *1 California Dr. (at Hwy. 29), Yountville. ☎ 707/944-2280.* *See p 144.*

Drive northeast on California Dr., then merge onto Hwy. 29 N.

2 ★★ Robert Mondavi Winery. The basic 1-hour production tour thoroughly covers all aspects of the winemaking process and gives you a look at the destemmer-crusher, the tank room, the bottling room, and the vineyard. Top-notch guides consistently make sure you know what you're looking at. Make reservations in advance. *7801 St.*

Helena Hwy. (Hwy. 29), Oakville. ☎ 707/226-1395. See p 155.

Keep heading north on Hwy. 29.

3 ★ St. Supéry Winery. This straightforward winery is a great place for first-timers to learn more about oenology. Its emphasis is education, and while here, visitors can experience "SmellaVision," an interactive display that teaches how to identify various wine aromas and attributes; there's also a demonstration vineyard where visitors learn about growing techniques. *8440 St. Helena Hwy. (Hwy. 29), Rutherford. ☎ 800/942-0809.* *See p 157.*

4 ★ Taylor's Automatic Refresher. For a quick bite, stop at this roadside burger shack with an impressive wine selection. *933 Main St. ☎ 707/963-3486. $.* *See p 85.*

Keep heading north on Hwy. 29.

5 ★★ Beringer Vineyards. This winery pioneered the idea of public tours in 1934, and it's obvious that Beringer has since perfected that brainchild. Today, Napa's oldest continually operating winery offers four tour options ranging from a basic introduction to a thorough exploration of Beringer's vintage legacy. *2000 Main St., St. Helena. ☎ 707/963-4812.* *For details, see p 136.*

Be sure to check out the stone mushrooms at Domaine Chandon.

Keep heading north on Hwy. 29 for about 4 miles (6.4km), then turn left on Larkmead Lane.

6 Frank Family Vineyards. Napa's least intimidating winery has exceptionally attentive staff members who take the time to explain anything you want to know about wine. *1091 Larkmead Lane, Calistoga. ☎ 800/574-9463.* *See p 146.*

7 ★★ All Seasons Bistro. The bistro/California-cuisine menu (fresh, local ingredients) matches wines to dishes, so you'll know what's just right for the entree you choose. *1400 Lincoln Ave., Calistoga. ☎ 707/942-9111. $$$.* *See p 105.*

Do oenophiles confuse you when they describe wine with words like grass or mineral? At Mondavi, you'll learn how to identify these aromas and flavors.

Wine Country for Nondrinkers

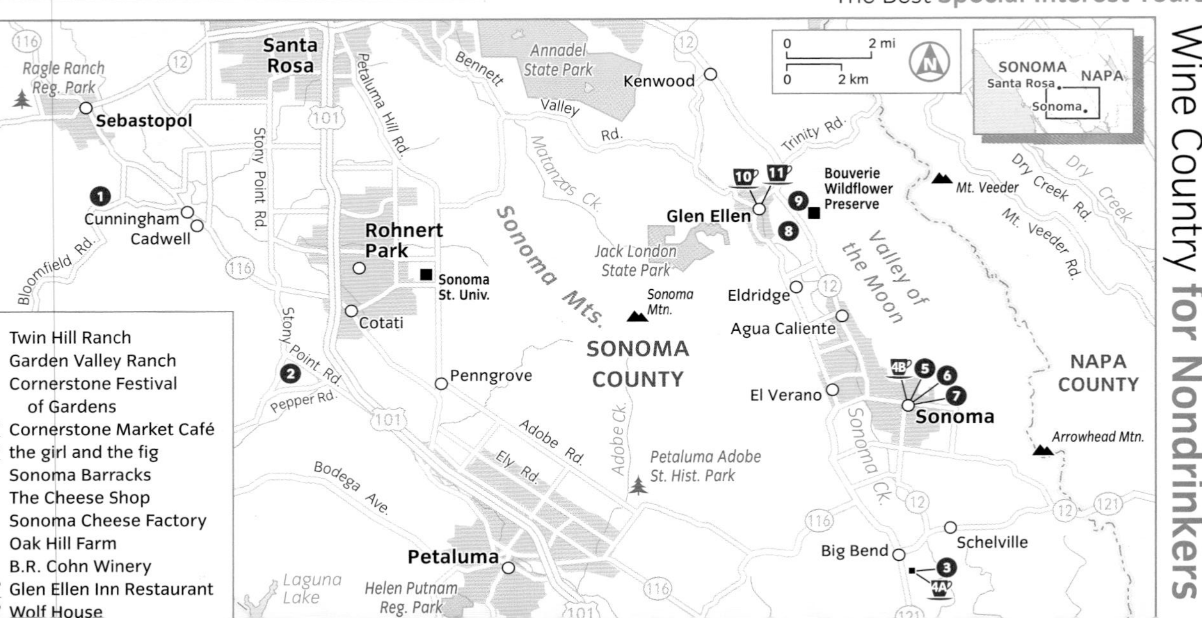

Want to visit wine country but are put off because you don't drink alcohol? Come anyway. Though wine initially put this region on the map, the tourism and agriculture industries have kept it there, ensuring that visitors are kept interested both before and after the tasting room. As a result, there's now a plethora of non-wine-related activities for those who just want to take a relaxing trip to the California countryside to do some nonalcoholic sampling and seeing. Here's how to get the wine country experience without the wine. ***Note:*** For nonalcoholic attractions in addition to these, also see the itineraries for foodies (p 32), history buffs (p 50), art aficionados (p 54), and outdoor enthusiasts (p 107). **START: Twin Hill Ranch, 1689 Pleasant Hill Rd., Sebastopol. Distance: About 40 miles (64km), doable in a day.**

1 ★ kids **Twin Hill Ranch.** Keep the doctor away with a visit to this Sebastopol operation that's been growing, packing, and shipping apples since 1942. In its country store (a perfect place to buy a gift for teacher), taste the ranch's signature apple bread, plus pies, cookies, juice, sauce, butter, and jelly, all made with the potassium-rich fruit grown on this ridiculously fertile land. Tours show you how the ranch produces and distributes 10 apple varieties, including Gravenstein, Gala, and Fuji. *1689 Pleasant Hill Rd., Sebastopol.* ☎ *707/823-2815. www.twinhillranch.com. Call ahead for tour appointments and pricing. Mon–Sat 8:30am–4:30pm (open Sun Thanksgiving to Christmas).*

Go west on Pleasant Hill Rd., which becomes Bloomfield Rd. Turn right on Lone Pine Rd., then right on Gravenstein Hwy./Hwy. 116. Turn right on Stony Point Rd., then right on Jewett Rd., then left on Pepper Rd.

2 ★★ **Garden Valley Ranch.** Did you know that apples are a member of the rose family? Continue the theme at this 9-acre (3.6-hectare) Victorian ranch, which has more than 8,000 rosebushes, a

An apple a day. . .

fragrance garden, and a test garden (where rosarians try to develop new species). On spring weekends, the ranch hosts tours ($35; call ahead to make an appointment), during which lunch is served alongside an assortment of teas in the fragrance garden, which overlooks thousands of roses. There's also a retail nursery where you can buy a variety of flowers, from antique, climbing, and miniature roses to floribundas, hybrid teas, and colorful annuals, as well as gardening supplies, seeds, and books. *498 Pepper Rd., Petaluma. ☎ 707/795-0919. www.gardenvalley.com. Self-guided tours ($5, including a descriptive booklet) Wed–Sun 10am–4pm; nursery open Wed–Sun 10am–5pm. Guided tours ($10, including a descriptive booklet) by appointment and require a minimum of 10 people.*

From Pepper Rd., get on Hwy. 101 S. Take Hwy. 116 E, then turn left on Frates Rd., which becomes Adobe Rd., which becomes Hwy. 116 again, then becomes Hwy. 121.

Indulge in a cheese plate at the girl and the fig.

3 ★★ Cornerstone Festival of Gardens. Nine acres (3.6 hectares) of 20 gardens were designed mostly by prominent landscape architects. These walk-through outdoor spaces are aimed at those interested in high-concept gardening—but they're enjoyable by all, as are the on-site shops and galleries. The **Barn Gallery** displays information about each installation and designer, while **A New Leaf Gallery** *(☎ 707/933-1300)* displays and sells beautiful indoor and outdoor modern sculptures by more than 50 artists. **Translations** *(☎ 707/938-0888)* sells outdoor furnishings and Asian-inspired landscape elements, and **Artefact Design & Salvage** *(☎ 707/933-0660)* offers antique garden pieces and found objects. *23570 Hwy. 121, Sonoma. ☎ 707/933-3010. www.cornerstonegardens.com. Free, though docent tours for groups of 10 or more cost $6 per person (reservations required).*

4A ★ Cornerstone Market Café. The seasonal lunch menu at this cute food shop lists pannini sandwiches, soups, and salads; order from that or put together a meal from the artisan foods sold in the grocery section. *23584A Hwy. 121, Sonoma. ☎ 707/935-1681. $.*

Take Hwy. 121 northwest, then turn right on Watmaugh Rd. and left on Broadway. Turn right on E. Napa St.

For a more comprehensive sit-down meal, **4B ★★ the girl and the fig,** just off Sonoma Plaza, is highly acclaimed. Cheese sampling at the restaurant's well-stocked *salon de* *fromage* is a great alternative to wine tasting. *110 W. Spain St.* ☎ *707/938-3634. $$.* *See p 81.*

5 ★★ kids **Sonoma Barracks.** Cross 1st Street again to get to this landmark, also part of Sonoma State Historic Park. Vallejo, whose assignment it was to secularize the mission, kept his Mexican troops here to guard against Native American tribes and rebuff possible threats (though none ever developed) from Russian settlers. During and after the revolt, these barracks were the Bear Flag Party's headquarters. When the U.S. took over, American soldiers moved in for a spell. Since then, it's been a winery, a law office, and a private residence, among other things. It became state property in 1958, and today there are two museum rooms and a theater in which you can catch the 22-minute video about General Vallejo. History buffs will appreciate the gift-shop merchandise. ***Tip:*** If possible, coincide your tour with the every-other-Saturday 2pm firing of the cannon. *E. Spain St. & 1st St. E.* ☎ *707/939-9420. www.parks.ca.gov. Daily 10am–5pm. $2 admission for adults. Children under 17 free. Admission also includes Mission San Francisco Solano.*

6 **The Cheese Shop.** Try everything from international artisanal cheeses to olive oils, hard-to-find spices, honey and other condiments. *423 Center St.* ☎ *707/433-4998. Call for hours.*

7 ★ **Sonoma Cheese Factory.** If you're not sick of sampling cheese yet (and, really, who could be?), walk across the plaza to this third-generation family enterprise, which was the first cheese producer west of the Mississippi to win a gold medal from the authoritative Wisconsin Cheese Makers Association. *2 E. Spain St., Sonoma.* ☎ *800/535-2855.* *See p 80.*

From Spain St., turn left on 1st St., then right on Napa St. Make a slight right on Sonoma Hwy./Hwy. 12.

8 ★★ **Oak Hill Farm.** Head to this 45-acre (18-hectare) farm and its **Red Barn Store.** This business has existed since the 1950s and still grows its amazing heirloom vegetables entirely sustainably. The real highlight here is the century-old dairy barn housing the Red Barn Store. More than just an old-fashioned farm stand (though it's that, too), this is a unique place to buy organic produce, fresh flowers, beautiful wreaths, and handmade gifts amidst the farm's bountiful fields. *15101 Hwy. 12, Glen Ellen.* ☎ *707/996-6643. www.oakhillfarm.net. Apr–Dec Wed–Sun 11am–6pm.*

9 **B. R. Cohn Winery.** Yes, this is a winery, but the estate also specializes in gourmet (and pricey) olive oils and handcrafted vinegars. Taste them in the small tasting room, which is filled with framed platinum albums from vintner Bruce Cohn's other job as manager of the Doobie Brothers. His property is graced with groves of rare olive trees, terraced hills of plush lawn, and several picnic tables. Many musical events happen here; check the website. *15000 Hwy. 12, Glen Ellen.* ☎ *800/330-4064. www.brcohn.com.* *See p 137.*

10 ★ **Glen Ellen Inn Restaurant.** This homey dining room serves seasonally changing cuisine. Reservations recommended. *13670 Arnold Dr., Glen Ellen.* ☎ *707/996-6409. $$$.* *See p 100.* Another local option is **11** ★ **Wolf House,** a classy-but-relaxed joint with local food and warm service. *13740 Arnold Dr., Glen Ellen.* ☎ *707/996-4401. Reservations recommended. $$.*

Wine Country for History Buffs

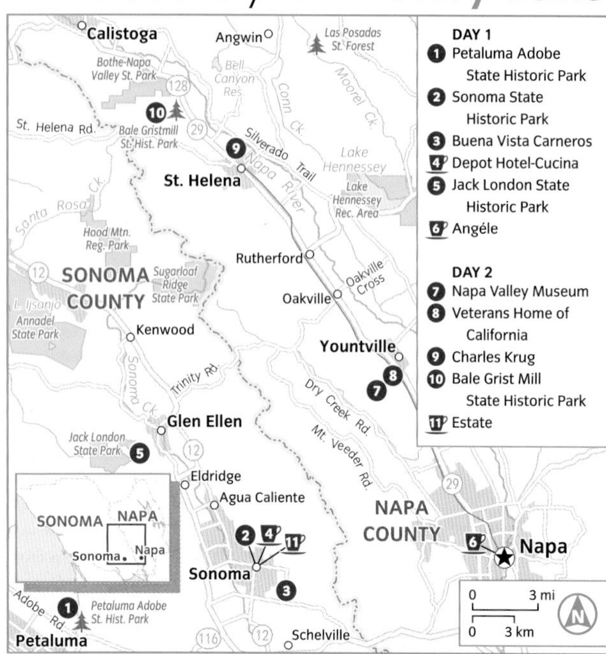

To get to the real roots of the land, beyond tasting rooms and newfangled tourist attractions, and to see why so many from so far came here with dreams of paradise so many years ago, follow this northwest-bound county-crossing tour. It'll give you a sense of wine country's rich cultural, political, and agricultural history, and will help you get to know Sonoma and Napa's most colorful historical characters, including General Mariano G. Vallejo (California's last Mexican governor), the Bear Flag Party, Agoston Haraszthy, American veterans, and Jack London. **START: Petaluma Adobe State Historic Park, 3325 Adobe Rd. Distance: About 40 miles (64km), doable in 2 days.**

1 ★★ kids Petaluma Adobe State Historic Park. What's now a state-owned site was, in the mid-1800s, General Vallejo's working rancho, which he used for commercial ventures like growing crops, rearing cattle, raising sheep, and breeding horses. After Vallejo was taken captive during the 1846 Bear Revolt, squatters took over. In the early 1900s, the state acquired the land and made it a historic park, refurnishing many of the rooms in the adobe-and-redwood main building with authentic artifacts to bring history alive for visitors. Start at the **visitor**

center to see exhibits portraying some of the agricultural and domestic activities that took place here. Then get maps to tour the historic Petaluma Adobe house. *3325 Adobe Rd. (off Hwy. 116), Petaluma. ☎ 707/762-4871. www.parks.ca.gov. Admission $2 (also good at the mission, barracks, and Lachryma Montis).*

Take Hwy. 116 east and turn left onto Watmaugh Rd. Turn left onto Broadway/Hwy. 12 and continue 1 mile (1.6km) until you hit Sonoma. Park at the Plaza.

2 ★★★ kids **Sonoma State Historic Park.** Less a park than it is a series of historic attractions throughout town, a thorough visit should include **Mission San Francisco Solano,** the **Bear Flag Monument,** the **Sonoma Barracks** (p 49), the **Blue Wing Inn** (p 80), and if you're in town at the right time, a tour of **Toscano Hotel** (p 80). *Main office: 363 W. 3rd St. (at W. Spain St.). ☎ 707/938-9560. www.parks.ca.gov. Admission $2 (includes all SHP sites), free for children under 17. Hours vary; call ahead.*

Also part of the park is **Lachryma Montis,** where Vallejo lived with his wife after he was deposed by the Bear Flag Party in 1846. In 1933, the state acquired the property and opened it to the public. Today, it (and an adjacent museum) continues to educate visitors. *W. Spain St., near E. 3rd St., Sonoma. ☎ 707/938-9559. Admission $2 (includes all SHP sites). Occasional free docent-led weekend tours; call ahead for schedule. Daily 10am–5pm.*

From 1st St., turn left on W. Spain St., then right on E. 2nd St. A left on E. Napa St. will bring you to Old Winery Rd. Turn left to get to:

3 ★★★ **Buena Vista Carneros.** The nation's oldest continuously operating winery's historical significance extends to the fact that this is essentially the birthplace of California wine: In 1851, Hungarian colonel **Agoston Haraszthy** planted a few vines here. A decade later, he further bolstered the local winemaking culture by returning from a trip to Europe with thousands of cuttings of hundreds of varieties, many of which he planted at this winery that he founded in 1857. *18000 Old Winery Rd., Sonoma. ☎ 800/926-1266.* *See p 137.*

Old houses and wagons are just a few of the historical items you'll see at Petaluma Adobe State Historic Park.

The Mission Solano is one of Sonoma's most famous landmarks.

4 ★★ Enjoy a sit-down lunch at **Depot Hotel-Cucina Rustica's** Northern Italian cuisine. Its historic stone building 2 blocks from the plaza was once a destination for 19th-century train passengers. *241 W. 1st St. ☎ 707/938-2980. $$.*

From Old Winery Rd., turn right on E. Napa St., then right onto Sonoma Hwy./Hwy. 12. Turn left onto W. Verano Ave., then right onto Arnold Dr., then left on London Ranch Rd.

5 ★★ kids **Jack London State Historic Park.** This is where the famous writer of *The Call of the Wild, White Fang,* and more than 50 other popular tales lived from 1905 until his 1916 death. In addition to 10 eucalyptus-laden miles (16km) of hiking trails, the park has a number of historic sites, including London's gravesite (a small copper urn), the remains of his burned-down dream house, the wood-framed cottage where London penned many of his later books, the stone House of Happy Walls, a museum dedicated to London's life (with a visitor center selling his books), an old distillery building, and more. ***Tip:*** Pick up the $1 self-guided tour map on arrival to get acquainted with the grounds. Picnic tables are available. *2400 London Ranch Rd., Glen Ellen. ☎ 707/938-5216. www.parks.ca.gov and www.jacklondonpark.com. Park admission $6 per car, $5 per car for seniors 62+. Park grounds daily 9:30am–7pm (during daylight saving), 10am–5pm (standard time). Museum daily 10am–5pm.*

6 ★★ **Angéle.** Finish the day at this rustic but upscale restaurant serving French country cuisine in the old boathouse of the Historic Napa Mill, built in 1884. Interior wood gives the restaurant a historic feel, as do beam ceilings and concrete flooring. *540 Main St., Napa. ☎ 707/252-8115. $$$.*

DAY 2

7 ★ **Napa Valley Museum.** Though it's housed in a modern building, this museum gives a great overview of Napa history; its mission is to promote the valley's cultural and environmental heritage. You'll learn how Chinese, Jews, and other ethnic groups contributed to valley life. Downstairs is a permanent multimedia exhibit demonstrating the winemaking process. Before you leave, check out the painting by Michael Keating and see how many winemakers you can spot in it;

among them are Robert Mondavi and Joe Heitz. *55 Presidents Circle, Yountville. ☎ 707/944-0500. www.napavalleymuseum.org. Admission $4.50 adults, $3.50 students & seniors, $2.50 kids 7–17, free for kids under 7. Wed–Mon 10am–5pm.*

8 Veterans Home of California. Napa Valley Museum is actually on the grounds of America's largest veteran's home, founded in 1884. It's the home of some 1,100 ex-soldiers, most 62 or older. Also on-site is the excellent 1,200-seat **Lincoln Theater** (☎ 707/944-1300), a 9-hole golf course, a 35,000-volume library, a baseball stadium, bowling lanes, and many other amenities. *100 California Dr., Yountville. ☎ 707/944-4600. www.cdva.ca.gov.*

Continue north on Hwy. 29.

9 ★ Charles Krug. Walking distance from Beringer is Charles Krug, the valley's oldest working winery; it was founded in 1861 but ceased operation during Prohibition. *2800 Main St. (Hwy. 29), St. Helena. ☎ 707/967-2229.* *See p 139.*

Continue north on Hwy. 29.

10 ★ kids Bale Grist Mill State Historic Park. This state park is worth a short stop for the sight of the massive wooden water-powered gristmill that was built in 1846 and used until the early 1900s. On weekends, you can see the mill in action as a miller performs demonstrations, then buy the stone-ground flour you watched being made. *3369 Hwy. 29, St. Helena. ☎ 707/942-4575. www.parks.ca.gov. Free admission to park; mill admission $2, free for kids under 17. Park daily 10am–5pm. Mill Sat–Sun 10am–5pm.* A 1-mile (1.6km) **History Trail** links this park to **★ Bothe-Napa Valley State Park** *(☎ 707/942-4575);* if you're motivated and have time, take it to see **★★ Pioneer Cemetery,** where many Napa settlers, including George C. Yount (p 94), are buried in a typical mid-1800s graveyard.

Now hop back in the car and head back to Sonoma for dinner. Follow Hwy. 29 southeast, turn right on Hwy. 12/Fremont Rd., then turn right onto 1st St north to Spain St:

11 ★★★ Estate is a beautiful dining room in Vallejo's daughter's early-1900s home. *400 W. Spain St. ☎ 707/933-3663. $$$.* *See p 81.*

At the House of Happy Walls in Jack London State Historic Park, you can take a peek into Mr. London's study.

A Day for Arts Aficionados

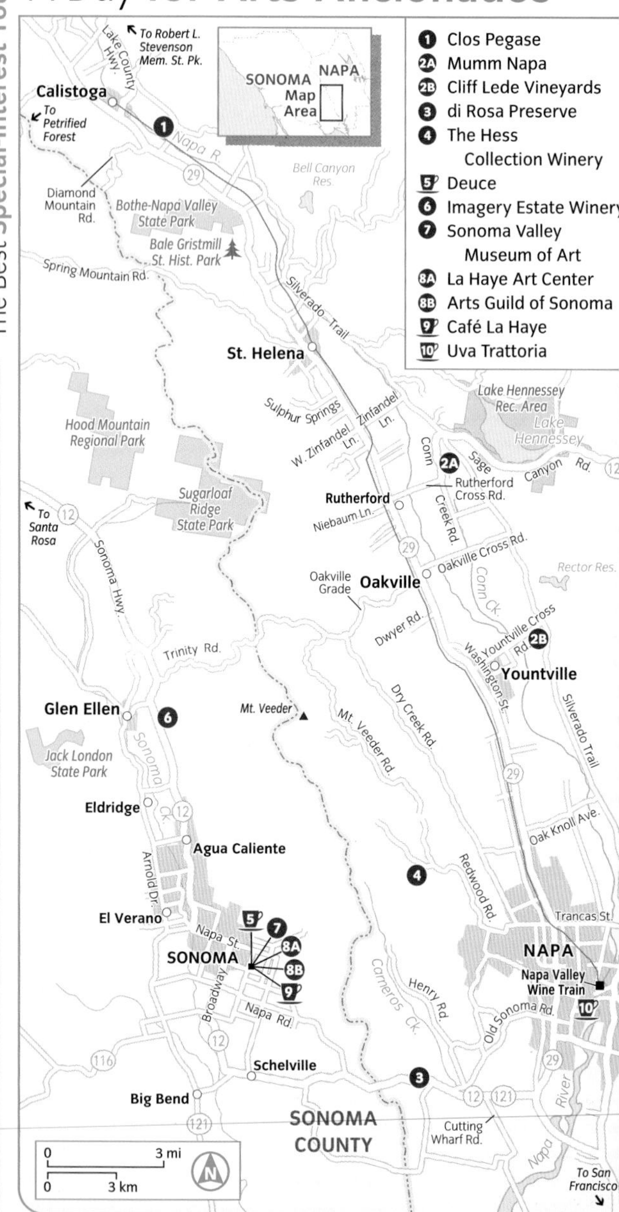

1 Clos Pegase
2A Mumm Napa
2B Cliff Lede Vineyards
3 di Rosa Preserve
4 The Hess Collection Winery
5 Deuce
6 Imagery Estate Winery
7 Sonoma Valley Museum of Art
8A La Haye Art Center
8B Arts Guild of Sonoma
9 Café La Haye
10 Uva Trattoria
SONOMA
NAPA
Map Area
To Robert L. Stevenson Mem. St. Pk.
Lake County Hwy.
Calistoga
To Petrified Forest
Napa R.
Diamond Mountain Rd.
Bothe-Napa Valley State Park
Bale Gristmill St. Hist. Park
Bell Canyon Res.
Spring Mountain Rd.
Silverado Trail
St. Helena
Sulphur Springs
W. Zinfandel Ln.
Zinfandel Ln.
Lake Hennessey Rec. Area
Lake Hennessey
Conn Creek Rd.
Sage Canyon Rd.
Rutherford Cross Rd.
Rutherford
Niebaum Ln.
Hood Mountain Regional Park
Sugarloaf Ridge State Park
To Santa Rosa
Sonoma Hwy.
Oakville Cross Rd.
Oakville Grade
Oakville
Conn Ck.
Rector Res.
Dwyer Rd.
Yountville Cross Rd.
Washington St.
Yountville
Trinity Rd.
Glen Ellen
Mt. Veeder
Mt. Veeder Rd.
Dry Creek Rd.
Silverado Trail
Jack London State Park
Sonoma Ck.
Eldridge
Agua Caliente
Arnold Dr.
Oak Knoll Ave.
Redwood Rd.
El Verano
Napa St.
SONOMA
Broadway
Napa Rd.
Trancas St.
NAPA
Napa Valley Wine Train
Old Sonoma Rd.
Henry Rd.
Carneros Ck.
Schelville
Big Bend
SONOMA COUNTY
Cutting Wharf Rd.
Napa River
To San Francisco
0 3 mi
0 3 km
N

Robert Mondavi wrote, "Wine is art. It's culture. It's the essence of civilization and the art of living." The land of viticulture also abounds with so many art forms, from the visual to the audible to the experiential. Though there's no way to list every wine country art venue—that's a whole other book—this tour gives you a taste of the many creative talents that find inspiration here. As novelist Jean Paul Richter wrote, "Art is indeed not the bread, but the wine of life." START: **Clos Pegase, 1060 Dunaweal Lane, Calistoga. Distance: about 90 miles (145km), doable in a day.**

1 ★★ Clos Pegase. Named for Pegasus, the mythological winged horse-god, this winery's winning design is a result of an architects' competition. Its stunning structures house a world-class fine-art collection, including a huge painting behind the tasting bar. There's also a remarkable sculpture garden. *1060 Dunaweal Lane, Calistoga.* ☎ *707/942-4981. See p 142.*

Take Dunaweal Lane south to turn left on Hwy. 128/29. Turn left on Deer Park Rd., then right on Silverado Trail.

2A ★★ Mumm Napa. Explore Mumm's photography gallery, which displays original Ansel Adams works in long Spanish-style hallways, then enjoy sparkling wine in the glass-enclosed tasting room. *8445 Silverado Trail, Rutherford.* ☎ *800/686-6272. See p 153.*

OR:

From Silverado Trail, turn right on Oak Knoll Ave., then left on Big Ranch Rd., then right back on Oak Knoll Ave. Turn left on Hwy. 29, then right on Hwy. 12/121 (Carneros Hwy.).

2B ★★ Cliff Lede Vineyards. This winery's gardens are graced with rosebushes and sculptures by artists like Keith Haring, Jim Dine, and Lynn Chadwick. A new winemaking facility opened in 2005, and the former one is now a modern art gallery displaying rotating 6-month shows of rising-star artists. *1473 Yountville Cross Rd., Yountville.* ☎ *800/428-2259. See p 140.*

From Mumm, head south on the Silverado Trail, turn right onto Yountville Cross Rd., and follow directions from Cliff Lede. From Cliff Lede, take Yountville Cross Rd., then turn left on Yount St. and turn right on Madison St. Turn left onto Hwy. 29 S. At Carneros Hwy./Hwy. 12/121, turn right.

3 ★★★ di Rosa Preserve. Yale-educated founder Rene di Rosa (he's now in his late 80s and lives on-site) opened his iconoclastic personal collection to the public in a confluence of art and bucolic nature. He started

Cliff Lede is known for the eclectic sculptures peppering its grounds.

Ansel Adams' works line the hallways at Mumm Napa.

buying works by young up-and-comers in the 1960s so that now he has more than 2,300 extremely avant-garde pieces by upwards of 900 artists, spanning media from canvas to stained glass to porcelain—even to old cars. The art spreads from three galleries (one housing a photography hall) out into the 217-acre (87-hectare) preserve with sculpture-laden meadows set against vineyards and a palm-tree-lined lake. There are no identifying labels on or near the art, so, according to di Rosa's intention, visitors have to contextualize pieces without reference to who made what when—though a folder in each gallery makes it clear for those that absolutely need to know. Don't miss the former di Rosa residence, where art is so pervasive that paintings are even hung on the ceiling. *5200 Carneros Hwy (Hwy. 12/121/Sonoma Hwy.), Napa. ☎ 707/226-5991. www.dirosapreserve.org. Admission $3, free on Wed. Gatehouse Gallery Tues–Fri 9:30am–3pm; tours of galleries ($12, free on Wed; reservations recommended) Tues–Fri 10, 11am & 12:30pm; tours of galleries ($15, reservations required) Sat 10, 11am & noon; tours of sculpture meadows ($12, reservations recommended) Apr–Aug Tues & Thurs 10am.*

Head east on Sonoma Hwy. (12/121). Turn left onto Old Sonoma Rd., left onto Buhman Ave., left onto Browns Valley Rd., and again left onto Redwood Rd.

4 ★★★ The Hess Collection Winery. Architectural design here is contemporary to match Donald Hess's museum-quality art collection, acquired over more than 30 years, on the upper levels of the 1903 stone winery. Works on display include paintings and sculptures by contemporary American and European artists. *4411 Redwood Rd., Napa. ☎ 877/707-4377.* *See p 149.*

Take Redwood Rd. southeast and turn right on Browns Valley Rd. Turn right on Buhman Ave., then right on Old Sonoma Rd. Turn right on Hwy. 12/121 and make a

A gallery and a winery? Yes, that's Hess.

slight right on Napa Rd., then right again on Broadway/Hwy. 12.

5 Deuce. You'll be crossing county lines now, so if you're hungry, enjoy European-inspired cuisine at this intimate restaurant, where new works by local artists are shown on a 3-month rotating basis. *691 Broadway, Sonoma. ☎ 707/933-3823. $$.*

6 ★ Imagery Estate Winery. Truly a winery for art lovers, each Imagery bottle label is a tiny version of an original painting commissioned specifically for the wine it hugs. Each must somehow include a replica of Benziger's Parthenon (Imagery is Benziger's sister winery). A curated collection of more than 175 artworks hangs in Imagery's gallery. *14335 Hwy. 12, Glen Ellen. ☎ 707/935-4515. See p 150.*

Take Hwy. 12 southeast and turn right on Broadway.

7 ★★ Sonoma Valley Museum of Art. Walking distance from the plaza, this excellent institution borrows local, international, and ethnic art of all media from private collections, artists, and other museums to create thematic exhibits. In the past, showings have ranged from the somewhat frivolous ("The Art of the Wine Label") to the deeply emotional, like "Faces of the Fallen," portraits of the thousands of soldiers killed in Iraq. The museum has also brought in works by Rodin as well as exotic showings, like cloths of Bali. However, SVMA prides itself on bringing to light lesser-known regional artists. *551 Broadway, Sonoma. ☎ 707/939-7862. www.svma.org. Admission $5, free for kids under 18. Occasional lectures, workshops, and music performances; check website for schedule. Wed–Sun 11am–5pm.*

Imagery's wine labels are works of art.

8A ★ La Haye Art Center. Walking distance from the museum is this nonprofit gallery cooperative that's open only when artists are in residence, or by advance appointment. *148 E. Napa St. ☎ 707/996-4373.*

OR:

8B Arts Guild of Sonoma. This small, no-frills gallery features mixed-media works by local artists. *140 E. Napa St. ☎ 707/996-3115. Sun–Mon & Thurs 11am–5pm; Fri–Sat 11am–9pm.*

9 ★★ Café La Haye. This self-appointed "place for food and art" is a small but smartly designed restaurant that enhances diners' experiences with big, ever-changing works of modern art. Reservations recommended. *140 E. Napa St., Sonoma. ☎ 707/935-5994. $$. See p 81.* If you're headed back to Napa for your lodging, head to **10 ★ Uva Trattoria** for after-dinner drinks and live music (usually jazz). Performances happen Wednesday to Sunday nights. *1040 Clinton St., Napa. ☎ 707/255-6646. $$.*

Wine Country for Health & Wellness

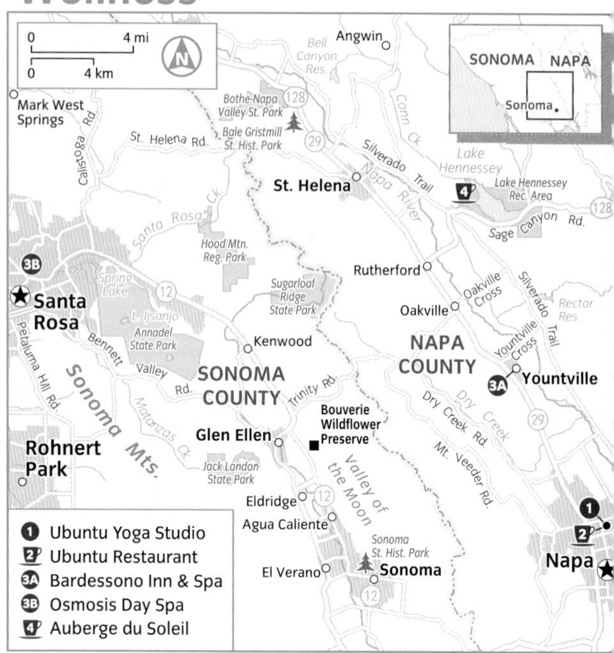

Napa Valley's calming setting makes it the perfect backdrop for a day focused on mind, body, and soul. Pamper yourself at a spa, eat for health, and expand your physical and spiritual horizons with yoga and meditation. Follow this itinerary to leave wine country feeling rested and reinvigorated. START: **Ubuntu Restaurant & Yoga Studio, 1140 Main St. Distance: about 90 miles (145km), doable in a day.**

1 ★ Ubuntu Yoga Studio. Start with a yoga session at this oasis in the heart of downtown Napa. Its name means "humanity toward others" in South Africa's Bantu language—fitting for a place that combines the ancient practice with gourmet, "vegetable-inspired" cuisine. More than 25 accomplished instructors teach yoga at all levels in a studio that sits in the center of a biodynamic garden. *1140 Main St.* ☎ *707/251-5656. www.ubuntunapa.com.*

Tired? Good news: You won't have to travel far for lunch:

2 Ubuntu Restaurant. The vegetarian menu tempts even steadfast carnivores. Chef Jeremy Fox uses fresh, local ingredients, changing the menu depending on what's in season. Try his signature cauliflower in a cast-iron pot. For dessert, try the vegan carrot cake cupcakes. *1140 Main St. ☎ 707/251-5656.* *See p 77.*

Head north on Hwy. 29, exit toward Yountville.

3A Bardessono Inn & Spa. This luxury hotel is not just one of California's greenest, it's also home to one of wine country's most decadent spas. Release tension with a Deep Tissue Bodywork Massage, or relax with a Hand, Foot and Ear Reflexology and Massage. Treatments are 60, 90, or 120 minutes, and cost between $125 and $295. *6526 Yount St. ☎ 707/204-6000. www.bardessono.com.*

OR:

If you're willing to make a longer trip, head to:

3B Osmosis Day Spa in Sonoma County. It's the only place in America where you can experience a Cedar Enzyme Bath, a Japanese heat treatment that's said to miraculously dissolve any aches and pains. You can also sip tea in the lush Japanese garden or indulge in a customized facial or Swedish massage. Single treatments start at $75 but packages cost up to $295. You'll have to travel more than an hour from Napa's town center to get here, so arrange your day accordingly. *209 Bohemian Hwy., Freestone. ☎ 707/823-8231. www.osmosis.com.*

From Yountville, get back on Hwy 29, heading north toward Rutherford.

4 ★ Auberge du Soleil. Finish your day with wine and dinner on a balcony providing one of the valley's best sunset views. It's on the pricey side, but between the delectable cuisine and one-of-a-kind vistas, you get what you pay for. ***Reservations required.*** *180 Rutherford Hill Rd. ☎ 707/963-1211.*

Osmosis Day Spa features a Zen tea garden.

Wine Country for Romance

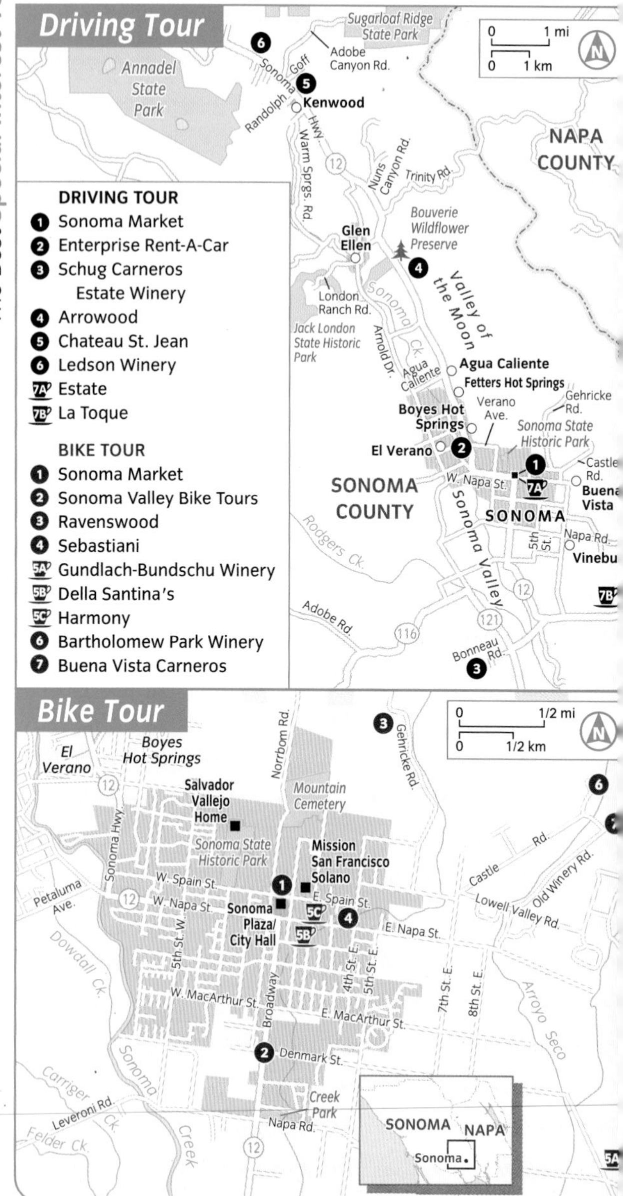
Driving Tour
DRIVING TOUR
1 Sonoma Market
2 Enterprise Rent-A-Car
3 Schug Carneros Estate Winery
4 Arrowood
5 Chateau St. Jean
6 Ledson Winery
7A Estate
7B La Toque
BIKE TOUR
1 Sonoma Market
2 Sonoma Valley Bike Tours
3 Ravenswood
4 Sebastiani
5A Gundlach-Bundschu Winery
5B Della Santina's
5C Harmony
6 Bartholomew Park Winery
7 Buena Vista Carneros
Annadel State Park
Sugarloaf Ridge State Park
Adobe Canyon Rd.
Kenwood
NAPA COUNTY
Glen Ellen
Bouverie Wildflower Preserve
Valley of the Moon
Jack London State Historic Park
Agua Caliente
Fetters Hot Springs
Boyes Hot Springs
El Verano
Sonoma State Historic Park
SONOMA COUNTY
SONOMA
Buena Vista
Vineburg
Bike Tour
El Verano
Boyes Hot Springs
Salvador Vallejo Home
Mountain Cemetery
Mission San Francisco Solano
Sonoma Plaza/ City Hall
Creek Park
SONOMA
NAPA
Sonoma

Whether you're trying to impress your new sweetie, seeking the perfect proposal moment, celebrating your honeymoon, or spending time with the longtime love of your life, wine country is the quintessential place for romance. This Sonoma-centric tour takes you to the wineries and restaurants most suitable for lovebirds. ***Note:*** Before you start this itinerary, the two of you need to decide whether you want to make this a biking or a driving tour. Then follow the appropriate travel plan below (the biking path is leisurely, mostly flat, and not too strenuous). START: **Sonoma Market, 500 W. Napa St., Sonoma. Distance: Biking: 13 miles (21km), doable in a day. Driving: 26 miles (42km), doable in a day.**

1 ★★ Sonoma Market. Whether you're biking or driving, make a morning stop here to assemble lunch for later from the full deli and sandwich bar. If you order 24 hours in advance, the market can have a boxed picnic, including a deluxe sandwich, salad, and fruit ready and waiting ($16). The market itself is locally loved for its upscale selection of specialty foods, fresh breads, and reasonably priced wines. *500 W. Napa St., Sonoma. ☎ 707/996-3411. Daily 6am–9pm.*

BIKE TOUR

From the market, take Napa St. east and turn right on Broadway.

Go ahead—give a tandem bike a try. You know you'll be laughing and smiling all day long.

2 Sonoma Valley Bike Tours. Sonoma's the perfect place to dually attempt a bicycle built for two—so rent a tandem bicycle. The experience is even more fun if you've never tried this kind of riding before; communication and listening are key to doing it successfully (just like in a relationship). *520 Broadway, Sonoma. ☎ 707/996-2453. www.sonomavalleybiketours.com. Tandem bikes $70 per day. Daily 8:30am–5pm.*

From the cyclery, pedal north on Broadway and turn right on E. Napa St., then left on E. 4th St. Turn right at Brazil St., then left on Gehricke Rd. (2½ miles/4km).

3 ★ Ravenswood. If strong wine makes for strong love, this is the place to bolster your affection. Take a tour together of the vineyards and cellar; barrel tasting is included. *18701 Gehricke Rd., Sonoma. ☎ 707/933-2332.* *See p 155.*

Head south on Gehricke Rd., turn right on Brazil St., then left on E. 4th St. (1⅓ miles/2.1km).

4 ★★ Sebastiani. The big tasting room might be crowded, but that'll just push the two of you closer together. Besides, after tasting the cabernet, merlot, and Barbera, and strolling the historic grounds hand in hand, you both will forget all about it. If you plan in

The stone press house at Buena Vista is just one of the structures that makes this winery so romantic.

advance, though, you can arrange for customized private tastings (call for pricing). *389 E. 4th St., Sonoma.* ☎ *707/933-3230. See p 157.*

To get to Gundlach Bundschu, take 4th St. south and turn left on Patten St., then right on E. 5th St. Turn left on Napa Rd. and left on Denmark St. (3 miles/4.8km).

5A ★★ **Gundlach Bundschu Winery.** Unfold the picnic you bought from Sonoma Market at any of Gundlach-Bundschu's many picnic grounds. The remote hillside tables and the olive grove near a pond both overlook the valley. If it's spring or summer, you might be able to catch an after-lunch Shakespeare or Mozart performance in the outdoor amphitheater (check the website for schedules). *2000 Denmark St., Sonoma.* ☎ *707/938-5277. www.gunbun.com. See p 148.* If you prefer a restaurant lunch on the plaza, there's a romantic outdoor patio at 5B ★★ **Della Santina's** *(133 E. Napa St., Sonoma;* ☎ *707/935-0576; $$)* or an elegant, love-inducing dining room at 5C ★★ **Harmony** *(480 E. 1st St.;* ☎ *707/996-9779; $$$; p 81).*

From Gundlach Bundschu, take Denmark St. northwest and turn right on E. 7th St. Turn right on Castle Rd., which becomes Vineyard Lane (3 miles/4.8km).

6 Bartholomew Park Winery. Share tastes of limited-production wines, then explore the historical museum, memorial park, and hiking trails. Or simply sit and enjoy the views; on a clear day, you can see to San Francisco. *1000 Vineyard Lane, Sonoma.* ☎ *707/935-9511. See p 134.*

Take Vineyard Lane, which becomes Castle Rd., then turn left on Lovall Valley Rd. Turn left on Old Winery Rd. (2 miles/3.2km).

7 ★★★ **Buena Vista Carneros.** This estate inspires romance with its ivy-covered buildings, antique fountains, and restored 1862 press house, which houses the tasting room. *18000 Old Winery Rd., Sonoma.* ☎ *800/926-1266. See p 137.*

For recommendations for dinner venues, refer to the driving tour below.

DRIVING TOUR

From Sonoma Market, take W. Napa St. west and turn right on Sonoma Hwy. 12.

2 Enterprise Rent-A-Car. Evoke romance-movie scenes by renting a convertible. Enterprise has a branch where you can rent open-top cars. They offer pickup service, too, so if you don't already have a car with you to get to the branch office, it won't be a problem. Additionally, all the gateway airports to wine country have many car-rental counters. *18981 Sonoma Hwy., Sonoma.* ☎ *707/938-0200.*

Take Sonoma Hwy. southeast to turn right on W. Verano Ave. Turn

left on Arnold Dr., then right on Stage Gulch Rd. Turn left on Hwy. 116, then right on Bonneau Rd.

3 ★ Schug Carneros Estate Winery. In the cozy tasting room, share sips of European-style wines, then stroll hand in hand to see the herb garden, the duck pond, and the spectacular view. If it's clear out, see whether your lover can spot Mt. Diablo in the distance. *602 Bonneau Rd., Sonoma. ☎ 800/966-9365. See p 157.*

For where to have lunch, refer to the biking tour above.

Take Bonneau Rd. northeast and turn left on Hwy. 116/Arnold Dr. Turn right on Madrone Rd., then left on Sonoma Hwy./Hwy. 12.

4 ★ Arrowood. More than 20 years ago, a married couple founded this winery on a hillside overlooking Sonoma. Today, their love for each other and for wine evidences itself in the bright tasting room. After tasting, go out onto the veranda and gaze upon Sonoma Mountain, its valley—and each other. *14347 Sonoma Hwy. (Hwy. 12), Glen Ellen. ☎ 800/938-5170. See p 133.*

Follow the highway northwest.

5 ★★ Chateau St. Jean. Romantic in the more academic sense of the word (it has a bit of a sentimental, nationalistic French feel about it, though "Jean" is pronounced the American way), this château, which includes a fancy visitors' center, a small art gallery, and a formal garden with pond, provides a nice setting for you and your amour. *8555 Sonoma Hwy. (Hwy. 12), Kenwood. ☎ 707/833-4134. See p 140.*

Keep following the highway northwest.

6 ★ Ledson Winery. Fairy-tale-like architecture, complete with a castle structure, regal gates, and a hyper-pruned fountain courtyard, is apt to evoke scenes of Prince Charming and his lovely maiden. If you're getting in the mood for an intimate dinner back at your hotel, pick up a to-go meal at this winery's gourmet market and picnic space—and don't forget a bottle of pinot noir or chardonnay. *7335 Sonoma Hwy. (Hwy. 12), Kenwood. ☎ 707/537-3810. See p 152.*

7A ★★★ Estate. One of Sonoma's most romantic restaurants (formerly called the General's daughter) is housed in an early-1900s Victorian that used to be General Vallejo's daughter's home. The atmosphere is intimate and discreet—and the food is sublime. *400 W. Spain St. ☎ 707/933-3663. $$$.* If you're headed back to Napa for your lodging, consider dining at 15-table **7B ★★ La Toque**, which has an utterly romantic setting complementing Chef Ken Frank's excellent French cuisine. *1314 McKinstry St., Napa. ☎ 707/257 5157. $$$$$.*

Ledson is both a castle and a winery.

Wine Country Without a Car

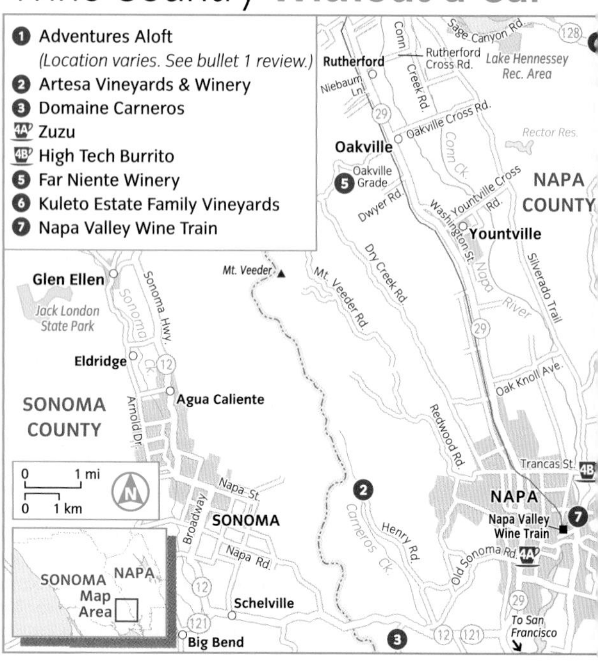

Traffic is an increasing problem in Napa, and, hey, you didn't plan this getaway just to sit in more gridlock. Besides, if you're planning to try all the wine you'd like to, getting behind the wheel just doesn't factor in. So let others shuttle you around while you sip to your heart's content. Take this opportunity to see far-apart wineries that are off the main drag and experience some of Napa's best alternative ways to get around. ***Note:*** This itinerary requires advance planning to secure reservations. ***Tip:*** For other non-car transportation ideas (bikes, bus, and so on), refer to "Savvy Traveler" (p 193); for walking tours, see "Charming Towns" (p 71).

1 ★★★ kids Adventures Aloft. Wine country's ultimate mode of transportation is the hot-air balloon; in fact, Napa Valley is the busiest hot-air balloon flight corridor in the world. Northern California's temperate weather allows for ballooning year-round and on clear summer weekends in the valley, it's a rare day when you don't see at least one of the colorful airships floating above the vineyards. One of the best companies providing rides is Adventures Aloft. Though the company's headquartered in Yountville, its employees will pick you up from your hotel as long as it's in Napa Valley south of Calistoga (when you call to make your reservation, make sure to ask whether

Up, up, and away!

your lodging is within shuttling range). You'll have to get up before the sun, but it'll be worth it for the breathtaking serenity you'll experience as you float 3,500 feet (1,050m) above some of the world's most spectacular scenery. Skilled pilots double as informative tour guides, creating a highly personalized adventure. You'll get pastries and coffee before the flight and a full champagne breakfast after. Delivery back to your hotel is also included. Reservations are required and should be made as far in advance as possible. ☎ *707/944-4408. www.nvaloft.com. $225 per person, including transportation.*

Another good choice is the highly reputable ★★★ **Bonaventura Balloon Co.** (☎ 800/FLY-NAPA; www.bonaventuraballoons.com; about $235 per person, including transportation). ***Tip:*** When the valley is foggy, companies drive passengers outside the valley to nearby areas to balloon. Though they cannot guarantee the flight path until hours before liftoff, they should refund your money if you decide not to partake.

Plan in advance for a chauffeured car to meet you back at your hotel after ballooning. **Beau Wine Tours and Limousine Service** *(☎ 707/938-8001; www.beauwinetours.com)* provides sedans, limos, vans, and SUVs; **California Wine Tours** *(☎ 800/294-6386; www.californiawinetours.com)* crafts personalized winery trips in town cars, SUVs, limos, and minibuses; **West Coach Limousine** specializes in luxury limos *(☎ 707/548-2329; www.westcoachlimo.net; around $75 per hour)*. See p 66 for more options.

❷ ★★ **Artesa Vineyards & Winery.** In a limo is a perfect way to visit the somewhat spread-out Carneros appellation. **Artesa** is one of the few wineries directly east of Napa's downtown. A dramatically modern tasting room makes this Spanish-owned winery the "jewel of Carneros." Try the small-lot chardonnay and pinot noir, then explore the Carneros Center, which includes an exhibit on the region's history, a winemaking museum, and an art exhibit. *1345 Henry Rd., Napa.* ☎ *707/224-1668.* *See p 134.*

❸ ★ **Domaine Carneros.** You can see this French-owned château beckoning you from the highway. Have your driver stop and ascend the grand staircase into the only tasting room to serve sparkling wines made exclusively with Carneros grapes. *1240 Duhig Rd.,*

The sculptures are funky and modern at Artesa.

Transportation Tips

Limos are the most luxurious transportation option, but they're not the only one. You can cab it too; we recommend Napa Valley Cab (☎ 707/257-6444; www.napavalleycab.com). If you've got your own car (rented or otherwise) but don't want to risk driving it yourself after a few tastings, **BeeDriven** will take the wheel. A knowledgeable local driver will chauffeur you in your own car, following any itinerary you choose (they'll also customize an itinerary for you, should you prefer). And it's cheaper than a limo. Four hours for a group of four runs up a tab of $125; 6 hours costs $225. Advance reservations recommended (☎ 707/251-0882; www.napabeedriven.com). Shuttles are yet another option, but only if you don't mind not being in charge of your own itinerary (☎ 707/257-1950; www.wineshuttle.com).

Napa. ☎ *707/257-0101, ext.108.* *See p 144.*

4A ★★ **Zuzu.** For lunch, direct your chauffeur to this locals' favorite. Mini-Mediterranean plates meant for sharing are served in a comfortable, warm, and not remotely corporate atmosphere. Since you're not driving, indulge at the small but friendly wine and beer bar. *829 Main St., Napa.* ☎ *707/224-8555. $.* *See p 77.* For a quick to-go alternative, tell your driver to shift gears toward 4B ★ kids **High Tech Burrito,** an excellent fresh-Mex chain. If you like, take your healthy, creatively concocted wrap in the limo with you as you head north. *641 Trancas St., Napa.* ☎ *707/224-8882. $.*

Vintage cars fill Far Niente's Carriage House.

5 kids **Far Niente Winery.** Yes, this one's on the beaten path, but it has a faraway feel, created by its stone structure and Southern-style gardens with 8,000 azaleas and 100 ginkgo trees. And just because you're not behind the wheel today doesn't mean you can't ogle the amazing collection of classic automobiles in the **Carriage House.** After, taste Far Niente's current releases and late-harvest Dolce dessert wine. Appointment required. *1350 Acacia Dr., Oakville.* ☎ *707/944-2861.*

6 **Kuleto Estate Family Vineyards.** Bordering the far-flung (for Napa) Chiles Valley District appellation is this lovely spot for touring and tasting. Few wineries offer this great a view of Lake Hennessey,

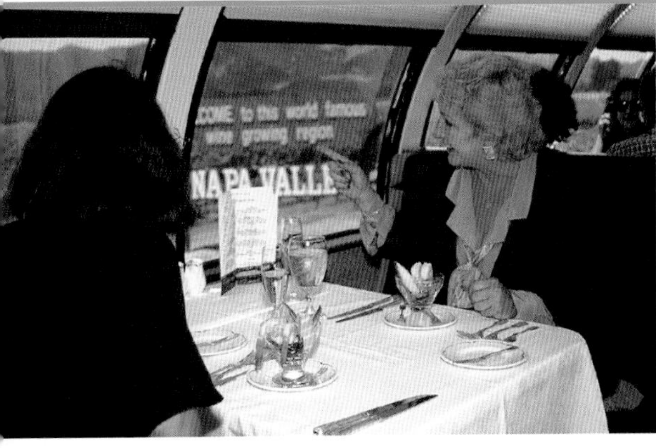

Take a ride on the Napa Valley Wine Train.

such mountainous scenery, or quite the possibility to glimpse wildlife. Appointment required. *2470 Sage Canyon Rd. (Hwy.128), St. Helena.* ☎ *707/963-9750.*

Hit Napa's McKinstry Street Depot for ❼ ★ kids **Napa Valley Wine Train's** 5:30pm check-in (boarding's at 6pm and the train departs for St. Helena at 6:30pm). Get to the station even earlier if you want to partake in the pre-boarding wine tasting. This rolling restaurant is a leisurely way to see Napa. The nonstop 3-hour journey through the vineyards of Napa, Yountville, Oakville, Rutherford, and St. Helena is a lazy 36-mile (58km) cruise on vintage-style cars finished with polished mahogany paneling and etched-glass partitions. The windows are slightly dirt-stained, but staffers are attentive, if not overly enthusiastic. Dinner's served with all the finery—linen, china, silver, and crystal—but the food itself is not quite memorable. The point here is the train ride, which means that this is a more interesting ride during daylight saving time. ***Tip:*** Sit on the west side for the best views. *1275 McKinstry St., Napa.* ☎ *800/427-4124. www.winetrain.com. Dinner packages $50–$129. Daytime rides, with or without meals, are available too; tickets range from $50–$124. Boarding times Mon–Fri 11am & 6pm; Sat–Sun 9am, noon & 6pm. (The dinner schedule is abbreviated in Jan and Feb.) Check the website for special events.*

Cabbing It

Napa Valley Cab (☎ *707/257-6444; www.napavalleycab.com).*

A tractor makes its way through vineyards at Domaine Carneros.

Wine Country **on a Budget**

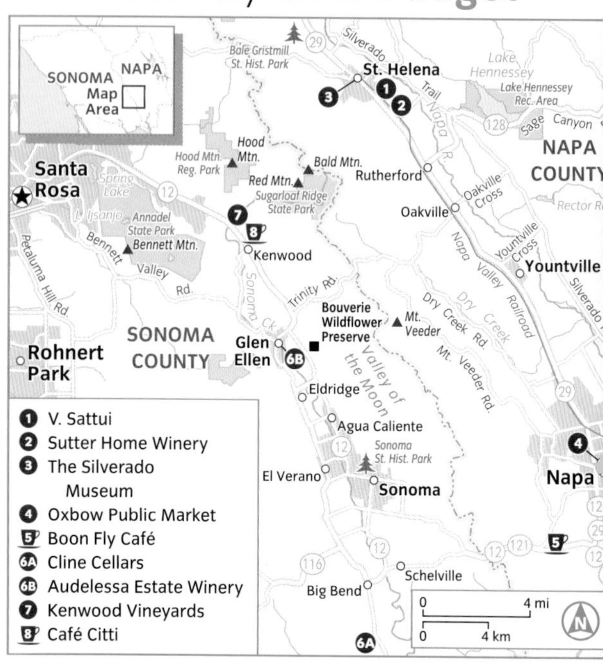

A budget traveler might not choose a region characterized by splurging and expensive taste. While Napa and Sonoma (especially Napa) are indeed those types of destinations, the budget-conscious can still come here, indulge, and leave without breaking the bank. Here's how. **START: V. Sattui, 1111 White Lane, St. Helena. Distance: 53 miles (85km), doable in a full day.**

1 ★★ **V. Sattui** offers free tastes (eight wines!) and self-guided tours all day. Explore the historic winery's aging cellars, museum, and outdoor spaces. At the deli and cheese shop, there are free samples aplenty. ***Tip:*** To fit everything in today, take advantage of V. Sattui's 9am opening time. *1111 White Lane, St. Helena. ☎ 707/963-7774.* *See p 160.*

Take White Lane southwest and turn right on St. Helena Hwy. (easy walking distance).

2 ★ **Sutter Home Winery.** Tastings are free; enjoy them in the original 1874 winery. Afterward, take a self-guided garden tour (also free) to see the estate's extensive gardens, which were modeled after Canada's **Butchart Gardens.** The organic White Zinfandel garden nurtures 125 rose species. *277 St. Helena Hwy. (Hwy. 29), St. Helena. ☎ 707/963-3104, ext. 4208.* *See p 159.*

Take St. Helena Hwy. northwest and turn right on Adams St. Turn left on Library Lane.

3 kids The Silverado Museum. Dedicated to the life of Robert Louis Stevenson, this room-sized museum houses more than 8,000 writerly artifacts, including original manuscripts, photographs, and the author's copies of his own books. Free admission. *1490 Library Lane, St. Helena.* ☎ *707/963-3757.*

Go southeast on Library Lane to turn right on Adams St. Turn left on Hwy. 29 and take the ramp toward Lincoln Ave. Turn right on Solano Ave., then right onto Lincoln Ave. Turn right on Soscol Ave., then left on 1st St.

4 ★★★ Oxbow Public Market. Downtown Napa's main attraction can be as cheap as you want it to be. Peruse the colorful stalls, people-watch and pick up free samples: try a bit of the gourmet ice cream at Three Twins, get free chocolate caramel sauce at Annette's, savor slivers of cheese, and chomp on charcuterie at the Fatted Calf. Still hungry? At Pica Pica, a satisfying Argentinian meal costs less than $10. *600 First St.* ☎ *707/963-1345. www.oxbowpublicmarket.com. Mon–Sat, 10am–6pm, Sun 10am–5pm (closed major holidays).*

To feel as though you've gone to an expensive restaurant, head to **5 ★★ Boon Fly Café,** which has upscale decor, white-linen tables, and classy California cuisine. *4048 Sonoma Hwy. (at Carneros Inn), Napa.* ☎ *707/299-4900. $$.*

From Oxbow Public Market, go west on 1st St. onto Hwy. 29 S. Turn right on Carneros Hwy. (Hwy. 121/12), and turn left to stay on it.

6A ★ Cline Cellars. Get here in time to take the 1 or 3pm free tour, or walk around yourself to see the quaint grounds, which include ponds, rosebushes, and the highlight: a small, woodsy museum (free

You'd never guess that V. Sattui's fancy grounds are home to free tastes!

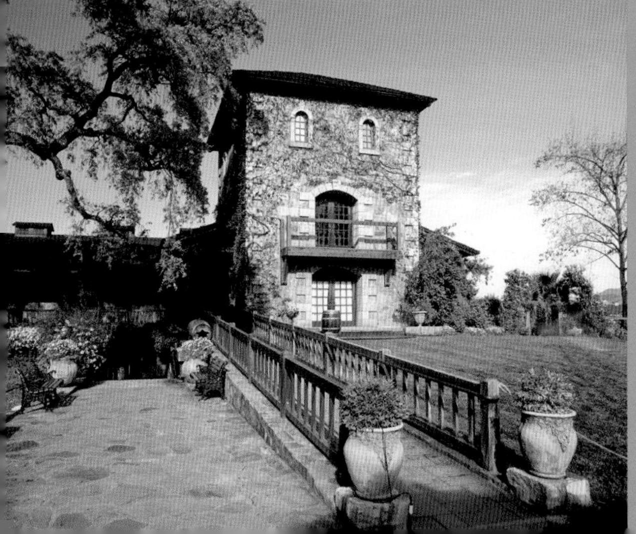

admission) housing dioramas of all 21 California missions. Tastings are free, too, and they happen in a rustic 1850s farmhouse. *24737 Carneros Hwy. (Calif. 121), Sonoma.* ☎ *707/940-4000.* *See p 140.*

OR:

From Oxbow Public Market, go west on 1st St. onto Hwy. 29 S. Turn right on Carneros Hwy. (121) N; it becomes Arnold Dr.

6B Audelssa Estate Winery. Though this winery doesn't generally show guests its vineyards, its storefront tasting room in central Glen Ellen gives free tastings. Ask for sips of chardonnay and pinot noir, then examine the historic relics and photos documenting Glen Ellen's history—see if you can spot authors Jack London and M. F. K. Fisher in the mix. *13647 Arnold Dr., Glen Ellen.* ☎ *707/933-8514.* *See p 134.*

From Cline, head east on Hwy. 121 and turn left (north) on Hwy. 12. From Audelssa, take Arnold Dr. northeast and turn left on Sonoma Hwy. (Hwy. 12).

7 ★ Kenwood Vineyards. The tasting room here is in a 1906 farmhouse, even though the winery's now a modern, high-production facility (most of it cleverly concealed in the original barnlike buildings). Though the winery looks modest, its output is staggering: nearly 500,000 yearly cases of wines well known throughout the U.S. Alas, tours aren't available, but free tastes include an array of varietals, including the popular sauvignon blanc, a crisp, light wine with hints of melon. *9592 Sonoma Hwy. (Hwy. 12), Kenwood.* ☎ *707/833-5891.* *See p 151.*

8 ★ Café Citti. The high-quality Northern Italian cuisine at Citti (pronounced "Cheat-ee"), a roadside trattoria, is delightfully inexpensive. Order from the huge menu board above the open kitchen, then grab a table (the ones on the patio are best on warm evenings) and a server brings your hearty meal. Wine is available by the bottle, the espresso is plenty strong, and everything on the menu board is available to go. *9049 Sonoma Hwy., Kenwood.* ☎ *707/833-2690. $$.* ●

Cline Cellars feels more like a home than a tasting room.

4

The Most **Charming Towns**

Napa

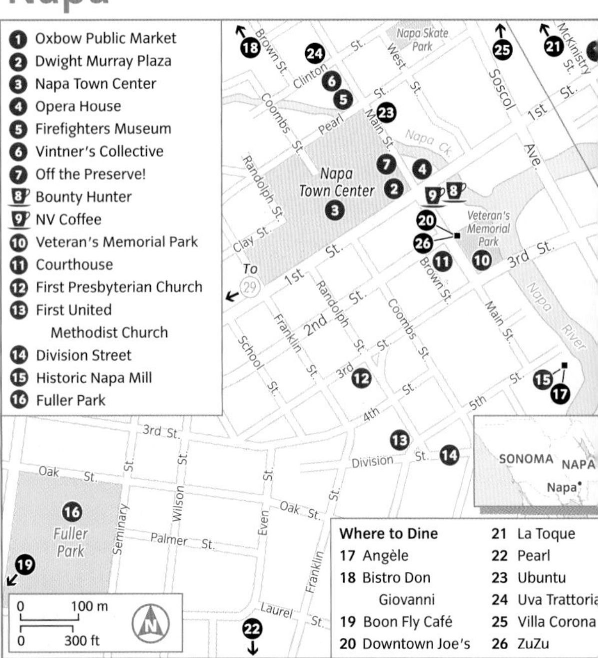

This walking tour takes you through the city of Napa—the town, not the region, valley, or county. The southern bookend to the ritzier towns above it, Napa is the more lived-in, real-life community that caters more to its ever-growing residential population than to its tourists. But that's exactly its charm: Visitors feel invited in rather than pandered to. Plant yourself here for a day, sip a glass of local cab, stroll among this riverside town's Victorian and Gothic landmarks, and mingle with Napans (or "Napkins," as locals call themselves). For more information, contact the Napa Downtown Association. *1556 1st St. No. 102. ☎ 707/257-0322. www.napadowntown.com or the Napa Valley Conference and Visitors Bureau (see 3 below).* START: **1st & Main sts. Distance: 1-mile (1.6km) of walking.**

1 ★ Oxbow Public Market. Start your day at one of the town's most talked-about new attractions, a sprawling marketplace filled with artisan foods and wine sellers. Dine at one of the eateries (**Pica Pica Maize Kitchen** serves Venezuelan cuisine), buy specialty food items and souvenirs, and do dessert at Kara's Cupcakes ($3.25 each).

Previous page: A house in the Old Western-style town of Calistoga.

2 Dwight Murray Plaza. Walk southwest on 1st Street, stopping just past Main to this community gathering spot replete with various shops, a fountain, and picnic tables. Check out the mural depicting the Napa River waterfront in its early-1900s heyday.

3 kids Napa Town Center. Head to this retail complex to grab a caramel apple at Rocky Mountain Chocolate Factory or gelato at Christopher's Fine Foods, and stroll past shops (don't miss the 50,000-sq.-ft./4,645-sq.-m McCaulou's Department Store, known for its selection of affordable clothes for the whole family). All the retailers are housed in historic buildings and connected by a pedestrian street. Look for the two huge oak trees that serve as town landmarks. Here you'll also find the overachieving **Napa Valley Conference and Visitors Bureau** (*☎ 707/226-7459; www.napavalley.org; Mon–Sat 9am–5pm, Sun 11am–5pm*). Stop in for a variety of local information, money-saving coupons, and pamphlets outlining self-guided walking tours of the town's historic buildings. *1290 Napa Town Center ☎ 707/255-9375. 1310 Napa Town Center.*

4 ★ Napa Valley Opera House. Cross the street to Main, and you'll see this Italianate-style building. Even if you don't see a show, this performance venue is worth a look for its historic value. Listed on the National Historic Register, it was originally built in 1879. Some nights, Jack London read aloud to rapt audiences; on others, traveling Vaudeville acts titillated delighted patrons. Due to poor attendance, however, it closed in 1914 and sat quiet and dilapidating until concerned local preservationists recently restored and reopened it—to the tune of $14 million. Today, operatic performances are still the minority at this 16-row venue, despite the establishment's name. Management prefers to bring in symphonies, musicals, and even country, rock, and R&B performers like Rosanne Cash, Los Lobos, and Boyz II Men. Occasionally, theatric

Napa's Main Street.

The Napa Valley Opera House is spectacular both night and day.

and dance troupes come through as well. Check the website for show times and schedules. *1030 Main St.* ☎ *707/226-7372. www.napavalleyoperahouse.com. Box office open Mon–Fri 10am–5pm, Sat noon–4pm.*

5 ★ kids **Napa Firefighters Museum.** Run by the Napa City Firefighters Association, this small museum is a loving tribute to the history of firefighting. Displays show antique and modern equipment used by lifesaving heroes. *1201 Main St., Napa.* ☎ *707/259-0609. Open Wed–Sat 11am–4pm. Free admission. Also see p 39.*

6 ★★ **Vintner's Collective.** Wine discoveries await at this 18-winery tasting room in the old Pfeiffer Building, which was built in 1875 and is Napa's first stone building (touch the native sandstone). After previous lives as a brewery, saloon, brothel, and Chinese-owned laundry, in 2002 it became an outlet for small, virtually unknown wineries like Judd's Hill, Melka, and Mi Sueno—in short, stuff you *won't* find at home. To boot, Keith Fergel (French Laundry's sommelier, also known as the wine expert at the region's most famous restaurant) named this tasting room his favorite stop for finding new wines. *1245 Main St.* ☎ *707/255-7150. www.vintnerscollective.com. Daily 11am–6pm. Tastings $25.*

7 **Off the Preserve!** Plucked from the modern art collection at the di Rosa Preserve (p 55), this gallery's contemporary exhibits are showcased in the circa-1886 Kyser-Williams building. *1142 Main St.* ☎ *707/226-5991. www.dirosapreserve.org. Wed–Fri 9:30am–3pm (Sat. by appointment only). Free admission.*

8 ★★ **Bounty Hunter Rare Wine & Provisions.** A combination wine bar/eating joint/retail shop/tasting room, Bounty Hunter has bottles that even devoted collectors would be hard-pressed to find elsewhere. The thinking here is, "Find your own cult wine." Or just enjoy on-tap Guinness with a hearty sandwich. Before walking into this saloonlike space, admire its exterior: The brick Semorile Building, embellished with decorative cast-iron railing, was built in 1888 and is on the National Historic Register. *975 1st St.* ☎ *707/226-3976. www.bountyhunterwine.com. Daily Sun–Thurs 11am–10pm (until midnight Fri–Sat). Tastings $2.50–$19.*

9 **Napa Valley Coffee Roasting Co.** For a sweet fix after Bounty Hunter, or if you just need a caffeinated pick-me-up, this roastery in the adjacent **Winship Building** (also on the Historic Register) sells small-batch custom roasts and a selection of pastries. *948 Main St.* ☎ *707/224-2233. $.*

10 **Veterans Memorial Park.** Savor your coffee on the river's edge at this tranquil park. On holidays like Independence Day and Labor Day, the site comes alive with music and festivities. And when Governor Arnold Schwarzenegger comes to town, he holds press conferences here. *Main & 3rd sts.*

⑪ ★ kids Courthouse. Napa's Renaissance-style courthouse, built in 1878, is still very much a working court, complete with a law library, hall of records, and mediation center. It's on the National Register of Historic Places for its 19th-century architecture and history—in 1897, for example, this courthouse was the site of California's last public hanging. Explore the first-floor pictorial hall for a visual depiction of Napa County history. On the east lawn (2nd St.) look for the 1893 flagpole modeled after the Eiffel Tower, as well as a Wappo Indian grinding rock. *825 Brown St.*

⑫ ★ First Presbyterian Church. Were it not for its protuberant steeple and ornamental doorway, this pyramidal church, built in 1874, would look like a big rooftop sitting on the ground. It is one of the county's best examples of Victorian Gothic architecture—no surprise, then, that this California Registered Historical Landmark is also in the National Register of Historic Places. *1333 3rd St. ☎ 707/224-8693. www.fpcnapa.org.*

Heading from downtown into the Napa Abajo District, you'll notice larger city blocks and a high concentration of residential architectural styles spanning the 1800s. The entire district is on the National Register of Historic Places.

⑬ First United Methodist Church. This mix of religious and secular architecture done in late-Gothic style is home to an elaborate sanctuary and gorgeous stained-glass windows. Be sure to try its small labyrinth. *601 Randolph St. ☎ 707/253-1411. www.napaumc.org. Labyrinth hours 11am–2pm ($3 suggested donation).*

Stroll riverward on **⑭ ★ Division Street,** so named because it divides Napa Abajo from downtown. All the turn-of-the-20th-century homes on this lane are historically significant, from the **Hayman House** *(1227 Division St.)* to the Greek Revival–style **Lamdin Cottage** *(1236 Division St).*

⑮ ★★ Historic Napa Mill. Abutting the Napa River are this complex's Hatt buildings, also on the National Register of Historic Places (sensing a theme here?)—they're good examples of the industrial false-front brick buildings that used to cluster the river's once-bustling wharves. The 1884 building used to house a grain mill (the old tin silos are still attached) and a roller-skating rink. These days, it's a smart commercial center including the "haunted" **Napa River Inn** (p 122) and a variety of shops: Stop at the upscale **Napa General Store,** the **Napa Valley Lavender Co.,** and the **Vintage Sweet Shoppe** for locally made non-wine souvenirs or gifts and ponder the exquisite mosaic fountain—its scenes portray Napa Valley's history. *500 Main St. ☎ 707/251-8500. www.napariverinn.com/napamill.php.*

Get a java jolt at the Napa Valley Coffee Roasting Co.

The Napa Valley Mill is home to a number of fun boutiques.

⓰ kids **Fuller Park.** Take a 15-minute stroll to Napa's first park, which boasts more than 83 tree species, many marked with plaques commemorating important events. Named after Napa's 1905 mayor, John A. Fuller, the shaded park is a great spot to rest and unwind; kids will love its fountain and large playground. ***Oak & Seminary sts.***

Where to Dine

★★ **Angèle** *FRENCH* This riverside spot has exciting food and surroundings to match; its combo of wood beams, concrete walls and floors, bright yellow barstools, and heated patio is great for intimate dining. The culinary ante is way up there: Think fabulous, crispy roast chicken with fresh corn and chanterelles or King salmon with arugula salad and heirloom tomatoes. If the chocolate soup's on the menu, it's a must-order for dessert. Reservations recommended. ***540 Main St. (at Historic Napa Mill). ☎ 707/252-8115. Entrees $10–$32. AE, MC, V. Lunch & dinner daily. Map p 72.***

★★★ **Bistro Don Giovanni** *ITALIAN* A bright, bustling restaurant highlighting quality ingredients and California flair. Entrees never disappoint, especially the thin-crust pizzas from the wood-burning oven and the house-made pastas. Begin with the salad of beets and *haricots verts*. If it's warm enough, dine alfresco in the vineyards. Reservations recommended. ***4110 Howard Lane. ☎ 707/224-3300. Entrees $12–$36. AE, DC, DISC, MC, V. Lunch & dinner daily. Map p 72.***

★ **Boon Fly Café** *AMERICAN* Along the rural Carneros Highway is a great bargain dining option: the gourmet roadhouse in front of the Carneros Inn. The slick and inviting interior is modern barn style, complete with a corrugated metal water-shed-like pizza oven and light, airy surroundings accented with dark wood. The food similarly balances rustic and chic with fancy renditions of comfort classics like killer beer-battered onion rings and flatbread pizzas. Breakfast options include satisfying omelets and pancakes. If you're passing by and in a hurry, there are tasty to-go items like donut holes and breakfast sandwiches. ***4048 Sonoma Hwy. ☎ 707/299-4900. Entrees $8–$27. AE, DC, DISC, MC, V. Breakfast, lunch & dinner daily. Map p 72.***

kids **Downtown Joe's** *AMERICAN* Foodies will want to steer clear, but those looking for a good heavy breakfast, a down-home atmosphere, and live entertainment during the evenings (Thurs–Sun) will appreciate this well-priced restaurant. Beers, such as the tart Golden Ribbon American, are made in-house, as are the breads and desserts. If the sun's out, request a table on the outside patio. Weekday happy hours feature specials such as $3 pints and half-price appetizers. ***902***

Main St. ☎ 707/258-2337. Entrees $11–$25. AE, DC, DISC, MC, V. Breakfast, lunch & dinner daily. Map p 72.

★★ La Toque *AMERICAN FRENCH* *Wine Spectator* deemed this one of America's best restaurants; it's known for unrivaled cuisine, warm ambiance, a long wine list, and accommodating waitstaff. Acclaimed Chef Ken Frank uses fresh, organic ingredients in his culinary masterpieces. Try the truffle menu. *1314 McKinstry St. ☎ 707/257-5157. Tasting menu $49–$88. AE, DC, DISC, MC. Dinner daily.*

★ Pearl *CALIFORNIA ECLECTIC* If you prefer to skip the destination restaurants and head for a casual but quality meal among locals, head to Pearl, which has a warm, friendly dining room and a lovely enclosed patio. The seasonally influenced menu includes a selection of salads, sandwiches, and main courses; an excellent choice is the soft polenta with sautéed vegetables. Reservations recommended. *1339 Pearl St., no. 104. ☎ 707/224-9161. Entrees $12–$27. MC, V. Tues–Thurs 11:30am–2pm, 5:30–9pm; Fri–Sat 11:30am–2pm, 5:30–9:30pm. Map p 72.*

Ubuntu *VEGETARIAN* Chef Jeremy Fox's "vegetable-based" cuisine is so good, even die-hard carnivores come away raving. And Ubuntu won't break the bank, either. *1140 Main St. ☎ 707/251-5656. Most entrees less than $15. AE, V, DISC, MC. Breakfast & lunch Mon–Fri, dinner daily. Map p 72.*

★ Uva Trattoria *ITALIAN* At this lively restaurant with a hopping music scene, jazz musicians perform almost every evening, making diners' reasonably priced meals a special occasion. To start, order *arancini* (breaded, fried basil-risotto balls filled with Teleme cheese); follow that with a gourmet pizza or house-made pasta. *1040 Clinton St. ☎ 707/255-6646. Entrees $11–$21. AE, MC, V. Tues–Thurs 11:30am–10pm, Fri 11:30am–midnight, Sat 5pm–midnight, Sun 4–9pm. Map p 72.*

★ Villa Corona *MEXICAN* A funky, colorful local favorite hidden in the southwest corner of a strip mall. Order at the counter, then wait for the huge burritos, enchiladas, and chimichangas to arrive at your table. *3614 Bel Aire Plaza (on Trancas St.). ☎ 707/257-8685. Entrees $6–$11. MC, V. Daily 10am–8pm. Map p 72.*

★★ ZuZu *TAPAS* If you've had it with French and Italian fare and wine-country-themed dining rooms, this neighborhood haunt will refresh and restore you. Enjoy shockingly affordable Mediterranean-inspired small plates, like tangy paella, paired with intriguing by-the-glass wines and a friendly attitude. Desserts aren't as interesting, but with a bottle of wine and more delicious plates than you could possibly devour, who cares? Reservations not accepted. *829 Main St., Napa. ☎ 707/224-8555. Tapas $3–$14. MC, V. Mon–Thurs 11:30am–10pm, Fri 11:30am–11pm, Sat 4pm–11pm, Sun 4–10pm. Map p 72.*

La Toque features a truffle mushroom menu.

Sonoma

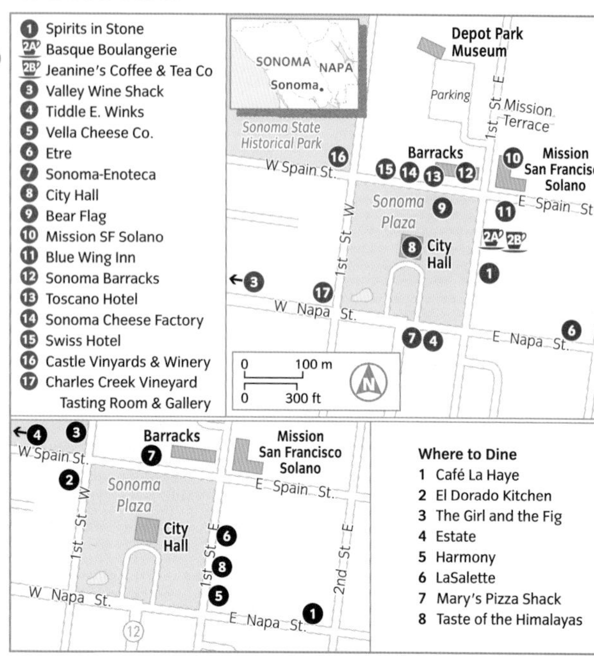

At the northern boundary of the Carneros District, along Highway 12, is the centerpiece of Sonoma Valley: the midsized town of Sonoma, which owes much of its appeal to Mexican general Mariano Guadalupe Vallejo. Vallejo fashioned this pleasant, slow-paced community after a typical Mexican village—right down to its central plaza, which still serves as Sonoma's geographical and commercial center. The plaza sits at the top of a "T" formed by Broadway (Hwy. 12) and Napa Street. Most of the surrounding streets form a grid pattern around this axis, making Sonoma easy to navigate. The plaza's Bear Flag Monument marks the spot where the crude Bear Flag was raised in 1846, signaling the end of Mexican rule; the symbol was later adopted by the state of California and placed on its flag. The 8-acre (3.2-hectare) park at the center of the plaza, complete with two ponds that are populated with ducks and geese, might make you want to take an afternoon siesta—but don't. There's too much to see here. Depending on your pace, allow a half- to a full day. START: **Sonoma Valley Visitors Bureau, 453 1st St. E. Distance: Less than a half-mile (.8km) of walking.**

❶ ★ **Spirits in Stone.** Cross the street to get to this gallery selling African sculptures, paintings, baskets, and ethnic jewelry. It'll make you want to go to Kenya. *452 1st St. E. ☎ 707/938-2200. www.spiritsinstone.com. Daily 10am–6pm (open until 8pm Fri–Sat).*

2A Basque Boulangerie. Grab lunch at this crowded little bakery with fresh sandwiches and good coffee. *460 1st St. E. ☎ 707/935-7687. Daily 7am–6pm. $.* Also offering exceptional coffee is tucked-away **2B Jeanine's Coffee & Tea Co.**, which roasts its own beans and shares a quirky storefront with a tobacconist. *464 1st St. E. ☎ 707/996-7573. $.*

❸ **Valley Wine Shack.** This little shop does offer bottles from the valley, but 80% of its wines come from Italy, Argentina, and elsewhere. The best part? Evening wine tastings cost just a dollar. *535 W Napa St. ☎ 707/938-7218. Daily 11am–7pm.*

❹ ★★★ kids **Tiddle E. Winks Vintage 5 & Dime.** A treasure trove of nostalgic paraphernalia. Marvel at the meticulously kept tchotchkes, including authentic college pennants (some date back to the 1940s), decades-old board games, and old-fashioned candies and sodas. This place is like a hands-on museum; kids love it as much as adults do. *115 E. Napa St. ☎ 707/939-6933. www.tiddlewinks.com. Sun–Thurs 11am–5pm, Fri–Sat 11am–6pm.*

❺ **Vella Cheese Co.** This store off the beaten path specializes in handmade cheeses. The friendly staffers are generous with the samples and always happy to educate you. *315 2nd St E. ☎ 707/938-3232. www.vellacheese.com. Mon–Sat 9:30–6pm.*

❻ ★★ **Etre.** Some store-design expert must've planned this delight-filled boutique; it's in a restored 1880s bungalow with a singular selection of hard-to-find home wares, books, cosmetics, fragrances, and other excellent ware. *156 E. Napa St. ☎ 707/939-2700. www.etresonoma.com. Mon–Fri 11am–6pm, Sat 10am–6pm, Sun 11am–5pm.*

❼ ★ **Sonoma-Enoteca.** Back on the plaza, a staffer behind this wine bar hands you a sheet listing the 20 wine selections of the day, all from small-lot wineries; your task is to select 6 to try. Also taste a variety of olive oils and browse the home decor selection. *35 E. Napa St. ☎ 707/935-1200. www.sonoma-enoteca.com. Wed–Mon 11am–6pm (last tasting at 5:30pm). $5 for 6 tastes, $10 with a cheese plate.*

Tiddle E. Winks is tchotchkes heaven.

Walk past 8 **City Hall,** which looks like something out of *Back to the Future,* and through a children's park, after which you'll see the 9 ★★ **Bear Flag Monument,** representing the end of Mexico's rule.

10 ★★★ kids **Mission San Francisco Solano.** The plaza's crowning jewel, and its reason for being, is this must-see landmark, known also as Sonoma Mission. *363 3rd St. W. ☎ 707/938-1519. www.parks.ca.gov. Daily 10am–5pm. $2 admission for adults. Children younger than 17 free. Admission also includes the Sonoma Barracks. For details, see p 49.*

11 ★ **Blue Wing Inn.** Across the street from the mission is this pleasantly dilapidated building, commissioned by Vallejo around 1840 to accommodate "emigrants and other travelers," as its inscription states. Notable guests included John C. Frémont (an explorer, general, senator, and presidential candidate) and

The Sonoma Mission and its trademark bell.

Western legend Kit Carson, as well as members of the Bear Flag Party—not to mention outlaws and bandits. Admire it from the outside. *133 E. Spain St.*

12 ★★ kids **Sonoma Barracks.** This Sonoma landmark is a must-see during your stroll through this historic town. *See p 49 for details.*

13 **Toscano Hotel.** Built in 1851 as a general store and library, this became a hotel in 1886. In 1972, the Sonoma League for Historic Preservation faithfully refurbished the building and opened it for public tours. *20 E. Spain St. ☎ 707/938-9560 (Sonoma State Historic Park). www.parks.ca.gov. Tours Sat & Sun 1–4pm, Mon 11am–1pm. Free.*

14 ★ **Sonoma Cheese Factory.** This huge marketplace, a 75-year-old institution, has more cheese varieties than conceivably imaginable. Many are available for sampling, alongside snacks and wine. There's also a small coffee and gelato bar. *2 E. Spain St. ☎ 800/535-2855. www.sonomajack.com. Daily 8:30am–5:30pm.*

15 **Swiss Hotel.** Built in 1840, the Swiss Hotel was home to Vallejo's brother and vintner. Though it has nothing to do with Switzerland (the name was adopted from another local hotel that burned down), it's been a hotel and restaurant since 1909. Step into the bar to see a bevy of historic Sonoma photos. *18 W. Spain St. ☎ 707/938-2884. www.swisshotelsonoma.com. See below for restaurant hours.*

16 **Castle Vineyards & Winery Tasting Room.** Tastings of

Sonoma Plaza marks the center of town.

European-style current releases are $5, but if you buy a bottle, the fee is waived. *122 W. Spain St. ☎ 707/996-1966. www.castlevineyards.com. Daily 10am–5pm.*

⑰ **Charles Creek Vineyard Tasting Room & Gallery.** Even if you're done tasting for the day, step in to see the cow made of corks. If you *are* tasting, it's $5 for about six samples—but that fee's refundable upon purchase. *483 1st St. W. ☎ 707/935-3848. www.charlescreek.com. Daily 11am–6pm.*

Where to Dine

★★ **Café La Haye** *CALIFORNIA/MEDITERRANEAN* Despite its limited hours and somewhat high prices, this tiny, artsy dining room is worth a visit for its top-notch food and wine. The baked almond-crusted goat cheese with roasted beets is a menu highlight. *140 E. Napa St. ☎ 707/935-5994. Entrees $17–$25. AE, MC, V. Dinner Tues–Sat. Map p 78.*

★★★ **El Dorado Kitchen** *CALIFORNIA* El Dorado Hotel's in-house establishment presents exquisite plates in a thoroughly comfortable space. The personalized six-course tasting menu is highly recommended. *405 1st St. W., Sonoma. ☎ 707/996-3030 or 800/289-3030. Entrees $21–$32; tasting menu $60. AE, MC, V. Lunch & dinner daily (bar after dusk). Map p 78.*

★★★ **Estate** *NEW AMERICA* Formerly called the General's Daughter, this turn-of-the-20th-century Victorian house was once the home of General Vallejo's daughter—but there's nothing passé about the all-organic menu and refined decor. An utterly romantic dining experience. *400 W. Spain St. ☎ 707/938-4004. Entrees $8–$22. MC, V. Dinner Tues–Sun. Map p 78.*

★★ **the girl and the fig** *FRENCH* This cozy restaurant's gotten a lot of attention, and for good reason: The food's fantastic and imaginative. After dining, sample cheeses at the *salon de fromage. 110 W. Spain St. ☎ 707/938-3634. Entrees $10–$25. AE, DISC, MC, V. Lunch & dinner daily. Brunch Sun. Map p 78.*

★★ **Harmony** *CALIFORNIA* Ledson Hotel's restaurant and lounge has marble decor and a seasonally changing menu. If it's available, try the ricotta-mint ravioli as an appetizer. *480 E. 1st St. ☎ 707/996-9779. AE, DISC, MC, V. Lunch & dinner Wed–Mon. Map p 78.*

★ **LaSalette** *PORTUGESE* One of wine country's only Portuguese restaurants has a pleasant dining room decorated with hand-painted tiles. Choose from a large selection of cheeses and ports for a perfect ending to the inspired dishes. *452 E. 1st St. ☎ 707/938-1927. Entrees $11–$25. AE, MC, V. Lunch & dinner daily. Map p 78.*

kids **Mary's Pizza Shack** *ITALIAN* Belying its name, this place has more pasta and sandwich choices than it does pizza options. Neither is it a shack; its bright, inviting interior is quite comfortable. *8 W. Spain St. ☎ 707/938-8300. Entrees $6–$15. Pizzas $6–$24. AE, DISC, MC, V. Lunch & dinner daily. Map p 78.*

Taste of the Himalayas *INDIAN/NEPALI/TIBETAN* This friendly restaurant, whose founders are descendents of Nepali sherpas, is a good place to try momos, curry, or tandoori. *464 E. 1st St. ☎ 707/996-1161. Entrees $9.50–$18. AE, MC, V. Lunch & dinner daily. Map p 78.*

St. Helena

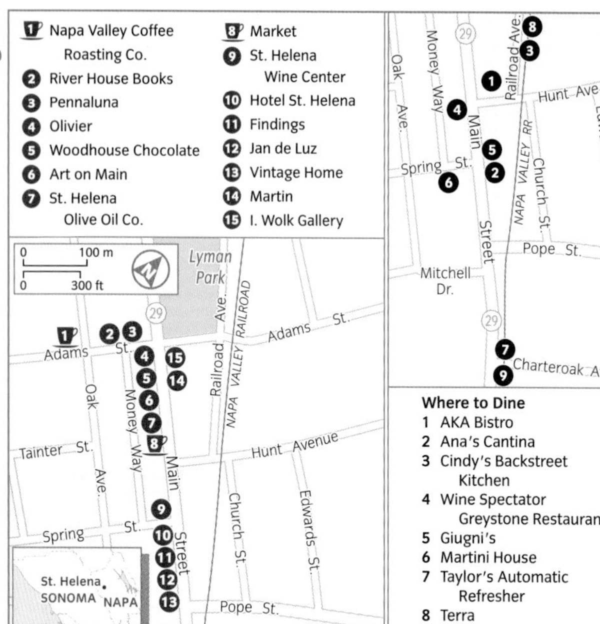

A first glance of St. Helena (say "Saint Hel-een-uh") gives the impression that this could be a pleasant Anytown, USA. But a step into any of its myriad boutiques, galleries, and showrooms reveals otherwise; their brand of ritziness couldn't be afforded many other places. This walking tour starts just off Main Street, then takes you through a foodie's delight. Crossing the street allows you to take in wine country's artsy side. Allow a half-day. START: **Napa Valley Coffee Roasting Co., 1400 Oak Ave. St. Distance: Less than a half-mile (.8km) walk.**

1 ★ Napa Valley Coffee Roasting Co. Coffee and pastries fuel you in this relaxing and sunny ambience, bettered by an antique coffee press on display in the back and a communal book swap in the front. *1400 Oak Ave. St. ☎ 707/963-4491. $.*

2 ★ River House Books. Peruse the well-rounded travel and architecture sections at this inviting bookstore. *1234 Adams St. ☎ 707/963-1163. www.riverhousebooksnapavalley.com. Mon–Sat 10am–5:30pm, Sun 11am–4pm.*

3 ★ Pennaluna. A unique and global selection of gifts, bedding, and kid stuff. *1220 Adams St.* ☎ *707/963-3115. Mon–Sat 10am–5pm, Sun 11am–5pm.*

❹ ★★★ **Olivier.** This beautiful French-style store is where to sample a wide array of epicurean savories. The big copper vats lining the walls are actually olive oil dispensers; feel free to mix your own. Olivier also offers bath goods, as well as upscale dishware imported from Provence. *1375 Main St.* ☎ *707/967-8777. www.oliviernapavalley.com. Mon–Sat 10am–6pm (5pm on Sun).*

❺ ★★ **Woodhouse Chocolate.** This salon showcases gorgeous handmade chocolates: Try the fan-shaped Thai ginger confection or the brown-butter *ganache* ($1.85 each). These decadent treats in delicate boxes can be shipped anywhere in America. *1367 Main St.* ☎ *800/966-3468. www.woodhousechocolate.com. Daily 10:30am–5:30pm.*

❻ **Art on Main.** A small gallery with striking art is a draw for fans of modern or wine-related works. *1359 Main St.* ☎ *707/963-3350. www.imagesnapavalley.com. Daily 10am–5pm.*

The road to St. Helena.

❼ ★★ **St. Helena Olive Oil Co.** Between stone walls, helpful staffers guide you through tastings of vinegars, honeys, fruit relishes, compotes, flavored salts, tapenades, syrups, sauces—oh, and olive oils. *1351 Main St.* ☎ *707/968-9260. Daily 10:30am–5pm.*

❽ ★ **Market.** This long restaurant with a wooden bar and stone walls has helpful waitstaff and playful American cuisine. Try the "Very Adult Macaroni and Cheese," and save room for desserts that'll take you back to childhood: homespun cotton candy (made at your table), s'mores, or butterscotch pudding. *1347 Main St.* ☎ *707/963-3799. Entrees $9.50–$20. AE, MC, V. Daily 11:30am–10pm. Map p 82.*

Sample olive oil at St. Helena Olive Oil Co.

❾ **St. Helena Wine Center.** More than your typical wine shop, this one has rare and high-end wines in the back (think Screaming Eagle), unique vodkas (like Charbay's green tea flavor), and yummy liqueurs. *1321 Main St.* ☎ *707/963-1313. www.shwc.com. Daily 10am–5:30pm (until 6pm during peak months).*

❿ **Hotel St. Helena.** Step into this dark B&B to see the eccentric, almost creepy, decor (old dolls and mounted animal heads abound) and maybe to sip coffee at the small wine bar. *1309 Main St.* ☎ *707/963-4388. www.hotelsthelena.com. Wine bar daily 3–8pm.*

Tra Vigne is a local favorite.

⓫ **Findings.** Eclectic offerings combine the antique and the new; check out the jewelry, frames, and furniture. *1269 Main St. ☎ 707/963-6000. Daily 10am–6pm (until 7pm Fri–Sat).*

⓬ ★ **Jan de Luz.** This impressive home-decor store features custom-embroidered table linens, upscale furnishings, even fountains and fireplaces. *1219 Main St. ☎ 707/963-1550. www.jandeluz.com. Daily 9:30am–5:30pm.*

⓭ ★ **Vintage Home.** An inspiring store with distinctive home goods like pillows, linens, candles, and books. *1201 Main St. ☎ 707/963-7423. Daily 10am–5:30pm (Sun until 4pm).*

Now that you've walked the most interesting part of Main Street's south side, cross the street and slip into ⓮ ★★ **Martin.** A true showroom, this lavish store displays everything from art books to large furnishings. *1350 Main St. ☎ 707/967-8787. Wed–Mon 10am–6pm (Sun until 4pm).*

⓯ ★ **I. Wolk gallery.** A sparse space with lighthearted art. *1354 Main St. ☎ 707/963-8801. www.iwolkgallery.com. Daily 10am–5:30pm.*

Where to Dine

AKA Bistro NEW AMERICAN This bistro from SoCal restaurateur Robert Simon is at once casual and sophisticated. It's got an impressive selection of local wines, and Chef Chris Kennedy is known for his modern takes on American classics. *☎ 707/967-8111. Entrees $31–$60. AE, DC, DISC, MC, V. Lunch & dinner Wed–Sat. Dinner only Sun–Tues.*

Ana's Cantina MEXICAN A friendly joint with great Mexican food, billiards, darts, beer, and a fun crowd. Live entertainment Wednesday through Saturday. *1205 Main St. ☎ 707/963-4921. Entrees $2–$7. MC, V. Lunch & dinner Thurs–Mon. Bar daily. Map p 82.*

★★ **Cindy's Backstreet Kitchen** *CALIFORNIA/AMERICAN* An upscale, down-home kind of place, this restaurant with a darling dining room presents unfussy yet creative dishes made with local ingredients. *1327 Railroad Ave. ☎ 707/963-1200. Entrees $11–$25. DC, DISC, MC, V. Lunch & dinner daily. Map p 82.*

Giugni's *SANDWICHES* Locals come here for a satisfying bite and an escape from pretense; there's always a long line at the counter. Don't be surprised if you get hit by a touch of nostalgia here: Historical political posters clutter the walls, and among the grocery items for sale are Cokes in glass bottles and old-time jawbreakers. *1227 Main St. ☎ 707/963-3421. Sandwiches $5.45–$6.45.*

No credit cards. Breakfast, lunch & dinner daily. Map p 82.

★★ **Martini House** *NEW AMERICAN* One of the area's more renowned restaurants, Martini House is well designed both in terms of decor and cuisine. Chef/owner Todd Humphries's comprehensive seasonal tasting menus ($59–$67) can be ordered with a sommelier wine pairing, which can bump the per-person price up to $100. There's also an excellent prix-fixe dinner ($49), or just order an a la carte entree with one of the divine soups or salads. *1245 Spring St. ☎ 707/963-2233. Entrees $25–$34. AE, DC, DISC, MC, V. Lunch & dinner daily. Map p 82.*

★ **Taylor's Automatic Refresher** *DINER* It isn't every day that a roadside burger shack gets a spread in **Food & Wine** magazine, but then, this outdoor diner built in 1949 isn't your average fast-food stop. Its excellent hamburgers on soft but sturdy buns are known the valley over. Vegetarians need not sigh when their dining companions opt for Taylor's: There are at least five veggie options, including a burger and a taco. *933 Main St. ☎ 707/963-3486. Entrees $5–$16. AE, MC, V. Lunch & dinner daily. Map p 82.*

★★ **Terra** *NEW AMERICAN* Terra manages to be humble even though it serves some of northern California's most extraordinary food. The dining room is rustic-romantic with stone walls. The menu, by James Beard Award–winning chef Hiro Sone, reflects the region's bounty as well as European and Japanese influences. Desserts are sublime, especially orange risotto in brandy snap with passion-fruit sauce. Reservations recommended. *1345 Railroad Ave. ☎ 707/963-8931. Main courses $19–$36. AE, DC, MC, V. Dinner Wed–Mon. Map p 82.*

★★ **Tra Vigne** *ITALIAN* Its combination of good food and high energy makes Tra Vigne a long-standing favorite among visitors and locals. Whether guests dine in the Tuscan courtyard or in the enormous dining room, they're treated to wonderful bread with house-made olive oils and robust California dishes cooked Italian-style. Try the heirloom tomato salad, the daily oven-roasted pizza special, or fresh pasta. Reservations recommended. Adjoining **Cantinetta** offers sandwiches and lighter meals. *1050 Charter Oak Ave. ☎ 707/963-4444. Main courses $16–$29. DC, DISC, MC, V. Lunch & dinner daily.*

★★ **Wine Spectator Greystone Restaurant** *CALIFORNIA* You know a restaurant at the Culinary Institute of America (where culinary pros go to become executive chefs) has got to be good—and is it ever. Watch as chefs prepare small plates, then try them with a new-to-you wine. *1304 Main St. ☎ 707/967-1010. Entrees $21–$40. AE, DC, DISC, MC, V. Lunch & dinner daily. Map p 82.*

The heirloom tomato and mushroom salad at Martini House.

Healdsburg

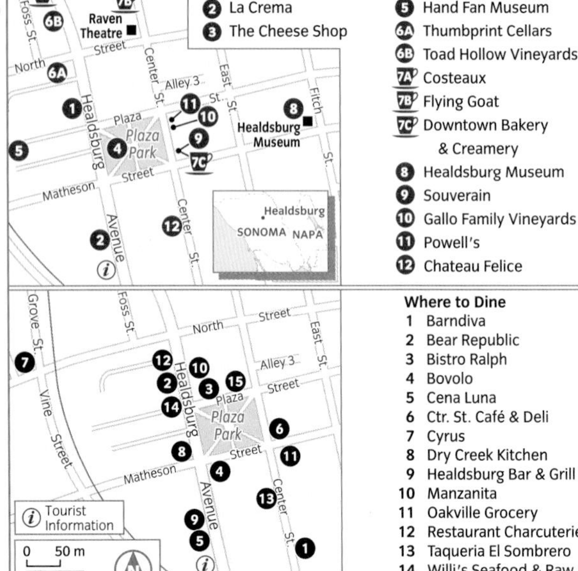

Healdsburg is a town on the rise. Not long ago, it was just another agricultural Sonoma borough, content to quietly produce some of the world's best food and wine. But word got out about where all that refined alimentation was coming from, and local tourism-minded entrepreneurs picked up on the excitement. Hence, recent arrivals of fancy hotels (especially Les Mars and Hotel Healdsburg) and their respective restaurants (Cyrus and Dry Creek Kitchen) drew big names like Martha Stewart and Bob Dylan, definitively stamping the town onto the jet-setter map. And Healdsburg's status just keeps rising, thanks to all the famous wineries that keep opening tasting rooms downtown, new shops targeting well-heeled patrons, and perennial attractions like the jazz festival each June and the twice-weekly organic farmers' market (p 20). Still, Healdsburg gracefully maintains a friendly small-town personality that also has reverence for the area's rich history—and just a touch of quirkiness. This full-day walking tour highlights the town's best tasting rooms and historical spots. START: **Toad Hollow Vineyards's tasting room, 409A Healdsburg Ave. Distance: Less than a half-mile (.8km).**

1 ★ **Kendall-Jackson.** Try one of America's most recognizable wine brands (p 151) in this tasting room. Your eyes will be drawn to the particleboard floor and the agreeable selection of wine-related merchandise, but once your nose whiffs the wines, your body and soul will be stationed at the expertly staffed bar. Print free tasting coupons from the website. *337 Healdsburg Ave. ☎ 707/433-7102. www.kj.com. Daily 10am–5pm. $5 for 4 tastes ($15 for reserves).*

2 ★★ **La Crema.** Modern design sets this tasting room apart, as do coastal artisan wines. The winery specializes in Burgundian varietals, so try chardonnay and pinot noir. *235 Healdsburg Ave. ☎ 707/431-9400. www.lacrema.com. Thurs–Tues 10:30am–5:30pm. Closed Wed. Free tastings.*

3 **The Cheese Shop.** An intimate shop just off the plaza that specializes in artisan cheeses from South America. There's also a variety of local *fromage* and a great olive selection. You can taste for free before purchasing. Mon–Sat 10am–6pm. *423 Center St. ☎ 707/433-4998.*

4 ★ **Plaza Park.** There are plenty of picnic benches in Healdsburg's acre-wide focal point. At this site of Healdsburg's fairs, festivals, and concerts, find the Olympic flame statue honoring local athletes. On the other end of the park is the 1847 millstone from Cyrus Alexander's gristmill. In between, there's a fountain and palm, pine, and redwood trees.

5 ★ **Hand Fan Museum.** Take a break from sampling wine in this tiny room, which displays a multicultural collection of beautiful hand fans, some dating back to the 1700s. *327A Healdsburg Ave. ☎ 707/431-2500. www.handfanmuseum.com. Wed–Sun 11am–4pm, or by appointment. Free.*

6A ★ **Thumbprint Cellars.** A tasting lounge with sleek furnishings, a youthful vibe, and handcrafted small-lot wines, Thumbprint holds occasional events like blending seminars and winemakers' dinners, so call (or go online) in advance to find out what's going on and whether you need a reservation. *36 North St. ☎ 707/433-2393. www.thumbprintcellars.com. Daily 11am–6pm. Free tastings.*

OR:

6B ★ **Toad Hollow Vineyards.** This tasting room is a playful place

The sidewalks of Healdsburg are perfect for a stroll.

Healdsburg's Best Shopping

Though they're not explicit stops on this tour, Healdsburg is packed with inspired shops; among the best are alluring **Evans Designs Gallery** (*☎ 707/473-0963*), exotic **Baksheesh** (*☎ 707/473-8008*) and **Spirits in Stone** (*☎ 707/723-1723*), haven-like **Toyon Books** (*☎ 707/433-9270*), and sleek **Lime Stone** (*☎ 707/433-3080*). For specialty wines, try **The Wine Shop** (*☎ 707/433-0433*) or **Thirty-Four North** (*☎ 707/473-0808*).

to start your day. Frog-themed everything is everywhere, but the wines served over a river-stone bar focus attention into your glass. A few food items, such as balsamic vinegar, are also available. *409A Healdsburg Ave. ☎ 707/431-8667. www.toadhollow.com. Daily 10:30am–5:30pm. Free tastings.*

7A ★★ **Costeaux French Bakery.** If the wine's leaving you in need of a midday coffee or pastry, you're in luck: Healdsburg has excellent cafes and bakeries. Costeaux, a sunny spot beloved by locals, has been a Healdsburg tradition since 1923, with its breads, soups, salads, and desserts. Fun fact: Costeaux claims the record for having baked the world's largest pumpkin pie. Look for the 6-foot-3-inch (1.9m) pie tin. *417 Healdsburg Ave. ☎ 707/433-1913. $.* Devotees consider 7B ★ **Flying Goat Coffee** California's best java; they'll drive miles for a cup. *324 Center St. & 419 Center St. ☎ 707/433-3599. $.* Aromatic 7C **Downtown Bakery & Creamery** sells fantastic sticky buns, fruity pastries, and fresh breads. *308A Center St. ☎ 707/431-2719. $.*

8 ★★★ kids **Healdsburg Museum.** From Center Street, turn right onto Matheson Street, and as you pass St. Paul's Episcopal Church, admire its stained-glass windows. A few steps farther and you're at Healdsburg's museum. Andrew Carnegie donated $10,000 in 1909 to make this neoclassical revival–style building a public library, so its entryway still bears his name. Inside, artifacts document local history, from Pomo Indian times to the town's former life as Rancho Sotoyome, to the squatter squabbles known as the "Westside Wars." One man who emerged victorious after the land conflicts became Healdsburg's founder in 1857: Ohio entrepreneur Harmon Heald. The museum also recounts the period after Healdsburg's incorporation with photos, period costumes, and even 19th-century shoes. Since it's also a historical society, hands-on research facilities with microfilmed newspapers and official county records are available. *221 Matheson St. ☎ 707/431-3325. www.healdsburgmuseum.org. Thurs–Sun 11am–4pm. Free.*

9 ★★ **Souverain.** Formerly called Cellar 360, this spot is now the boutique tasting room for winemaker Souverain. Drop in to taste a variety of Alexander Valley wines either at the bar or at a cocktail tables. *308B Center St. ☎ 707/433-2822. www.worldwineestates.com. Daily 11am–6pm. Tastings around $10 (various tasting options, one includes a*

How often do you get to walk to several tasting rooms all within blocks of each other?

cheese pairing); refundable with purchase.

10 ★★ Gallo Family Vineyards. At this new tasting room, try a three-wine flight or enjoy individual tastes while eager employees explain what you're sipping. If you're tired of standing over a bar, there are sit-down tables. *320 Center St. ☎ 707/433-2458. www.gallofamily.com. Daily 10am–6pm. Tastings free–$12. Also see p 146.*

11 ★★ kids Powell's Sweet Shoppe. Even grown-ups will feel like a kid in this neon-bright candy store. The term "sweet memories" turns literal here, since Powell's sells candies that haven't been seen since the 1950s. While nostalgic confections define the merchandise, they're interspersed with enduring favorites like bubble-gum cigars, jump-rope-length licorice ropes, and, of course, ice cream. The 1971 version of ***Willy Wonka & the Chocolate Factory*** plays continuously in the back. *322 Center St. ☎ 707/431-2784. www.powellssweetshoppe.com. Daily 10am–9pm (Sun until 8pm). $.*

12 ★★ Chateau Felice. This funky tasting room presents Chalk Hill wines made in the French tradition. The boutique winery makes only 3,000 cases per year; taste their contents over the copper bar (check out the collection of antique bottle openers) or settle in with a glass on the patio. *223 Center St. ☎ 707/431-9010. www.chateaufelice.com. Daily 11am–7pm. Free tastings; wines by the glass $3–$8.*

Where to Dine

★★ Barndiva *CALIFORNIA* The philosophy here is "eat the view." Barndiva's deep-red exterior looks like a tidy barn; inside is a flower-and-art-filled space with modern decor. Out back is a walled dining garden. The restaurant insists on using only sustainably produced, seasonally available ingredients from local sources. Potpies are good, but save room for the spicy, out-of-this-world chocolate orbit cake. *231 Center St. ☎ 707/431-0100. Entrees $10–$28. AE, MC, V. Lunch & dinner Wed–Sun. Map p 86.*

★ kids Bear Republic Brewing Co. *AMERICAN* A lively, casual brewpub with appetizers galore, creative sandwiches, and a huge selection of handcrafted ale. Decor includes old bicycles hanging from the ceiling and a California-themed agricultural mural. *345 Healdsburg Ave. ☎ 707/433-2337. Entrees $8.95–$17. MC, V. Lunch & dinner daily. Map p 86.*

★ Bistro Ralph *FRENCH* In this minimalist white restaurant, the ever-changing menu features globally influenced starters, pricy meat-oriented entrees, and a Healdsburg-based wine list. Reservations recommended. *109 Plaza St. ☎ 707/433-1380. Entrees $17–$36.*

Thai marinated lobster, avocado, melon, and fresh hearts of palm at Cyrus.

MC, V. Lunch & dinner Mon–Sat. Map p 86.

★ **Bovolo** *BREAKFAST & ITALIAN* A cute 24-seat spot in Plaza Farms makes everything, including gelato, from scratch. Breakfast options are unique—try the lavender-buttermilk waffle—as are antipasti (like quinoa caponata), sandwiches, pasta, and pizza. No escargot, although Bovolo is Italian for "snail." ***106 Matheson St.*** ☎ ***707/431-2962. Entrees $6.50–$12. MC, V. Breakfast, lunch & dinner daily. Map p 86.***

★★ **Cena Luna** *ITALIAN* Classy with dark-wood furnishings, Cena Luna changes its menu weekly, but fresh homemade pasta is always amazing. The husband-and-wife chefs know what they're doing. ***241 Healdsburg Ave.*** ☎ ***707/433-6000. Entrees $14–$22. AE, DC, MC, V. Dinner Mon–Sat. Map p 86.***

★ kids **Center Street Café & Deli** *AMERICAN* Step in here and be swept back to the 1950s; whimsical knickknacks and nostalgic what-have-yous are playfully placed all over this big, fun dining room. Breakfasts are delish, deli lunches are made to order, and an old-fashioned soda fountain serves luscious shakes. ***304 Center St.*** ☎ ***707/433-7224. Entrees $4.50–$12. AE, DISC, MC, V. Breakfast & lunch daily. Dinner in the summer. Map p 86.***

★★★ **Cyrus** *CALIFORNIA-FRENCH* The county's latest shining-star chef, young Douglas Keane, formerly of SF's lauded Gary Danko, is making a loudly heard splash in his new kitchen; there are whispers that he may be giving French Laundry—and Napa—a run for their money. In beautiful Les Mars Hotel this sophisticated restaurant named for pioneer Cyrus Alexander offers prix-fixe cuisine, but you can mix and match the amount and kinds of courses you order. Order wine; the food pairs exceptionally well. Reservations recommended. ***29 North St.*** ☎ ***707/433-3311. Tasting menus $102–$130. AE, MC, V. Dinner daily. Map p 86.***

★★★ **Dry Creek Kitchen** *CALIFORNIA* Celeb chef Charlie Palmer's only California venture is a successful melding of splendid cuisine and excellent service. Within hip Hotel Healdsburg, the kitchen turns out inspired, well-presented dishes based on what's seasonally relevant and available. ***317 Healdsburg Ave.*** ☎ ***707/431-0330. Entrees $26–$39. AE, MC, V. Dinner Mon–Thurs. Brunch & dinner Fri–Sun. Map p 86.***

kids **Healdsburg Bar & Grill** *AMERICAN* This all-American restaurant has a thorough menu for kids and a refreshing on-tap selection (Guinness and Sierra Nevada included) for parents. There's a strong do-it-yourself vibe, from ordering at the kitchen to making your own Bloody Mary (Sat & Sun). Sporadic live music really gets the place going. ***245 Healdsburg Ave. ☎ 707/433-3333. Entrees $10–$14. MC, V. Lunch & dinner daily. Map p 86.***

★★ Manzanita *CALIFORNIA* Named after a type of tree and accented with woodsy elements amid stylish modernity, the mood's set as soon as you walk in. Once seated, an inspired menu (which changes weekly) and gracious owners take care of the rest. Try anything wood-fired. ***336 Healdsburg Ave. ☎ 707/433-8111. Entrees $12–$28. AE, DISC, MC, V. Lunch & dinner Wed–Sun. Map p 86.***

★★ Oakville Grocery *CALIFORNIA* One of four stores bearing this name this outpost has an al fresco eating area that's always packed on sunny days. Before settling on your order, browse in awe at the fascinating gamut of colorful gourmet options in this small but impressive market. Try a sandwich or pizza with wine from the tasting bar. ***124 Matheson St. ☎ 707/433-3200. Entrees $8–$16. AE, MC, V. Breakfast, lunch & dinner daily. Map p 86.***

★ Restaurant Charcuterie *FRENCH-MEDITERRANEAN* A small restaurant whose offerings center around cured pork. Decor consists of hundreds of cute piggy figurines, which is slightly disconcerting. Still, service is friendly and there are enough options if pig's not your preference. ***335 Healdsburg Ave. ☎ 707/431-7213. Entrees $9–$25. AE, MC, V. Lunch & dinner daily. Map p 86.***

★ Taqueria El Sombrero *MEXICAN* This low-key joint, popular with locals, has all the expected Mexican fare, plus breakfast and seafood. ***245 Center St. ☎ 707/433-3818. Entrees $2–$10. DISC, MC, V. Breakfast, lunch & dinner daily. Map p 86.***

★ Willi's Seafood & Raw Bar *SMALL PLATES* An energetic vibe permeates Willi's dining room, bar, and outdoor patio. If you want to hunker down with your own big meal, this isn't the place—but if you want to swap tastes of fancily prepared seafood like miso-glazed sturgeon, Willi's fits the bill. ***403 Healdsburg Ave. ☎ 707/433-9191. Small plates $10–$15. DISC, MC, V. Lunch & dinner Wed–Mon. Map p 86.***

★★ Zin *NEW AMERICAN* With exposed concrete walls hung with big semi-abstract vineyard paintings, Zin is a stylish place to eat. Chef Jeff Mall trained under Bradley Ogden, a fact reflected in his culinary creations. Ask about blue-plate specials or try staples like beer-battered green beans and egg-noodle pappardelle. To go with your meal, order—you guessed it—zin. ***344 Center St. ☎ 707/473-0946. Entrees $15–$29. AE, MC, V. Lunch & dinner Mon–Fri. Dinner Sat–Sun. Map p 86.***

After Dark: Raven Theater

The 500-seat pulse point of the town's performing arts scene stages uproarious theatric and stirring music performances. Check the website for show times. ***115 North St. ☎ 707/433-6335. www.raventheater.org & www.ravenplayers.org.***

Guerneville

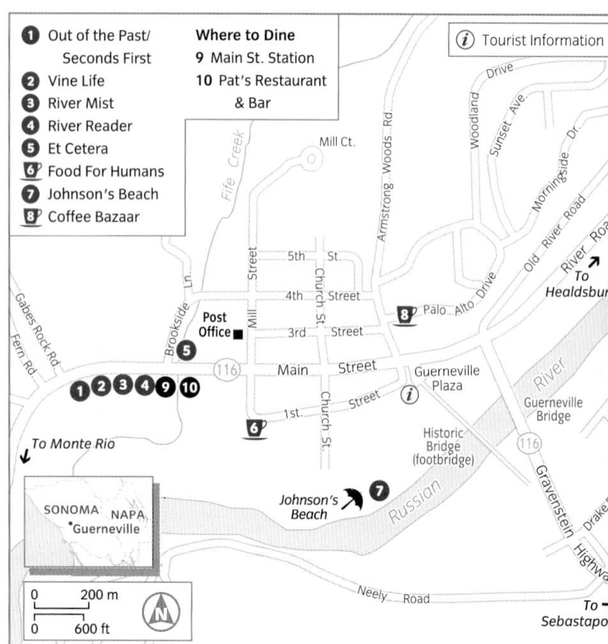

A mystical redwood forest enchants visitors as they make the winding drive into Guerneville. The town itself (say "Gurn-ville," or risk identifying yourself as an out-of-towner by elongating the middle "e") is a throwback to everything small-town America used to be—except for its progressive orientation. Rainbow flags and signs proclaiming "This is a hate-free zone" adorn many businesses—a testament to the village's largely gay and lesbian population. Many storekeepers keep their pets beside them as they regale tourists with little-known facts about the area. This half-day walking tour, rather than a hyper-structured itinerary, is more a leisurely stroll down Main Street; part of your fun should be wandering into boutiques that appeal directly to you in addition to the ones listed here. START: **Where Highway 116 becomes Main Street, just after the Safeway grocery store. Walk east. Trip Length: Less than a half-mile (.8km).**

1 Out of the Past and **Seconds First** are two businesses housed in one incense-scented storefront. You'll find oddities like Betty Boop light-switch covers and hilarious fridge magnets, plus peculiar posters and vintage clothes. *16365 Main St. ☎ 707/869-2211. Daily 11am–6pm.*

❷ ★★ **Vine Life.** A haven for interior decorating fanatics, oenophiles, and foodies, this shabby-chic boutique sells specialty food items, hand-printed stationery, local wines, and other little surprises. *16359 Main St. ☎ 707/869-1234. www.vinelifegifts.com. Daily 11am–5pm (6pm during summer).*

❸ **River Mist.** Wares here include artsy jewelry and decorative collectibles. Even if you don't intend to buy, step inside to see the mural depicting the town and to pat Yip, the resident Pomeranian. *16357 Main St. ☎ 707/869-0475. Summer hours Mon–Thurs 11am–5pm, Fri–Sun 11am–7pm. Winter hours Wed–Mon 11am–5pm.*

❹ ★ **River Reader.** This simple, straightforward bookshop has an excellent collection of progressive and alternative literature, a small kids' section, a local-author shelf, and a newsstand with gay-themed magazines front and center. A few ethnic gifts, too. Be sure to give Callie the calico cat some attention; she basks in it. *16355 Main St. ☎ 707/869-2240. Daily 10am–6pm (5pm on Sun).*

❺ ★ **Et Cetera.** Et Cetera showcases an inspired mix of ethereal Asian-inspired homewares and earthy furnishings. *16270 Main St. ☎ 707/869-5808. www.etcetc1.com. Daily 10am–6pm.*

Guerneville is a small town with a big, open mind.

Veer off Main Street to find:

❻ **Food For Humans,** a natural foods market that stocks organic produce, snacks, and eco-friendly merchandise. *16385 1st St. ☎ 707/869-3612. $.* Buy a sandwich or a wrap, crackers, cheese, and fruit, then tote your picnic down to ❼ kids **Johnson's Beach** on the Russian River, where you can take a dip or admire Guerneville Bridge. There's a kiddie pool, so bring the little ones. *16241 1st St. www.johnsonsbeach.com. Daily 10am–6pm, mid-May to early Oct.* For a pick-me-up after your riverside picnic, try the java or ice cream at eclectic ❽ **Coffee Bazaar.** *14045 Armstrong Woods Rd. ☎ 707/869-9706.*

Where to Dine

Main Street Station *ITALIAN* This corner restaurant is undeniably upbeat. Menu options include pizza, sandwiches, salads, and pasta. Don't miss the evening jazz performances. *16280 Main St. ☎ 707/869-0501. Entrees $6–$16. AE, MC, V. Lunch & dinner daily. Map p 92.*

Pat's Restaurant & Bar *AMERICAN* This basic down-home diner has an adjoining woodsy bar. Don't let the tough-looking staff fool you; they're as sweet and professional as can be. *16236 Main St. ☎ 707/869-9904. Entrees $4–$11. Cash only. Breakfast & lunch daily. Map p 92.*

Yountville

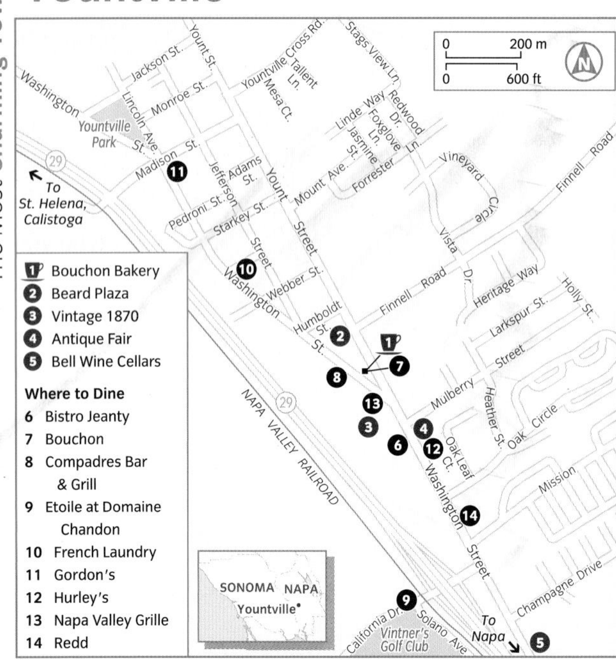

Pioneer George C. Yount, known for having planted the valley's first grapevine, is this town's namesake and founder. Since before its 1855 inception, Yountville (say "Yont-ville") has been a premier winemaking region. In 1973, prestigious French champagne house Moët et Chandon chose Yountville as the site for its U.S. expansion, and Domaine Chandon was born. About 20 years later, chef Thomas Keller bought a small restaurant called The French Laundry. Much of the sophistication that now defines Yountville sprang up around these two institutions; since their establishment, other prominent winemakers and chefs have moved in so that the mile-long walking town is now an unparalleled dining destination. When visiting, notice the locals; there are about 3,000 of them, and they range from world-famous chefs to immigrant grape pickers to young skateboarders to patriotic veterans who live at America's largest veterans home, right here in town. After dark, bars become lively. This tour is relatively short, because tiny Yountville's main attractions are unarguably its restaurants. (See "Where to Dine," below, to plan your dining experiences.) **START: Bouchon Bakery, 6528 Washington St. Distance: Less than a mile (1.6km) of walking.**

Yountville is tiny, but worth a visit and a stroll.

Grab a morning pastry at Thomas Keller's 1 ★ **Bouchon Bakery.** Buying from the small, usually packed boulangerie is an affordable way to sample the creations of America's most famous chef. The confections here are as much a treat for the eyes as they are for the palate; even if you don't partake, at least gaze at the perfectly laid-out sweets in the glass case. There's no inside seating, so sit outside on a bench or stroll while savoring a buttery croissant, a signature chocolate bouchon, or impossibly fresh bread. *6528 Washington St. ☎ 707/944-2253. $.*

As you walk out of Bouchon Bakery, turn right to explore:

❷ **Beard Plaza.** The myriad art galleries in this courtyard complex were built in the late 1980s by the Beard family. The works for sale in these intimate exhibition spaces (like **RAS** and **Images**) are the creations of talented glass artists, painters, sculptors, jewelers, and ceramicists. Much of the art is modern or wine-inspired. *6540 Washington St.*

Walk southward down Washington and on your left, you'll soon see:

❸ **Vintage 1870.** This swap-meet-style shopping center is in a historic brick building; the onetime Groezinger Winery was built in 1870 and at its height was California's largest winery. Foodies will want to check out **Cravings,** which offers an array of food items, including many mustard varieties. Among the other shopping options: several art galleries, a fun shoe shop, a kids' clothing store, and a wine room. *6525 Washington St., ☎ 707/944-2451. www.vintage1870.com. Daily 10am–5:30pm.*

Continue down Washington and you'll hit:

❹ **Antique Fair.** This gem of an antiques store showcases nostalgic artifacts from bygone eras. Though pricey, seeing these fascinating items that look like they could have come out of a wealthy 19th-century manor is worth stepping in for. *6512 Washington St. ☎ 707/944-8440. www.antiquefair.com. Daily 10am–6pm.*

Walk far down Washington and a bit off the beaten path (consider driving) to:

❺ ★ **Bell Wine Cellars.** This small artisanal winery has a tasting bar in a warehouselike room among casks and barrels. But the wine's excellent, and so's the company: South African owner/winemaker Anthony Bell is quite liable to come out and converse about the ardent passion he has for crafting each wine he'll have you taste. Reservations recommended. *6200 Washington St. ☎ 707/944-1673. www.bellwine.com. Daily 10:30am–4pm.*

Where to Dine

★ **Bistro Jeanty** *FRENCH* This casual, warm bistro, with muted buttercup walls and a patio area, serves seriously rich French comfort food for legions of fans. Think tomato soup in a puff pastry, crème brûlée (made with a thin layer of chocolate cream), and rib-gripping free-for-alls including coq au vin, cassoulet, and a thick-cut pork chop with jus. Quality has suffered since Jeanty has branched out to three restaurants, but when the kitchen is on, it's still a fine place to sup. *6510 Washington St. ☎ 707/944-0103. Entrees $18–$38. AE, MC, V. Lunch & dinner daily. Map p 94.*

★★ **Bouchon** *FRENCH* Dark and rich surroundings complement attentive service and a refined menu developed by Thomas Keller. The *gnocchi a la parisienne,* made with wheat instead of potato, melt in your mouth. Don't neglect the superlative wine list. A bonus, especially for restless residents and off-duty restaurant staff, is the late hours, although the menu becomes more limited when the crowds dwindle. *6534 Washington St. ☎ 707/944-8037. Entrees $17–$34. AE, MC, V. Lunch & dinner daily. Map p 94.*

★ **Compadres Bar & Grill** *MEXICAN* A casual spot at which to enjoy a margarita or local microbrew on the outdoor patio with Adirondack chairs and two wood-burning fire pits. Bonus: nightly marshmallow roasts (free!). *6539 Washington St. ☎ 707/944-2406. Entrees $8–$20. AE, DC, DISC, MC, V. Breakfast, lunch & dinner daily. Map p 94.*

★★ **Etoile at Domaine Chandon** *CALIFORNIA FRENCH* Domaine Chandon, one of very few wineries that offers on-site fine dining, maintains a classy, conservative dining room as well as a gorgeous outdoor space. The vanilla-scented kabocha squash ravioli, paired with 1997 Chandon Vintage Brut, is unlike anything you've ever tasted. Cap off your meal with a chocolate crepe made with coconut cream

Bouchon is a bread heaven straight from Thomas Keller.

Bistro Jeanty is a Yountville staple.

and caramelized bananas—pair it with Chandon Riche bubbly, and you'll leave walking on air. *1 California Dr. ☎ 707/204-7529. Entrees $15–$30. AE, DC, DISC, MC, V. Lunch & dinner Thurs–Mon. Map p 94.*

★★★ The French Laundry AMERICAN-FRENCH Not much has been left unsaid about what's often called the world's best restaurant. The interior is small and fancy, service is unparalleled, and the food—well, let's just say it can be described in two words: Thomas Keller. The chef's signature nine-course degustation or vegetarian tasting menu changes daily based on his ingenious whims; book well in advance—the waiting list to dine here is months long. *6640 Washington St. ☎ 707/944-2380. Typical dinner for 2: $480. AE, MC, V. Dinner daily. Lunch Fri–Sun. Dress code enforced. Map p 94.*

Gordon's CALIFORNIA Part country store, part deli, and part casual restaurant. One wall is lined with an intriguing collection of jams, mustards, olive oils, wines, and other gourmet goods for sale. Breakfast (oatmeal, omelets, and homemade pastries), lunch (soup, salads, and sandwiches), and real homemade flavor come from an open kitchen. Perfect if you want to escape the town's high-falutin' restaurants for an intimate brush with locals. *6770 Washington St., Yountville. ☎ 707/944-8246. Entrees $5–$15. MC, V. Breakfast, lunch & dinner daily. Map p 94.*

★★ Hurley's Restaurant and Bar CALIFORNIA Chef Bob Hurley is passionate about presenting balanced cuisine that pairs well with wine. Here, you get elite food without the matching attitude. The bar, which serves cocktails and snacks until midnight, is a local favorite. *6518 Washington St. ☎ 707/944-2345. Entrees $18–$29. AE, DISC, MC, V. Lunch & dinner daily. Bar menu available until midnight. Map p 94.*

★ Napa Valley Grille CALIFORNIA The theme at this chain restaurant is, well, Napa Valley. Entrees are listed on the lunch menu according to their Napa town of origin (Calistoga, St. Helena, and so forth). Try the pastas or items off the "Oakwood Grille." *6795 Washington St. ☎ 707/944-8686. Entrees $14–$27. AE, DC, DISC, MC, V. Lunch & dinner daily. Map p 94.*

★★ Redd CALIFORNIA Richard Reddington, an alumnus of NY's Daniel and Beverly Hills's Spago, incorporates ethnic influences into his regionally inspired seasonal menu. The dining space is clean and modern with chic accoutrements. *6480 Washington St. ☎ 707/944-2222. Entrees $13–$29. Tasting menus $75–$120. AE, DC, DISC, MC, V. Lunch & dinner daily. Map p 94.*

Glen Ellen

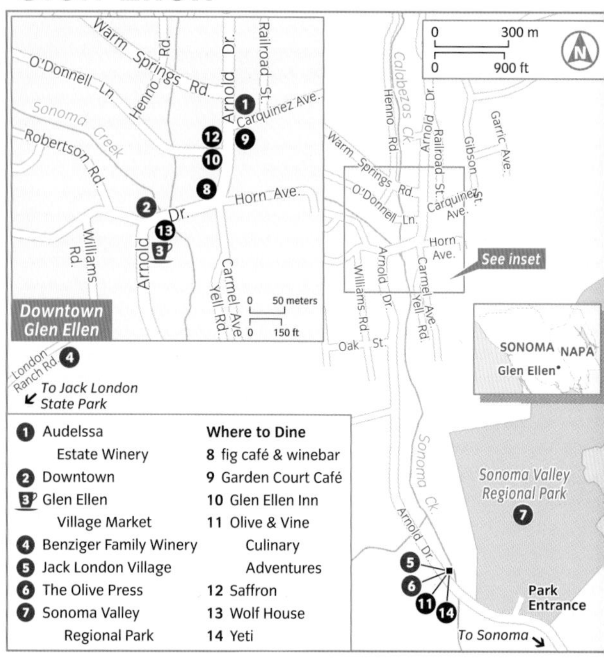

Glen Ellen, a small and sweet unincorporated Sonoma town, is home to fewer than 5,000 people, which makes it a tight-knit community. Local characters are many, from earthquake predictor Jim Berkland to Pixar's John Lasseter (often called today's Walt Disney) to Jack London's relatives—and, indeed, Jack London himself. Yes, the man is dead and gone (you can see his gravesite at the state park dedicated to him), but he's still very much present—not in a woo-woo kind of way, but in the form of extreme local reverence bordering on obsession. Though some would argue that Glen Ellen's too spread-out for a proper walking tour (unlike other Sonoma towns, there's no true town center), it's doable if you're not averse to occasionally walking about a mile along scenic byways. Otherwise, consider driving. This tour, depending on your pace, can be done in a half- or a full day. ***Tip:*** There's not much in the way of streetlights, so if you're going out after dark, several local inns supply flashlights to guests upon request.

START: **Navillus Birney Tasting Room, 13647 Arnold Dr. Distance: About 1.5 miles (2.4km).**

Jack London's Saloon in downtown Glen Ellen.

❶ ★ **Audelssa Estate Winery.** At the town's first intersection (Arnold Dr. and Warm Springs Rd.) in the 1920s mercantile Glen Ellen Square structure is this small country-style tasting room showcasing Audelssa wines. Though the wines are good and tastings are free, history buffs may be more interested in the exhibit documenting Glen Ellen's rich past; look for the photos of Jack London and M. F. K. Fisher. *13647 Arnold Dr.* ☎ *707/933-8514. See p 134.*

❷ ★ **"Downtown."** What locals call "downtown" is really just a 2-block stretch of Arnold Drive that runs from Warm Springs Road to London Ranch Road. It has about 20 buildings (many of them historic), a few old bridges, a Civil War cannon, and the convergence of the Sonoma and Calabasas creeks. The heyday here was about a century ago when trains brought in tourists. Still, the town hasn't changed much since the days when Jack London lived, wrote, and farmed nearby—it received its first traffic light in 2006 and still has virtually no sidewalks.

❸ ★ **Glen Ellen Village Market.** This very gourmet market (without the gourmet attitude) has hot and cold cases, delicious panini, a fabulous salad bar alongside an impressive produce section, and an excellent wine and cheese selection. Snack here or stock up on supplies for a picnic at **Sonoma Valley Regional Park.** *13751 Arnold Dr.* ☎ *707/996-6728. Daily 6am–9pm.*

Walk about a mile (1.6km) uphill on London Ranch Rd.

❹ ★★ kids **Benziger Family Winery.** Known for having the valley's best tour (it draws tourists around by a tractor, for heaven's sake), this biodynamic winery is one of the region's most welcoming. *1883 London Ranch Rd.* ☎ *888/490-2739. See p 136.*

Walk or drive another half-mile (.8km) up London Ranch Rd.

The fog rolls over the vineyards at Benziger.

5 ★ **Jack London Village.** This quaint little shopping spot houses an eclectic selection of restaurants and small shops, including a brand-new chocolate shop and cheesemonger, the **Eric Ross Winery** tasting room, as well as the **Olive Press** (see bullet **6**). *14301 Arnold Dr.*

6 **The Olive Press.** At this cooperative press, locals come to mill their own oil in the hopper (this is where Beltane Ranch makes its gourmet batches) and tourists come to taste the freshest extra-virgin flavor-infused blends they've ever tried—for free. But it's not as socialist as it sounds: Even if you bring your own bottle, a gallon of oil can go for $128. A better deal, perhaps, are the olive-themed gift items, foods, and books. *14301 Arnold Dr. No. 1. ☎ 707/939-8900. www.theolivepress.com. Daily 10am–5:30pm.*

Just past the Jack London Village and across Calabasas Creek is an entrance to:

7 **Sonoma Valley Regional Park.** This 162-acre (65-hectare) park has beautiful biking and walking paths, numerous easy hiking trails (some paved and some dirt), and a fenced dog park. It's most beautiful in spring, when the wildflowers bloom, but fall's magnificent colors, just before the oaks shed their leaves, rank a close second. There's a pretty picnic and lawn area at the trail head. *13630 Sonoma Hwy. ☎ 707/565-2041. www.sonoma-county.org/parks. Open daily from sunrise to sunset. Parking $5.*

Where to Dine

★★★ **the fig café & winebar** *CALIFORNIA-MEDITERRANEAN* the girl and the fig's (p 81) sister restaurant (which also refuses to capitalize its name) is more casual than its Sonoma Plaza sibling, but don't let the rustic neighborhood vibe fool you. The plates that come out of the open kitchen represent the kind of sophistication more commonly associated with urban restaurants. Start with a thin-crust pizza, a cheese plate, or the signature fig and arugula salad; end with the lavender crème brûlée. A huge perk here is the lack of a corkage fee, so bring along a bottle. If you didn't bring your own, wine is available by the flight, glass, or bottle—and there's a nice list to choose from. Reservations not accepted. *13690 Arnold Dr. ☎ 707/938-2130. Entrees $10–$19. AE, DISC, MC, V. Dinner daily. Sat–Sun 10am–2:30pm. Map p 98.*

kids **Garden Court Café** *AMERICAN* A sunny, genial place with savory breakfasts and lunches, as well as Sonoma wines and occasional special Friday-night dinners. At breakfast, order eggs done any which way. Lunch offerings consist mostly of sandwiches and salads. There's a pet-friendly umbrella-shaded terrace outside; owners can order meals for their dogs off a three-option menu. *13647 Arnold Dr. ☎ 707/935-1565. Entrees $6–$11. MC, V. Breakfast & lunch Wed–Mon. Map p 98.*

★★ **Glen Ellen Inn Restaurant** *CALIFORNIA-FRENCH* A locals' favorite for its warm, romantic atmosphere. The beautiful presentations that emerge from the open kitchen here change with the seasons. Garden seating is the favorable choice on sunny days, but the covered patio is also welcoming. The 550-selection wine list offers numerous bottles from Sonoma, and more than a dozen wines by the glass. For dessert, don't miss the fabulous house-made sundae: Coconut-encrusted French-vanilla ice cream floats in bittersweet caramel sauce. Reservations recommended. ***Tip:*** There's a small parking lot behind the restaurant. *13670 Arnold Dr. ☎ 707/996-6409. Main courses $9–$25. AE, DISC, MC, V. Lunch & dinner Fri–Tues. Dinner Wed–Thurs. Map p 98.*

Olive & Vine Culinary Adventures *CALIFORNIA* This pretty cafe-deli has a small sit-down area, but most of its business comes from its extensive catering offerings, so to-go picnics and box lunches ($14–$16) are superb. Offerings also include simple breakfasts (mostly pastries), coffee options, and wine-tasting. *In Jack London Village. 14301 Arnold Dr. ☎ 707/996-9150. Entrees $10–$15. MC, V. Breakfast & lunch Wed–Mon. Map p 98.*

★★ **Saffron** CALIFORNIA This narrow, intimate room beckons you in from the street. Once inside, you'll enjoy creative cuisine and an interesting wine list highlighting Spanish wines, plus an impressive selection of beers and ales (more than 20 selections span the globe). *13648 Arnold Dr. ☎ 707/938-4844. Entrees $13–$25. MC, V. Dinner Tues–Sat. Map p 98.*

★★ **Wolf House** *NEW AMERICAN* One of Glen Ellen's most famous establishments, in Jack London Lodge, serves food in a saloon or out on the terrace, which overlooks a serene creek. The lunch menu adds fancy flourishes to old American favorites, while Chef Jay Veregge's dinners emphasize locally procured ingredients, some even culled from the Lodge's garden. A reasonably priced Sonoma-centric wine list offers many by-the-glass options. ***Reservations recommended.*** After dinner, head to the Lodge's fun saloon, which is filled with colorful folks, TVs broadcasting sports games, and Jack London photos and memorabilia. *13740 Arnold Dr. ☎ 707/996-4401. Entrees $8.50–$27. AE, MC, V. Lunch & dinner daily. Map p 98.*

Glen Ellen's fig café & winebar is the casual version of the famous Sonoma restaurant, the girl and the fig (p 81).

Yeti INDIAN/PAKISTANI For a taste of the Himalayas in one of wine country's tinier towns, Yeti doesn't disappoint. Sit indoors to watch Chef Narayan Somname work his magic behind the long bar, or enjoy a view of Sonoma Creek from the large outdoor patio. The succulent, authentic dishes are reasonably priced. *14301 Arnold Dr. ☎ 707/996-9930 AE, DISC, MC, V Entrees $15–$20. Lunch & dinner daily.*

A burger is tiered and speared at the Glen Ellen Inn.

Calistoga

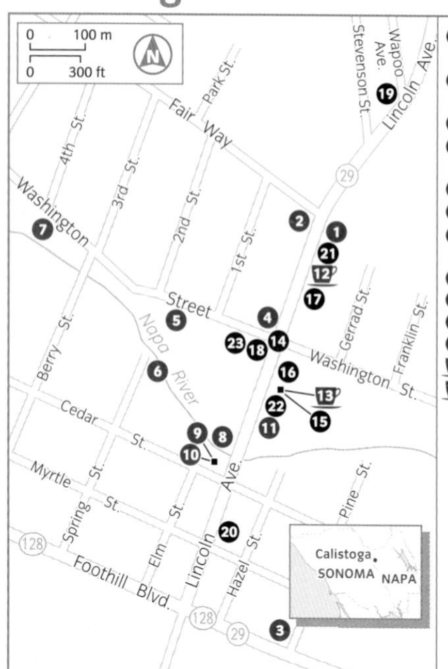

1 Napa Valley Railroad Depot
2 Dr. Wilkinson's Hot Springs Resort
3 Calistoga Pottery
4 American Indian Trading Co
5 Sharpsteen Museum
6 Napa River
7 Holy Assumption Monastery
8 Main Element Gallery
9 Hurd Beeswax Candles
10 Ca'toga Galleria d'Arte
11 Mudd Henns
12 Calistoga Roastery
13 Calistoga Creamery & Bakery

Where to Dine
14 All Seasons Bistro
15 Bosko's Italian
16 Brannan's
17 Checkers
18 Hydro Grill
19 Kitani Sushi
20 Pacifico
21 Stomp
22 Soo Yuan
23 Wappo Bar & Bistro

Calistoga is an Old Western–style town with more than a touch of California eccentricity. Its people are still obsessed with Sam Brannan, a Maine-born pioneer who became California's first millionaire by selling gold-mining tools after stoking frenzy for the precious metal (he ran through San Francisco shouting of its discovery in the American River). When he came to this formerly Wappo, then Spanish, area, he was so taken with its hot springs that he bought thousands of acres on which to develop a spa resort town similar to what already existed in Saratoga, New York. In 1885, meaning to say that he would transform this into the Saratoga of California, he instead (perhaps due to his demising penchant for alcohol) proclaimed, "I will make this the Calistoga of Sarafornia!" The name stuck, and more than 120 years later, pleasure seekers still come to enjoy the tiny town's therapeutic mineral water and mud baths. The waters here are so coveted that they're bottled and sold for a handsome profit: The next time you see Crystal Geyser or Calistoga Water at your local market, remember your visit here. This tour highlights downtown Calistoga's history and cultural diversity, with stops at the town's best stores and galleries. **START: The Historic Calistoga Depot, 1458 Lincoln Ave. Distance: Less than a half-mile (.8km) of walking, doable in a half to a full day.**

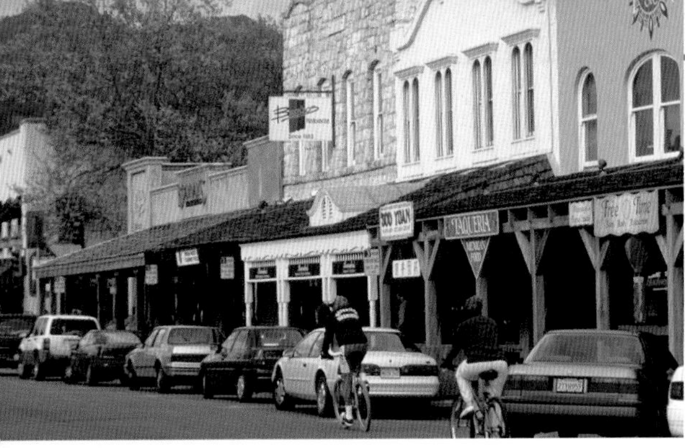

Lincoln Avenue is Calistoga's main drag.

1 ★ **kids** **Napa Valley Railroad Depot.** In 1868, it became possible to take the train into Calistoga, making it a gateway destination for wine country. This depot, California's second oldest, is on the National Register of Historic Places. Its site now supports six restored rail cars that still look as though they've just docked at the station. Inside the cars is a variety of quirky businesses, including a psychic from India, a florist, a wine store—and the **Calistoga Chamber of Commerce and Visitors Bureau:** Stop in to get insightful advice about the area, including current happenings. *1458 Lincoln Ave.* ☎ *707/942-6333. www.calistogachamber.com. Mon–Fri 10am–5pm, Sat 10am–4pm, Sun 11am–3pm (closed daily from 12:30–1pm).*

2 ★★ **Dr. Wilkinson's Hot Springs Resort.** You can get a massage at any old spa, but only at Dr. Wilkinson's, one of Calistoga's many hot-spring resorts, can you detoxify in a volcanic-ash mudbath with a facial mask and cucumbers over your eyes, then soak in a wildly bubbling mineral bath, then get wrapped in a blanket, *then* have a muscle-melting 1-hour massage. It's called "The Works," and it's not for everyone (refrain if you're sensitive to heat or think you might not like being surrounded in mud—though it's better than it sounds), but those who like it *adore* it. Sure, the spa might not win any awards for its decor anytime soon (it's rather bland), but it gets first prize for its ability to relax clients. Named for the late Dr. John Wilkinson, an ahead-of-his-time chiropractor who provided alternative therapies in the 1940s, the resort is now co-managed by his children, Mark and Carolynne. *1507 Lincoln Ave.* ☎ *707/942-4102. http://drwilkinson.com. "The Works" $149.*

3 **Calistoga Pottery.** A block south of Lincoln Ave, this shop showcases a colorful array of pieces you'll find in use at restaurants and wineries all over the valley. *1001 Foothill Blvd.* ☎ *707/942-0216. www.calistogapottery.com. Daily 9:30am–5pm.*

4 **American Indian Trading Co.** Another notable local store is this narrow showcase. The owners,

Treat yourself to a mud bath at Dr. Wilkinson's.

Learn about Napa's past at the Sharpsteen Museum.

working in conjunction with Native American tribes, sell stunning turquoise-and-silver jewelry, kachinas, dreamcatchers, medicine bags, and other crafts made by descendents of Calistoga's original residents. *1407 Lincoln Ave. ☎ 707/942-9330 or 877/735-7755. www.aitcoc.com. Daily 10am–6pm.*

❺ kids ★★ **Sharpsteen Museum.** The Sharpsteen chronicles northern Napa County's natural and cultural history. The definite highlight is the painstakingly created diorama depicting Brannan's resort as it was in 1868. The 32-foot-long (9.6m) town replica took nearly 3 years to build and sits under the panoramic photo on which it's based. Other exhibits display Wappo artifacts, Robert Louis Stevenson paraphernalia, a geothermal demonstration, a restored stagecoach, and a re-created barn. Ben Sharpsteen, the museum's founder, was an Academy Award–winning Disney filmmaker; the museum also contains one of his Oscars. *1311 Washington St. ☎ 707/942-5911. www.sharpsteen-museum.org. Daily 11am–4pm. Suggested donation: $3+ for adults.*

Just to the left of the museum is the beautiful:

❻ **Napa River,** home to a threatened population of steelhead and Chinook salmon. Right here, you can actually cross the river on foot—there's a shallow barrier across which adults and kids can easily wade to get to the playground on the other side.

Back out on Washington Street, pass the mint-green Community Presbyterian Church (3rd and Washington sts.) to find the fairy-tale-like:

❼ ★★ **Holy Assumption Monastery & Orthodox Religious Center.** Founded in the 1940s by Russian and Chinese refugee nuns, this peaceful religious center was originally a hotel. They built one of its woodsy chapels to replicate the one at Fort Ross. Surrounding the quaint buildings are fountains, a koi pond, and Asian-inspired gardens. If you keep your eyes peeled, you may spot the friendly resident one-eyed cat. The parish welcomes visitors of all backgrounds. *1519 Washington St. ☎ 707/942-6244. Hours vary; call ahead. Free, but donations accepted.*

Turn right to get back on Lincoln Avenue, cross a bridge over the river, and enter:

8 **Main Element Gallery,** a store with exquisite artworks and upbeat staff. *1333A Lincoln Ave. ☎ 707/942-6347. Daily 10am–6pm (5pm on Fri).*

At 9 ★ kids **Hurd Beeswax Candles,** the store's fast-talking owner, Mary Sue Frediani, explains her various wares; she stocks hand-rolled, honeycomb, and long-burning candles for all occasions. For a real treat, though, ask to see the observation beehive through a hidden window in the wall. Frediani points out the queen bee, who lays 1,500 eggs each day. In the same retail space is **OnThEdge Winery's** tasting bar, where fourth-generation vintners pour you a free taste of their heritage Charbono. If you want more, pay $2 per taste or buy a bottle for about $30. *1255A Lincoln Ave. ☎ 800/977-7211. www.hurdbeeswaxcandles.com. Daily 10am–5:30pm (8pm Fri–Sat).*

In the same shopping complex is:

10 **Ca'toga Galleria d'Arte,** a gorgeous space showcasing the works of Venice-born artist Carlo Marchiori. His Renaissance, baroque, and neoclassical styles are evidenced here in the form of porcelain plates, acrylic paintings, original furniture—and a fantastic cosmological ceiling mural that you can marvel at by merely looking up. Look down, and you'll see a glittering terrazzo floor that charts the pre-Copernicus universe. Find the Latin inscription "Hic Es" ("You are here"), and you'll know you've found Earth. *1206 Cedar St. ☎ 707/942-3900. www.catoga.com. Thurs–Mon 11am–6pm (opens 10am on Sat).*

11 **Mudd Henns.** End your tour by buying an only-in-Calistoga souvenir: mud. Yes, you can actually purchase the therapeutic local muck pre-packaged and ready to take home. A favorite is the detoxifying Fango Mud bath powder, made with volcanic ash, salicylic powder, and pine-needle extract, to relieve achy muscles and joints. *1348C Lincoln Ave. ☎ 800/793-9220. www.muddhens.com. Daily 10am–9pm.*

Calistoga's not exactly a high-stress place, but take time anyway to unwind at either of the town's best coffee shops: 12 **Calistoga Roastery** for its fresh single-bean varietal coffees. *1426 Lincoln Ave. ☎ 707/942-5757. $.* Also try 13 **Calistoga Creamery & Bakery** for rich brownies and good old-fashioned ice cream. *1353 Lincoln Ave. ☎ 707/942-0777. $.*

Where to Dine

★★ **All Seasons Bistro** *AMERICAN* This cleanly decorated bistro is very white, save for a red ceiling accented with Art Deco–style fans. As the name might imply, the menu changes seasonally; order from it or ask about Chef Thomas Halligan's tasting menus. *1400 Lincoln Ave. ☎ 707/942-9111. Entrees $19–$29. DISC, MC, V. Lunch & dinner Tues–Sun. Lunch Fri–Sun. Map p 102.*

★ **Bosko's** *ITALIAN* This trattoria with rock walls, wood-fired pizza, and fresh homemade pasta has a relaxing atmosphere. Save room for dessert; the tiramisu is stupendous. *1364 Lincoln Ave. ☎ 707/942-9088.*

Entrees $8.75–$22. AE, MC, V. Lunch & dinner daily. Map p 102.

★ **Brannan's** *NEW AMERICAN* A large Arts and Crafts–style restaurant with a classy fireplace dining room for chilly evenings and *al fresco* seating for warm days. Big salads, substantial sandwiches, and well-spiced specialties. *1374 Lincoln Ave. ☎ 707/942-2233. Entrees $10–$34. AE, MC, V. Lunch & dinner daily. Map p 102.*

kids **Checkers** *ITALIAN* Though entrees are mostly Italian (think pastas, pizzas, and calzones), the menu also lists unexpected options like Thai noodle salad. Start with a hot, garlicky appetizer like spinach and artichoke dip. *1414 Lincoln Ave. ☎ 707/942-9300. Entrees $8–$15. AE, DISC, MC, V. 11:30am–9:30pm (10pm Fri–Sat). Map p 102.*

★ **Hydro Grill** *AMERICAN* The more casual counterpart of All Seasons Bistro (see above), Hydro Grill has brick walls, lots of mirrors, and a great bar scene. Twenty on-tap beers make the Friday and Saturday evening entertainment more fun: Live music encompasses genres from blues to rock 'n' roll to swing.

JoLe combines modern style and family recipes.

1403 Lincoln Ave. ☎ 707/942-9777. Entrees $8–$17. DISC, MC, V. Breakfast, lunch & dinner daily. Map p 102.

JoLe *NEW AMERICAN* Serving small plates with huge flavor, chefs Matt and Sonjia Spector (a husband-and-wife team) employ local, organic ingredients whenever they can. Many of their recipes are updates of dishes originally conceived by Sonjia's mom and grandmother. Peruse the eclectic selection of wines from small producers. *1457 Lincoln Ave. ☎ 707/942-5938. Entrees $15–$50. V MC AE DISC. Dinner daily.*

★ **Kitani Sushi** *JAPANESE* A selection of Japanese specialties (udon, tempura, and the like) complement a long sushi list in this small, traditionally decorated restaurant. *1631 Lincoln Ave. ☎ 707/942-6857. Entrees $4–$23. MC, V. Lunch & dinner Wed–Mon. Map p 102.*

★ **kids** **Pacifico** *MEXICAN* At this festive restaurant, try a grilled fajita or one of the many traditional dishes with a pitcher of bright-blue Cabo Waborita. Friday nights, a mariachi band plays; on Saturdays, it's live Latin jazz. *1237 Lincoln Ave. ☎ 707/942-4400. Entrees $10–$18. MC, V. Lunch & dinner daily. Map p 102.*

Soo Yuan *CHINESE* This low-key joint with a long MSG-free menu offers Mandarin and Szechwan soups, platters, and moo-shu. *1354 Lincoln Ave. ☎ 707/942-9404. Entrees $4.25–$15. AE, DISC, MC, V. Lunch & dinner daily. Map p 102.*

★ **Wappo Bar & Bistro** CONTINENTAL This nook has an extensive wine list accompanying creative concoctions like chile relleno stuffed with currants and pine nuts and accented with walnut-pomegranate sauce. If it's warm out, dine on the brick patio. *1226 Washington St. ☎ 707/942-4712. Entrees $14–$24. AE, MC, V. Lunch & dinner Wed–Mon. Map p 102.* ●

5 The Great **Outdoors**

The Wine Country **by Bike**

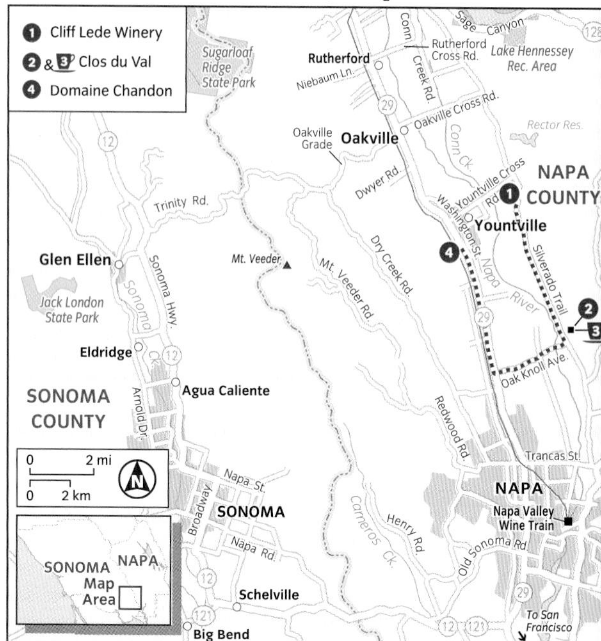

With incomparable scenery and relatively flat terrain, Napa and Sonoma are consummate bikers' destinations. Touring on two wheels while inhaling fresh country air is by far the most exhilarating way to appreciate wine country. This route, appropriate for those in moderate physical condition, cycles through Napa Valley and stops at some of its best wineries. ***Tip:*** Temper your intake and eat well, since biking under the influence is illegal. If you only want to imbibe at two wineries, picnic but don't taste at Clos du Val. START: **Yountville's Washington Street. Trip Length: Half a day (allow a full day if you like lingering at wineries). For where to rent bikes (they'll deliver 'em to you) see p 200.**

Head north on Washington, then turn right on Yount St., then right again on Yountville Crossroad. After 3 miles (4.8km), look for the first stop on your right.

1 ★★ **Cliff Lede Winery** is the northernmost winery in the famous Stag's Leap District. In the tasting room, young, energetic staffers eagerly tell all about their rich Bordeaux-focused varietals. After tasting, relax and examine works by famous artists on an outdoor terrace with views of vineyards and the Vaca

Previous page: You can rent canoes at River's Edge (p 114).

Food & Safety Along the Way

You'll want to eat sometime along the ride; to assemble your own picnic, stop at Yountville's family-owned **Ranch Market Too** (6498 Washington St.; ☎ 707/944-2662) beforehand to buy food (bring a backpack if you do this). Alternatively, book with ★★ **Napa Valley Bike Tours** (6488 Washington St.; ☎ 800/707-BIKE or 707/944-2953), a company that will cater lunch at any local winery with picnic grounds. Another benefit of going with Napa Valley Bike Tours: Its experts, who helped us devise this tour, follow clients with a van. That way, if you want to buy wine as you taste, ***you don't have to haul bottles (or cases) around.*** Vans also contain first-aid kits and bicycle maintenance tools. Not least of all, NVBT provides a knowledgeable guide, so you won't have to worry about looking down to read directions as you ride.

Mountains. *1473 Yountville Cross Rd.* ☎ *707/944-8642. See p 140.*

Turn right out of Cliff Lede's parking lot; after a fifth of a mile (.3km), Yountville Crossroad will end. Turn right on historic Silverado Trail and pedal the 3.7 stunning miles (6km) to glamorous

2 ★ **Clos du Val.** Be sure to try this French-influenced winery's signature cabernet. A peek at Clos du Val's rose garden and a game in its lovely pétanque (French bocce) court will round out your visit; this is also your picnic stop (see below). *5330 Silverado Trail, Napa.* ☎ *707/259-2200. See p 141.*

Enjoy lunch at **3 Clos du Val,** which has two picnic areas. For the prettiest surroundings, choose the olive grove.

Continue south on Silverado Trail. Turn right on Oak Knoll, cross Hwy. 29 and the railroad tracks, turn right on Solano Ave., and follow it north 4 miles (6.4km) until it ends in an intersection, where you'll find your next stop.

Cycle up **4** ★★ **Domaine Chandon's** long, vineyard-flanked driveway and across a creek bridge to the winery's entrance. Because Domaine Chandon was founded by French champagne house Moët & Chandon, there are many luxurious amenities here. Enjoy an educational presentation in a 28-seat theater before tasting the valley's most renowned bubbly. *1 California Dr., Yountville.* ☎ *707/944-2280. See p 144.*

To get back to this tour's starting point, bike to the end of Domaine Chandon's driveway to take a left onto California Dr. Cross the railroad tracks, go under a bridge, and ride until California Dr. ends. Take a left on Washington St.

Bike your way through wine country.

The Best Wine Country **Hike**

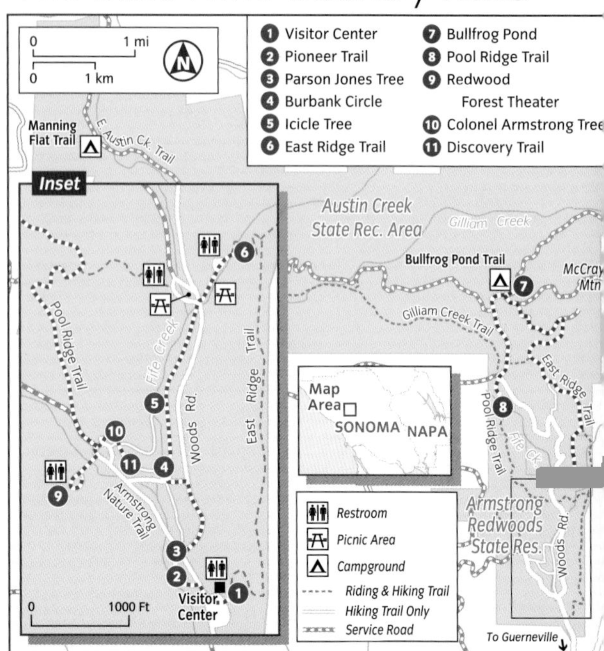

The Armstrong Redwoods State Reserve is the natural California you always see in photos: majestic, millennia-old redwoods through which only slivers of sunlight slice in. The adjacent Austin Creek State Recreation Area, by contrast, is more of an open forest with a greater variety of indigenous trees and wildlife. This loop hike highlights the park's biology and history and takes you among the giant redwoods. It's suitable for those in moderate physical condition. Purchase your picnic the day before. **17000 Armstrong Woods Rd., Guerneville. ☎ 707/869-2015. www.parks.ca.gov. Distance: About 4 miles (6.4km). Trip Length: Half a day.**

Travel Tip

Stock up the night before on picnic supplies at **Oakville Grocery** (in Healdsburg and Oakville; see p 91).

1 Visitor Center and follow signs to **2 Pioneer Trail,** a mulch path surrounded by first-generation redwoods. Notice the green carpeting flanking the trail. That's not clover, but oxalis—identifiable by its compound leaves with three leaflets and colored flowers. After passing a number of downed trees swept over by strong winds (redwood has a surprisingly shallow root system), you'll find the still-sturdy

❸ **Parson Jones Tree.** This is a prime example of the Coastal Redwood, the tallest of the tree species—and at 310 feet/93m, Parson Jones is the reserve's tallest tree. In shady, cool conditions, redwoods can grow 3 feet (.9m) per year, but once their top is exposed to sunlight, that rate slows to only an inch. This impressive organism, more than 1,300 years old, was named for Rev. William Ladd Jones, an ardent supporter of saving the grove from logging. He was also the husband of Lizzie Armstrong Jones (see below).

Where the trail splits at the creek, take the right fork and look for ❹ **Burbank Circle,** a perfect circle of centuries-old trees—it's a mystery how they got that way.

Stay on Pioneer Trail and on your left, you'll see the ❺ **Icicle Tree,** so named because of the massive icicle-like burls that used to hang off it. Burls occur when a tree repeatedly buds over in the same spot. Unfortunately, vandals have sheared the tree of most of its protrusions; redwood is highly valued for furniture-making and can fetch a pretty penny—a sad example of how short-term commercial gain can trump long-term sustainability.

Take a rest and savor the goodies you picked up from **Oakville Grocery.**

With a renewed sense of energy following your meal, veer right onto ❻ **East Ridge Trail.** Foliage becomes more diverse here: You'll notice that cool shadiness changes to open forestry highlighted by a serene mix of redwoods, oaks, firs, and madrones. If it's springtime, wildflowers like buttercups, iris, lupines, and poppies will enhance your hike. At the paved road, turn right and you'll encounter ❼ **Bullfrog Pond.** Listen for the singing bullfrogs.

Walk back down the way you came, but make a right onto ❽ **Pool Ridge Trail,** which ends in a paved loop with a parking area. Veer right here and go down a short path to ❾ **Redwood Forest Theater,** a natural amphitheater that used to seat more than 2,000 people for outdoor concerts and weddings. It's no longer used because the surrounding ecosystem is too delicate.

On the other side of the paved loop is the enormous ❿ **Colonel Armstrong Tree,** which has stood for about 1,400 years, making it the preserve's oldest tree. It's 308 feet (92m) high and has a diameter approaching 15 feet (4.5m; stand in front of it for a picture—its size versus yours will make you gasp). Colonel James B. Armstrong was an Ohio-born lumberman with ironically conservationist instincts—it was his efforts that kept this reserve preserved. He bought the land in 1875 and fought to make it a state park. Though he died before that happened, his daughter, Lizzie Armstrong Jones, saw to it that a county initiative was passed to ensure her father's dream.

Finally, take the short ⓫ **Discovery Trail.** It'll merge with the Pioneer Trail to lead you back to your car.

Ponder the tall trees at Armstrong Redwoods State Reserve.

From the **Russian River** to the **Pacific Coast**

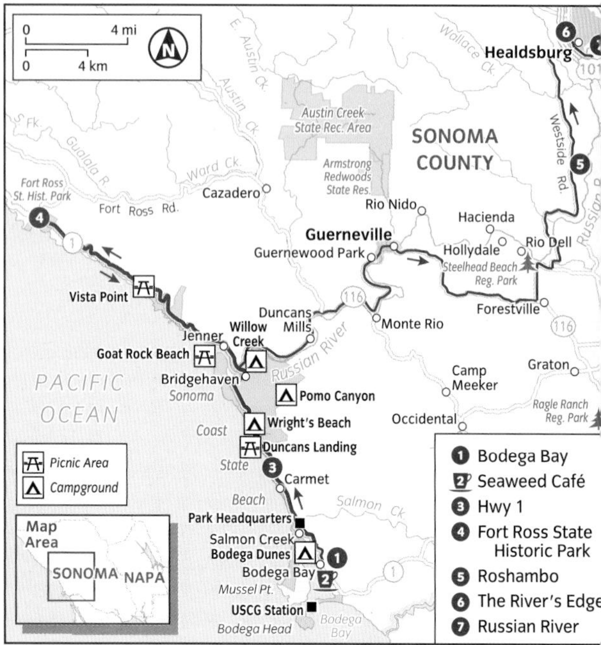

Sonoma's dazzling Pacific coastline and tranquil Russian River never fail to remind me why I live in California, and why Sonoma is a hydrophile's haven. Spend the morning at a breathtaking beach and the afternoon floating on a freshwater river to find yourself wondering whether life can get much better. This tour also takes you for a drive along the famously rugged, cliff-hugging Pacific Coast Highway 1 ("PCH" to locals). Start the day early (8:30am) so you can comfortably fit everything in. ***Tip:*** Dress in layers for the ever-changing coastal weather, and wear shoes in which you'd be comfortable walking on wet ground. START: **Bodega Bay. Trip Length: 1 day.**

❶ ★★ **Bodega Bay's** seascapes and breezes are a refreshing escape from everyday life. Stroll around for about 10 minutes to get a feel for this fishing village's permeating coastal culture. Hitchcock fans will be intrigued by ***Potter Schoolhouse;*** the film director's eye for so-innocent-they're-creepy locations must have been on high alert when he spotted this 1873 building—he gave it a significant role in ***The Birds.*** It's a private residence, so simply stroll by. *17110 Bodega Lane.* ☎ *707/876-3257. www.bodegaschool.com.* ***Note:*** The tiny town of Bodega Bay is not to be confused with the town of Bodega, which is a bit farther southeast *(www.bodegabay.com).*

2 ★★ **Seaweed Café.** The dining room here is an art-filled space with a fireplace and handcrafted furnishings—but as nice as the interior is, the real highlight is the view of the bay paired with the global menu, which focuses on organic coastal cuisine. The seasonal dishes are made "slow food"–style with ingredients from Sonoma ranches and farms, and a rotating selection of specials complements a la carte entrees. As for wine, you won't be able to order anything made west of Highway 101, a result of local pride. However, there's a wide selection of whole-leaf teas from around the world. *1580 Eastshore Rd., Bodega Bay.* ☎ *707/875-2700.*

The Pacific Coast is an awesome sight.

3 ★★★ kids **Hwy. 1 along Sonoma Coast State Beach.** This 21-mile (34km) drive represents some of California's most dramatic coastal lands. You'll pass rugged shale bluffs, coves, headlands, and offshore reefs. More than 300 bird species populate this stretch. If it's spring, look for capacious sprays of wildflowers like blue lupine and verbena. There are plenty of pullouts for photo ops, and beaches—many of which have tide pools teeming with invertebrate life—are accessible from more than a dozen points. Veer left when you reach Goat Rock Road to visit the peninsula's tip, **Whale Point,** so named because the annual grey whale migration passes through here from

A picnic, Sonoma style.

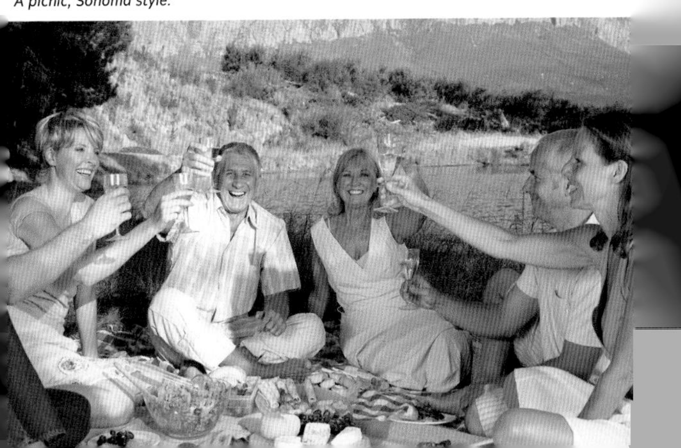

December to April, and because humpbacks are here year-round. Whale Point is also the site of **Goat Rock Beach,** the Russian River's mouth and home to hundreds of harbor seals (pups are born here from Mar–June). *Sonoma Coast State Beach.* ☎ *707/875-3483. www.parks.ca.gov.*

4 ★★ kids **Fort Ross State Historic Park.** On a wave-cut marine terrace, Fort Ross is comprised of steep bluffs, old-growth redwoods, and many points at which you can see impact of the San Andreas Fault, which comes ashore 2 miles (3.2km) south of the fort and through the old Russian orchard—look for sag ponds, escarpments, damaged trees, and off-kilter fences, all evidence of the notorious 1906 earthquake. *19005 Hwy. 1, Jenner.* ☎ *707/847-3286. www.parks.ca.gov. Park grounds open daily a half-hour before sunrise & close a half-hour after sunset. Historical buildings, the visitor center & the bookstore are open daily 10am–4:30pm. Parking fee: $6.*

Travel Tip: Rain

If the day turns out to be rainy, gray, and cold (and kayaking is the last thing you want to do), stop at funky **Guerneville** on your way back from the coast. For a detailed tour, see p 92.

5 Roshambo Winery. Stop off for a quick sip at Roshambo. The free tastes come with a view of the Russian River Valley. *3000 Westside Rd., Healdsburg.* ☎ *888/525-WINE.* *See p 156.*

Rent a canoe or kayak from the experts at **6 River's Edge** in Healdsburg, and buy a box lunch here for later. Choose from a basic $12 lunch (with a choice of sandwiches, chips, a cookie, and a fruit) or the $35 gourmet option (a locally procured affair of cheese, fruit, crackers, cold cuts, and dessert). Canoes and double kayaks cost $65 for a half-day; single kayaks run $35 for a half-day. Reservations recommended. Rentals include paddles, life vests & shuttle rides. Guided trips are available upon request. *13840 Healdsburg Ave., Healdsburg.* ☎ *800/345-0869. www.riversedgekayakandcanoe.com.*

7 ★★★ kids **The Russian River.** Take a relatively leisurely float on this rain-fed river—a ride that's appropriate for those in moderate physical condition, as well as children. Glide through the lush Alexander Valley past vineyards and arboreal private property interspersed with unnamed-but-inviting beaches on which you can break out your picnic. Keep an eye out for glimpses of wildlife like river otters, turtles, great blue heron, osprey, and egrets. Finish at either Rio Nido (a shorter, 11-mile/18km journey) or the Healdsburg Beach (longer at 15 miles/24km)—you'll recognize Rio Nido by the congregation of River's Edge boats, and the Healdsburg Beach is a dead end, so it's impossible to miss. River's Edge shuttles you back to your car from either finishing point. *Allow 4–5 hours.* ●

Kayak down the Russian River.

6 Napa & Sonoma Lodging

Where to Stay in Wine Country

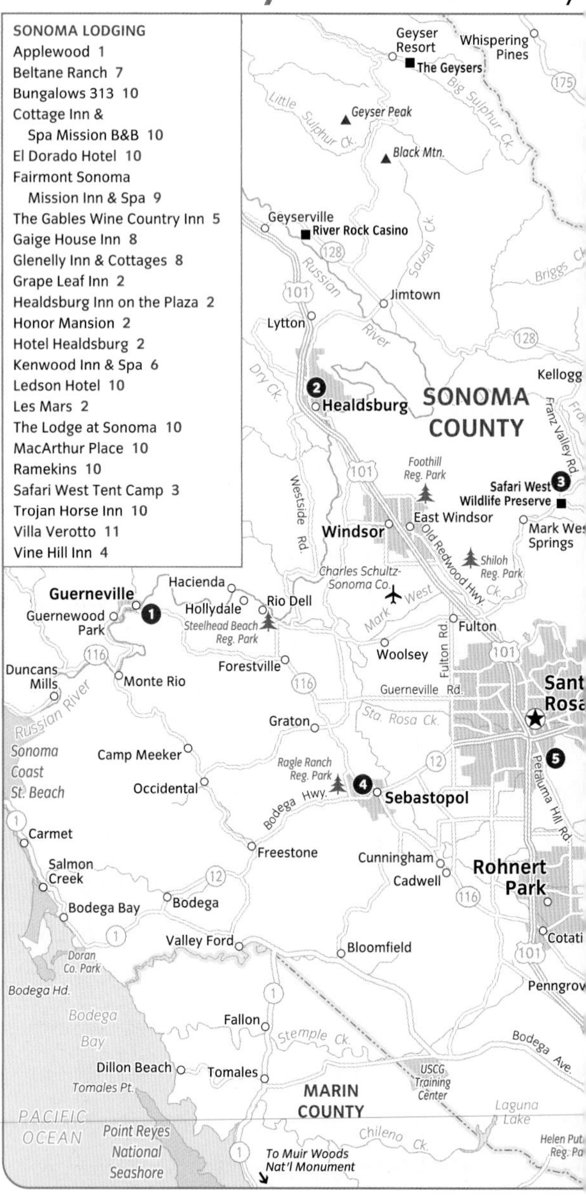

Previous page: After a day at the vineyards, soak in a luxurious tub at the Gaige House (p 125) in Glen Ellen.

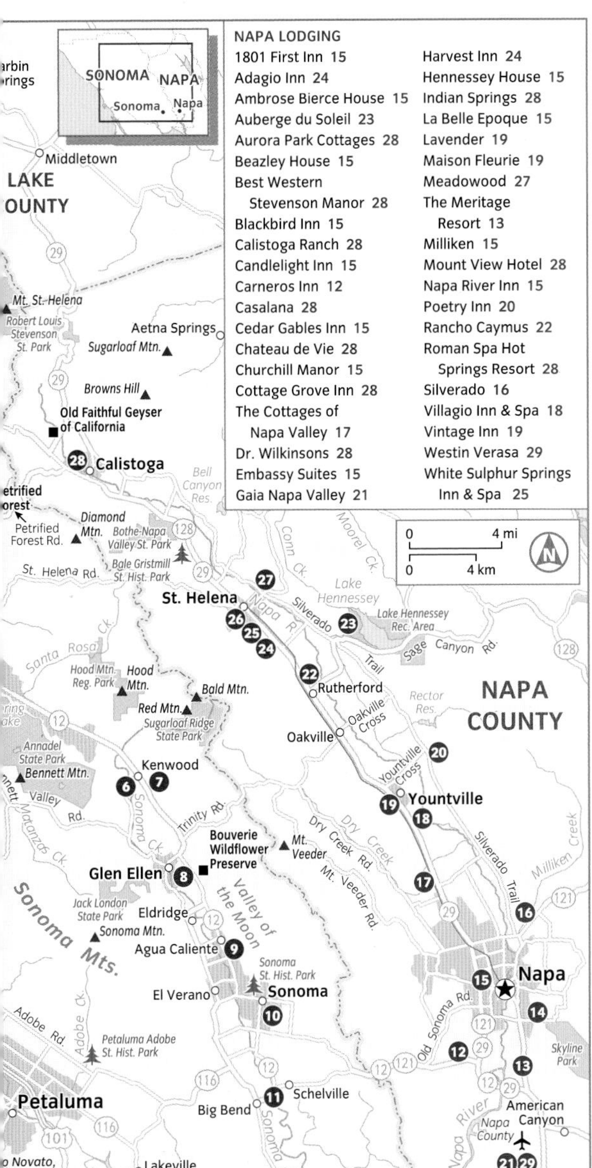
NAPA LODGING
1801 First Inn 15
Adagio Inn 24
Ambrose Bierce House 15
Auberge du Soleil 23
Aurora Park Cottages 28
Beazley House 15
Best Western Stevenson Manor 28
Blackbird Inn 15
Calistoga Ranch 28
Candlelight Inn 15
Carneros Inn 12
Casalana 28
Cedar Gables Inn 15
Chateau de Vie 28
Churchill Manor 15
Cottage Grove Inn 28
The Cottages of Napa Valley 17
Dr. Wilkinsons 28
Embassy Suites 15
Gaia Napa Valley 21
Harvest Inn 24
Hennessey House 15
Indian Springs 28
La Belle Epoque 15
Lavender 19
Maison Fleurie 19
Meadowood 27
The Meritage Resort 13
Milliken 15
Mount View Hotel 28
Napa River Inn 15
Poetry Inn 20
Rancho Caymus 22
Roman Spa Hot Springs Resort 28
Silverado 16
Villagio Inn & Spa 18
Vintage Inn 19
Westin Verasa 29
White Sulphur Springs Inn & Spa 25
SONOMA
NAPA
Sonoma
Napa
Middletown
LAKE COUNTY
NAPA COUNTY
Mt. St. Helena
Robert Louis Stevenson St. Park
Aetna Springs
Sugarloaf Mtn.
Browns Hill
Old Faithful Geyser of California
Calistoga
Bell Canyon Res.
Diamond Mtn.
Petrified Forest Rd.
Bothe-Napa Valley St. Park
Bale Gristmill St. Hist. Park
St. Helena Rd.
St. Helena
Lake Hennessey
Lake Hennessey Rec. Area
Sage Canyon Rd.
Silverado Trail
Rutherford
Rector Res.
Oakville
Oakville Cross
Yountville Cross
Yountville
Hood Mtn. Reg. Park
Hood Mtn.
Bald Mtn.
Red Mtn.
Sugarloaf Ridge State Park
Annadel State Park
Bennett Mtn.
Kenwood
Trinity Rd.
Bouverie Wildflower Preserve
Mt. Veeder
Dry Creek Rd.
Mt. Veeder Rd.
Glen Ellen
Jack London State Park
Eldridge
Sonoma Mtn.
Sonoma Mts.
Valley of the Moon
Agua Caliente
Sonoma St. Hist. Park
Sonoma
El Verano
Napa
Old Sonoma Rd.
Skyline Park
Adobe Rd.
Petaluma Adobe St. Hist. Park
Petaluma
Schelville
Big Bend
American Canyon
Napa County
Napa River
Lakeville
0 4 mi
0 4 km

Napa Lodging A to Z

★ Adagio Inn ST. HELENA Rooms in this quiet Edwardian B&B feature stained-glass windows and reading nooks. Amenities include a decadent breakfast, king beds, Wi-Fi, and evening wine and cheese. *1417 Kearny St. ☎ 707/963-2238. www.adagioinn.com. 3 units. $275–$385. MC, V. Map p 117.*

★ Ambrose Bierce House ST. HELENA Once the home of author Ambrose Bierce, this 1872 Victorian's comfortable rooms feature canopied beds, Jacuzzi tubs, and fireplaces. A champagne breakfast also awaits, and it's walking distance from downtown. *1515 Main St. ☎ 707/963-3003. www.ambrosebiercehouse.com. 4 units. $199–$299. MC, V. Map p 117.*

★★★ Auberge du Soleil RUTHERFORD With interior decor that's nearly unsurpassed in the region (it's contemporary Spanish-Mediterranean), Auberge is upscale enough to belong to Relais & Châteaux. Rooms feature sublime linens on oversized beds, outdoor terraces, flatscreen TVs, and Wi-Fi. Visit the superb restaurant, the luxuriant spa, and the open-air art gallery. *180 Rutherford Hill Rd. ☎ 707/963-1211. www.aubergedusoleil.com. 50 units. Doubles $550–$3,500. AE, DC, DISC, MC, V. Map p 117.*

★ Aurora Park Cottages CALISTOGA This retreat's homey cottages sport outside decks where you can savor a basket of pastries and fruit. Innkeepers are local experts, so ask them to customize a tour plan. *1807 Foothill Blvd. ☎ 707/942-6733. www.aurorapark.com. 6 units. $230–$305. AE, MC, V. Map p 117.*

★★ Beazley House NAPA Open since 1981 and still run by its original owners, this pet-friendly, wood-shingled property stakes its claim as Napa's first B&B. Offerings include country-style rooms (no TV), gardens, Wi-Fi, and Friday wine tastings. *910 1st St. ☎ 800/559-1649. www.beazleyhouse.com. 11 units. Doubles $199–$339. MC, V. Map p 117.*

Auberge du Soleil is the luxury-lodging choice in Napa.

Sublime scenery surrounds Calistoga Ranch.

Best Western Stevenson Manor Inn CALISTOGA Close to town center, this value-oriented inn's large rooms have a fireplace, kitchenette, or balcony. Amenities include breakfast, a pool, hot tub, sauna, and steam room. Check the website for deals. *1830 Lincoln Ave. ☎ 707/942-1112. www.stevensonmanor.com. 34 units. Doubles $145–$245. AE, DC, DISC, MC, V. Map p 117.*

★★ **Blackbird Inn** NAPA A stay at this well-located B&B includes afternoon wine tastings, Wi-Fi, and DVDs to borrow. Craftsman elements give the exterior a lodge feel, while rooms are country-style with spa tubs and fireplaces. *1755 1st St. ☎ 707/226-2450. www.blackbirdinnnapa.com. 8 units. $200–$285. AE, DC, DISC, MC, V. Map p 117.*

★★★ **Calistoga Ranch** CALISTOGA Operated by the prestigious Auberge brand, this quiet, airy ranch amidst the pines combines modern luxury with natural earthiness. Freestanding, pet-friendly lodges display elegant decor and a setup blurring the line between indoor and outdoor. A superior spa and restaurant impress. *580 Lommel Rd. ☎ 707/254-2800. www.calistogaranch.com. 46 units. Doubles $475–$1,225. AE, DC, DISC, MC, V. Map p 117.*

★★ **Candlelight Inn** NAPA A Tudor mansion on Napa Creek, this B&B in the redwoods (2 miles/3.2km from downtown) is a perennial favorite. Country-style rooms are equipped with a private balcony, a marble fireplace, or a two-person Jacuzzi tub. Don't miss the three-course breakfast. *1045 Easum Dr. ☎ 707/257-3717. www.candlelightinn.com. 10 units. Doubles $229–$369. AE, DISC, MC, V. Map p 117.*

★★ **The Carneros Inn** NAPA This cluster of private residences epitomizes clean design. Delve into 27 acres (11 hectares) of vineyards, a spa, restaurants (p 76), and an infinity pool. *4048 Sonoma Hwy. (Hwy. 12). ☎ 707/299-4900. www.thecarnerosinn.com. 104 units. Doubles $435–$555. AE, DC, DISC, MC, V. Map p 117.*

★ **CasaLana** CALISTOGA If you're a gourmand, you'll be enticed by the hands-on cooking classes held here. Even if you're not, you'll be minutes from downtown in a country-style room with a private entrance and Wi-Fi. *1316 S. Oak St. ☎ 707/942-0615. www.casalana.com. 2 units. $189–$319. AE, DISC, MC, V. Map p 117.*

★★ **Cedar Gables Inn** NAPA This Shakespeare-inspired 1892

manor's Renaissance-era artifacts mix with rich textures and colors. Rooms have whirlpool baths and fireplaces, and come with a three-course breakfast and an evening wine reception. Ask owners Ken and Susie Pope for a tour of the secret staircases. Three blocks from downtown. *486 Coombs St. ☎ 800/309-7969. www.cedargablesinn.com. 9 units. $156–$359. AE, DISC, MC, V. Map p 117.*

★ **Chateau de Vie** CALISTOGA The "house of life" is a B&B on a small working winery (try the cabernet). Highlights include a generous breakfast, refined rooms, a pool, and a view of Mt. St. Helena. *3250 Hwy. 128. ☎ 877/558-2513. www.cdvnapavalley.com. 4 units. $229–$429. AE, MC, V. Map p 117.*

★★ **Churchill Manor** NAPA This B&B a few blocks from downtown is a beautiful 1889 Victorian mansion bolstered by columns. Intricately decorated rooms feature vintage tubs and huge showers; outside, there's a fountain courtyard, rose gardens, and a capacious veranda. Borrow a tandem bike before heading out. *485 Brown St. ☎ 800/799-7733. www.churchillmanor.com. 10 units. Doubles $165–$335. AE, DISC, MC, V. Map p 117.*

★★ **Cottage Grove Inn** CALISTOGA Calm permeates these cottages set in an elm grove at the end of Calistoga's main strip. Relax by a fireplace or under a skylight in a two-person Jacuzzi tub. Furnishings are homey and cozy, and a stay includes breakfast and evening wine. *1711 Lincoln Ave. ☎ 800/799-2284. www.cottagegrove.com. 16 units. Doubles $250–$395. AE, DC, DISC, MC, V. Map p 117.*

★★★ **The Cottages of Napa Valley** NAPA Originally a 1929 motel, this sheltered complex was remodeled to embody country-style chic. A stay here is utterly gratifying, in part because of the amenities: a breakfast basket with delights from Bouchon, Wi-Fi, and weekend wine receptions. Each exceptionally comfortable cottage features a king bed, fireplace, kitchenette, Jacuzzi tub, and a front and back patio. *1012 Darms Lane. ☎ 707/252-7810. www.napacottages.com. 8 units. $255–$525. AE, MC, V. Map p 117.*

★ **Dr. Wilkinson's Hot Springs Resort** CALISTOGA Calistoga's longest family-owned business (established 1952) still has character. A mud bath here is a must; equally enjoyable are massages, facials, and mineral pools (p 103). Easy access to shops and restaurants. *1507 Lincoln Ave. ☎ 707/942-4102. www.drwilkinson.com. 42 units. Doubles $129–$299. AE, MC, V. Map p 117.*

★★ **1801 First Inn** NAPA Named for its downtown address, this Queen Anne Victorian blends contemporary touches with classic European decor. An in-house chef prepares delectable three-course breakfasts and gourmet hors d'oeuvres for evening wine tastings. *1801 1st St. ☎ 707/253-1331. www.1801first.com. 8 units. $199–$475. AE, DISC, MC, V. Map p 117.*

Embassy Suites NAPA Effort went into giving this chain a local feel. Touches include a swan pond with a wooden mill, a pool, and a large atrium where breakfast (included) is cooked to order and cocktails (also included) are served each evening. The suites' layout is such that the bedroom closes off from the living room, which is equipped with a pullout couch—meaning that a single reservation could work comfortably for a family of four. *1075 California Blvd. ☎ 707/253-9540. www.napavalley.embassysuites.com. 205 units. Doubles $159–$299. AE, DC, DISC, MC, V. Map p 117.*

Gaia Napa Valley Hotel & Spa ANDERSON One of the world's eco-friendliest hotels, Gaia is also luxurious; you'll enjoy breakfast in bed, a spa, and a heated outdoor pool. Only thing is, it's at a bit of a distance from wine country's main attractions. If you stay here, rent a car (preferably a hybrid) and plan your itinerary accordingly. *600 Broadway St. ☎ 888/798-3777. www.gaianapavalleyhotel.com. 122 rooms. $75–$279. AE, DC, DISC, MC, V.*

★★ **Harvest Inn** ST. HELENA This upscale property offers rustic country charm, daily wine tastings, and gorgeous gardens. Breakfast is included, and many suites feature fireplaces, spa tubs, Wi-Fi, and private terraces. Try a treatment at the spa. *1 Main St. ☎ 800/950-8466. www.harvestinn.com. 74 units. Doubles $256–$600. AE, DISC, MC, V. Map p 117.*

★ **Hennessey House** NAPA This downtown B&B's rooms are flowery and Wi-Fi-equipped. The main house is an 1889 Victorian and its six units are less pricey than the four in the Carriage House. A stay includes a sumptuous breakfast, afternoon tea, and evening wine. *1727 Main St. ☎ 707/226-3774. www.hennesseyhouse.com. 10 units. Doubles $119–$319. AE, DC, DISC, MC, V. Map p 117.*

★★ **Indian Springs** CALISTOGA Deriving its name from Calistoga's previous life as a Native American healing ground, this resort with comfortable bungalows is where you can detoxify in a volcanic-ash mudbath and soak in a naturally heated 1913 Olympic-size, thermal-geyser-fed mineral pool. *1712 Lincoln Ave. ☎ 707/942-4913. www.indianspringscalistoga.com. 16 units. Doubles $210–$315. DISC, MC, V. Map p 117.*

★ **La Belle Epoque** NAPA This plush B&B and its two-unit sister property across the street, the Buckley House, are century-old Queen Anne Victorians standing as

Meadowood has something for anyone who is willing to shell out a pretty penny.

stately testament to Napa's rich architectural history. Rooms boast elegant antiques and high-grade linens. Indulge in the candlelit breakfast and the nightly wine-and-cheese reception. *1386 Calistoga Ave. ☎ 800/238-8070. www.napabelle.com. 7 units. $159–$439. AE, DISC, MC, V. Map p 117.*

★ **Lavender** YOUNTVILLE A homey 1870 B&B with wooden floors and French-tinged country furnishings, Lavender's small touches include lavender sachets, chocolate upon turndown, Wi-Fi, and afternoon snacks. Borrowing the inn's bicycles makes exploring fun (though local attractions are within walking distance). *2020 Webber Ave. ☎ 707/944-1388. www.foursisters.com. 8 units. $150–$300. AE, DC, DISC, MC, V. Map p 117.*

★ **Maison Fleurie** YOUNTVILLE The "flowering house" certainly is. This garden property offers rooms with country-style decor and stone fireplaces, breakfast each morning, and wine and hors d'oeuvres each afternoon. *6529 Yount St. ☎ 800/788-0369. www.maisonfleurienapa.com. 13 units. Doubles $140–$300. AE, DC, DISC, MC, V. Map p 117.*

★★★ **Meadowood Napa Valley** ST. HELENA That George W. Bush stayed here during his most recent Napa visit says it all. This exclusive Relais & Châteaux property, also a private club for local leaders, is reminiscent of a grand country estate; its personalized service, luxury spa, tennis courts, croquet lawns, pools, and golf course set it apart. Lodging is amid oaks in a private 250-acre (100-hectare) valley. *900 Meadowood Lane. ☎ 800/458-8080. www.meadowood.com. 85 units. Doubles $450–$2,650. AE, DISC, MC, V. Map p 117.*

★ **The Meritage Resort** NAPA The Meritage, 4 miles (6.4km) from downtown Napa in the Carneros region, claims the world's only underground-cave spa. Also onsite are wine caves, vineyards, and tastings. Siena restaurant's Tuscan cuisine accompanies a comprehensive wine list. Rooms offer Wi-Fi, plasma TVs, and fireplaces. *875 Bordeaux Way. ☎ 866/370-6272. www.themeritagehotel.com. 338 units. Doubles $269–$489. AE, DC, DISC, MC, V. Map p 117.*

★★★ **Milliken Creek Inn & Spa** NAPA This garden property is known for luxury and attention to detail. Earth-toned rooms are graced with king canopy beds, fireplaces, fresh orchids, and private decks with river views. Marble bathrooms feature hydrotherapy tubs and rain showers. Breakfast is gourmet, and an evening wine-and-cheese reception is attended by vintners. Don't forego an aromatherapy massage at the spa. *1815 Silverado Trail. ☎ 707/255-1197. www.millikencreekinn.com. 12 units. Doubles $350–$675. AE, DC, DISC, MC, V. Map p 117.*

★★ **Mount View Hotel** CALISTOGA Smallish, romantic rooms with European-style antiques are set in a downtown 1917 building. Highlights include a pool and Jacuzzi, a lobby fireplace, Stomp Restaurant, and Wi-Fi. Breakfast snacks are delivered each morning, and there's an onsite spa. *1457 Lincoln Ave. ☎ 800/816-6877. www.mountviewhotel.com. 32 units. Doubles $169–$339. AE, DISC, MC, V. Map p 117.*

★ **Napa River Inn** NAPA In the 1884 Napa Mill complex, this downtown inn overlooks the Napa River. Pet-friendly rooms feature Wi-Fi and historical, nautical, and country stylings. In-room breakfast service and two restaurants, Celadon and Angèle, are superb. *500 Main St.*

☎ *707/251-8500. www.napariverinn.com. 66 units. Doubles $169–$499. AE, DC, DISC, MC, V. Map p 117.*

★★★ **Poetry Inn** YOUNTVILLE Cliff Lede Vineyards (p 140) has Stags Leap District's only public lodging—and what lodging! Posh rooms sit 500 feet (150m) above the valley; vineyard views are spectacular. Decor is classy and private outdoor showers add uniqueness. At breakfast (included), try the brie-and-strawberry French toast, then enjoy an open-air massage, lounge by the pool, or marvel at the wine cellar's rarities. *6380 Silverado Trail.* ☎ *707/944-0646. www.poetryinn.com. 3 units. $460–$1,400. AE, DC, MC, V. Map p 117.*

★ **Rancho Caymus Inn** RUTHERFORD This Spanish hacienda–style inn has a rich history, cozy-funky decor, and architecture that incorporates adobe fireplaces, 100-year-old timber, stucco walls, and clay tile. Amenities include Wi-Fi, breakfast, and a romantic garden courtyard. Some rooms come with kitchenettes, whirlpool tubs, or private balconies. Pay the property's La Toque restaurant a visit. *1140 Rutherford Rd.* ☎ *707/963-1777. www.ranchocaymus.com. 26 units. Doubles $169–$439. AE, MC, V. Map p 117.*

Roman Spa Hot Springs Resort CALISTOGA Though this is a spa resort, rooms are modest. The grounds contain three mineral-water pools (two are onsite) and two Finnish saunas. *1300 Washington St.* ☎ *707/942-4441. www.romanspahotsprings.com. 60 units. Doubles $130–$360. AE, DISC, MC, V. Map p 117.*

Silverado Resort NAPA This resort is a country club, so it's great for golf (two courses) but lacks the intimacy of many other wine-country inns. Suites have kitchenettes and undersized bathrooms. Decor is low-key—more practical than aesthetic. Highlights include the spa and The Grill. *1600 Atlas Peak Rd.* ☎ *707/257-0200. www.silveradoresort.com. 280 units. Doubles $315–$335. AE, DC, DISC, MC, V. Map p 117.*

★★★ **Villagio Inn & Spa** YOUNTVILLE Yountville's fanciest lodging has a distinctly Mediterranean feel, from the water features to the Roman-style "ruins." Rooms are luxurious, and a stay comes with a bottle

The Embarcadero suite comes with a fireplace at the Napa River Inn.

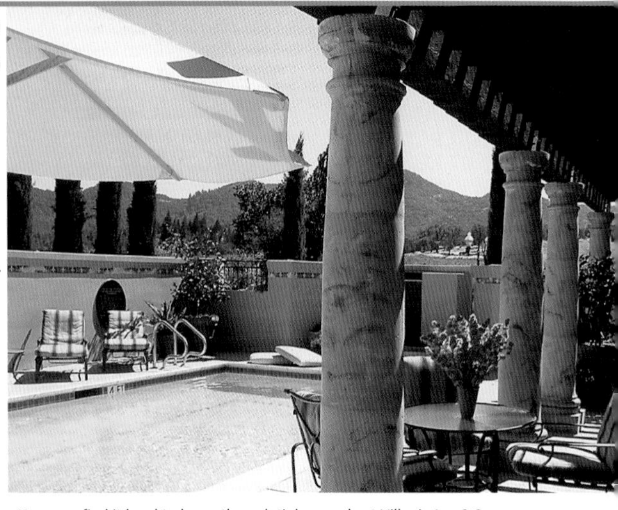

You may find it hard to leave the palatial grounds at Villagio Inn & Spa.

of Beringer and a superb breakfast buffet. Staffers are hospitable, and the spa's river-stone massage may well be Napa's best treatment. *6481 Washington St. ☎ 707/944-8877. www.villagio.com. 138 units. Doubles $340–$775. AE, DISC, MC, V. Map p 117.*

Vintage Inn & Spa YOUNTVILLE Villagio's older downtown sister property has spacious rooms with generous tubs and balconies. Amenities like free wine and breakfast make guests feel welcome. Ask for a room overlooking Domaine Chandon. *6541 Washington St. ☎ 800/351-1133. www.vintageinn.com. 92 units. Doubles $340–$740. AE, DISC, MC, V. Map p 117.*

★★★ **Westin Verasa** NAPA Rooms here are so spacious, so extravagant, so chock-full of amenities that you might end up wanting to stay inside. But don't—the hotel sits right on the Napa River and is within walking distance of the town's best landmarks, including Oxbow Public Market and 12 tasting rooms. It's also home to Michelin-starred restaurant, La Toque. *1314 Mckinstry Street. www.starwoodhotels.com. ☎ 707/257-1800. 180 suites. Doubles from $409–$819. AE, DISC, MC, V.*

Sonoma Lodging A to Z

★ **Applewood Inn** GUERNEVILLE This sweet 1922 mission revival–style mansion's individually decorated rooms are Wi-Fi-equipped. Outside, there's a pool, hot tub, and organic herb garden for the onsite restaurant (a stay includes breakfast). It's a 2-minute drive to Main Street, but feels forested and remote. *13555 Hwy. 116. ☎ 707/869-9093. www.applewoodinn.com. 19 units. Doubles $195–$345. AE, MC, V. Map p 116.*

★★ **Beltane Ranch** GLEN ELLEN This B&B in a pastel-yellow 1892 manor has everything a country ranch should: clean, antiques-furnished rooms with private entrances (no TV or phone); a big, delectable breakfast; a wraparound porch; hiking trails; a tennis court; and lots of greenery. Enjoy the drive up from the highway and request an upstairs room with a view. *11775 Sonoma Hwy. (Hwy. 12). ☎ 707/996-6501. www.beltaneranch.com. 6 units. $150–$220. Check or cash only. Map p 116.*

★ **Bungalows 313** SONOMA These private, spacious downtown cottages have kitchens, though a tasty breakfast is provided. There's also a fountain courtyard and the option of staying in the romantic 1906 brick house. Attention to detail reveals itself in small and large touches like fresh flowers and inviting interiors. *313 1st St. ☎ 707/996-8091. www.bungalows313.com. 5 units. $160 and up. DISC, MC, V. Map p 116.*

★★ **The Cottage Inn & Spa Mission B&B** SONOMA This well-loved retreat proximal to Sonoma's mission incorporates Cal-Med architecture and gardens. Individually decorated rooms have private entrances, fireplaces, spa tubs, and big, comfy beds. Also included are a pastries-and-fruit breakfast and access to a fitness club. *302 1st St. ☎ 800/944-1490. www.cottageinnandspa.com. 8 units. $225–$415. DISC, MC, V. Map p 116.*

★★ **El Dorado Hotel** SONOMA El Dorado's strong points are its chic decor—more town than country—and excellent plaza location. Small but sunny rooms feature four-poster beds, fine linens, and small balconies. Outside, there's a heated lap pool. The hip El Dorado Kitchen (p 81) is a must-try; chef Ryan Fancher was formerly at French Laundry. *405 1st St. ☎ 707/996-3030. www.eldoradosonoma.com. 27 units. Doubles $175–$225. AE, DC, MC, V. Map p 116.*

★★★ **Fairmont Sonoma Mission Inn & Spa** BOYES HOT SPRINGS Established in 1927, this Sonoma institution gets better with age. Rooms are charming; many have fireplaces. The mineral-water-fed spa is divine, as is the cuisine at upscale Santé. Though it's in a drab area 3 miles (4.8km) from Sonoma, guests don't want to leave; free wine tastings add to the desire to stay. The resort offers excursions like free hiking and biking tours and access to a nearby 18-hole golf course. *100 Boyes Blvd. ☎ 707/938-9000. www.fairmont.com/sonoma. 226 units. Doubles $209–$1,500. AE, DC, DISC, MC, V. Map p 116.*

★ **The Gables Wine Country Inn** SANTA ROSA This cozy B&B looks like a dollhouse from the outside and, inside, a Victorian manor. Rooms feature claw-foot tubs and historical appointments. Enjoy the lavender garden and sample wine in the evening. Splurge on the quiet creekside cottage, which has a hot tub. *4257 Petaluma Hill Rd. ☎ 800/422-5376. www.thegablesinn.com. 8 units. $175–$250. AE, DISC, MC, V. Map p 116.*

★★★ **Gaige House Inn** GLEN ELLEN Though this creekside inn was built in 1890, it's been entirely remodeled, including an addition of eight Asian-themed suites with decor rivaling that of five-star hotels. The superb breakfast is served in a light-filled space by friendly attendants. There's also an in-house spa, plus a pool and hot tubs. *13540 Arnold Dr. ☎ 800/935-0237. www.gaige.com. 23 units. Doubles $295–$590. AE, DISC, MC, V. Map p 116.*

A tempting pool is only one of the features that makes the Fairmont an oasis in Boyes Hot Springs.

★ Glenelly Inn & Cottages
GLEN ELLEN At this 1916 inn, try to stay in the cute country cottages in a wooded oak niche as opposed to the suites, which are also nice but a bit darker and smaller. Breakfast is included. *5131 Warm Springs Rd.* ☎ *707/996-6720. www.glenelly.com. 9 units. $119–$299. AE, DISC, MC, V. Map p 116.*

★★ Grape Leaf Inn HEALDSBURG Country chic (very chic) with stained-glass touches, this refined B&B is a century-old Queen Anne Victorian offering luxury amenities, soothing gardens, an exceptional four-course breakfast, and cozy rooms with skylights, fireplaces, and spa tubs. The speak-easy tasting room (hidden behind a bookcase!) hosts nightly wine-and-cheese tastings. *539 Johnson St.* ☎ *707/433-8140. www.grapeleafinn.com. 12 units. Doubles $285–$395. MC, V. Map p 116.*

★ Healdsburg Inn on the Plaza
HEALDSBURG Clean, comfortable rooms have high ceilings, fireplaces, and flourishes hearkening back to when the inn was built: 1901. A stay includes breakfast and afternoon wine. Since the inn is in the middle of town, request a room in the quieter back. *112 Matheson St.* ☎ *800/431-8663. www.healdsburginn.com. 12 units. Doubles $275–$375. AE, DISC, MC, V. Map p 116.*

★★★ Honor Mansion HEALDSBURG More than $1.5 million went into developing this property, resulting in an indulgent retreat. Plush suites in an Italianate Victorian building are surrounded by more than 120 rosebushes and a quarter-acre (.1-hectare) vineyard. A talented chef culls herbs from onsite gardens to concoct magnificent breakfasts. Also outdoors are a lap pool; jogging trail; croquet lawn; putting green; and tennis, bocce, and basketball courts. *14891 Grove St.* ☎ *707/433-4277. www.honormansion.com. 13 units. Doubles $355–$510. AE, MC, V. Map p 116.*

★★★ Hotel Healdsburg
HEALDSBURG A modern option

amid Healdsburg's more traditional properties, this $21-million hotel offers rooms with hardwood floors and Tibetan rugs, private balconies, deep bathtubs, and Frette linens. Outside, there's a pool and green lounging spaces. Cuisine is divine throughout, from breakfast to dinner at Charlie Palmer's inspired Dry Creek Kitchen (p 90). At the small spa, try the Combination Massage. *25 Matheson St. ☎ 707/431-2800. www.hotelhealdsburg.com. 55 units. Doubles $260–$790. MC, V. Map p 116.*

★★ The Kenwood Inn & Spa KENWOOD Gorgeous mission-style architecture houses rooms with textured decor. Other features include fountain courtyards, a tasting room, three Jacuzzis, and a pool. Try a bath or facial at the "vinotherapy" spa. Though it's a bit close to Highway 12, it maintains romance and privacy. Breakfast is included. *10400 Sonoma Hwy. (Hwy. 12). ☎ 707/833-1293. www.kenwoodinn.com. 30 units. Doubles $425–$825. AE, MC, V. Map p 116.*

★★ Ledson Hotel SONOMA This perfectly located hotel built by a fifth-generation winemaker transports guests to a time when antiques were new. Grand decor and modern amenities accent excellent service. Luxuriate by the fireplace while listening to live music at the hotel's Harmony Restaurant (p 81). *480 1st St. ☎ 707/996-9779. www.ledsonhotel.com. 6 units. $350–$395. AE, DISC, MC, V. Map p 116.*

★★★ Les Mars Hotel HEALDSBURG The ultimate in old-Europe-style luxury. Gracious service awaits each guest, as do inspired touches like Louis XV armoires, lavish four-poster beds, and Bain Ultra soaking tubs. A gourmet three-course breakfast and nightly cheese tastings are included, and dinner at the hotel's Cyrus—Healdsburg's "it" restaurant—is a real treat (p 90). *27 North St. ☎ 707/433-4211. www.lesmarshotel.com. 16 units. Doubles $475–$1,050. AE, MC, V. Map p 116.*

★★ The Lodge at Sonoma SONOMA At this comfortable resort, an inviting lobby welcomes guests before they retreat to a well-appointed room, suite, or cottage. A treatment at Raindance Spa invigorates, while a meal at Carneros surpasses even high expectations. *1325 Broadway. ☎ 707/935-6600. www.thelodgeatsonoma.com. 182 units. Doubles $169–$389. AE, DC, MC, V. Map p 116.*

★★ MacArthur Place SONOMA On one of Sonoma's main thoroughfares (so factor in some noise) is this country-style inn with pretty grounds. Breakfast is included, as is a wine-and-cheese reception in the library, where you can borrow a movie or book. Rooms are flowery and, if you upgrade to a suite, spacious. *29 E. MacArthur St. ☎ 707/933-2929. www.macarthurplace.com. 64 units. Doubles $199–$475. MC, V. Map p 116.*

★ Ramekins SONOMA This B&B and culinary school is the perfect stay for foodies. Packages include a bottle of wine and discounts on cooking classes that take place downstairs. Individually decorated rooms are Wi-Fi-equipped and have antique pine furniture and oversized bathrooms. Breakfast features homemade granola and pastries. *450 W. Spain St. ☎ 707/933-0452. www.innatramekins.com. 6 units. $135–$250. AE, DISC, MC, V. Map p 116.*

★★ Safari West Tent Camp SANTA ROSA Central to both valleys is this ultimate family getaway. The 400-acre (160-hectare) preserve, home to hundreds of African animals, maintains a cluster of safari

The perfect spot to curl up after a long, arduous day of wine-tasting: a room with a fireplace at Les Mars Hotel.

tents with hardwood floors. From each accommodation, guests can watch giraffes, zebras, and cheetahs. Breakfast is included, and the safari drive is a must-do (p 24). *3115 Porter Creek Rd. ☎ 707/579-2551. www.safariwest.com. 32 units. $170–$295. AE, MC, V. Map p 116.*

★ **Trojan Horse Inn** SONOMA This 1887 Victorian farmhouse is romantic and comfortable. Rooms feature antique furnishings and memory-foam mattresses sheathed in Frette. Pleasantries include a multi-course breakfast, a hot tub, bikes to borrow, and wine receptions. *19455 Sonoma Hwy. (Hwy. 12). ☎ 707/996-2430. www.trojanhorseinn.com. 6 units. $190–$250. AE, DISC, MC, V. Map p 116.*

★ **Villa Verotto** CARNEROS Elusive, exclusive, and exquisite, this vineyard estate has a pool, a hot tub, and three smartly decorated bedrooms. The owners of the gated property keep its address confidential until booking to ensure guests' privacy—but it's about 5 miles (8km) from Sonoma Plaza. *☎ 415/225-3027. www.verotto.com. 1 unit. $600–$1,275. MC, V. Map p 116.*

Vine Hill Inn SEBASTOPOL Once an 1897 farmhouse, this romantic B&B still keeps a barn with chickens, goats, and a blind pony. Rooms have private decks, Jacuzzi tubs, hardwood floors, and warm decor. A tasty breakfast, swimming pool, and vineyards add to the appeal. *3949 Vine Hill Rd. ☎ 707/823-8832. www.vine-hill-inn.com. 4 units. $170. AE, DISC, MC, V. Map p 116.* ●

7 The Best Wineries

Napa Valley Wineries

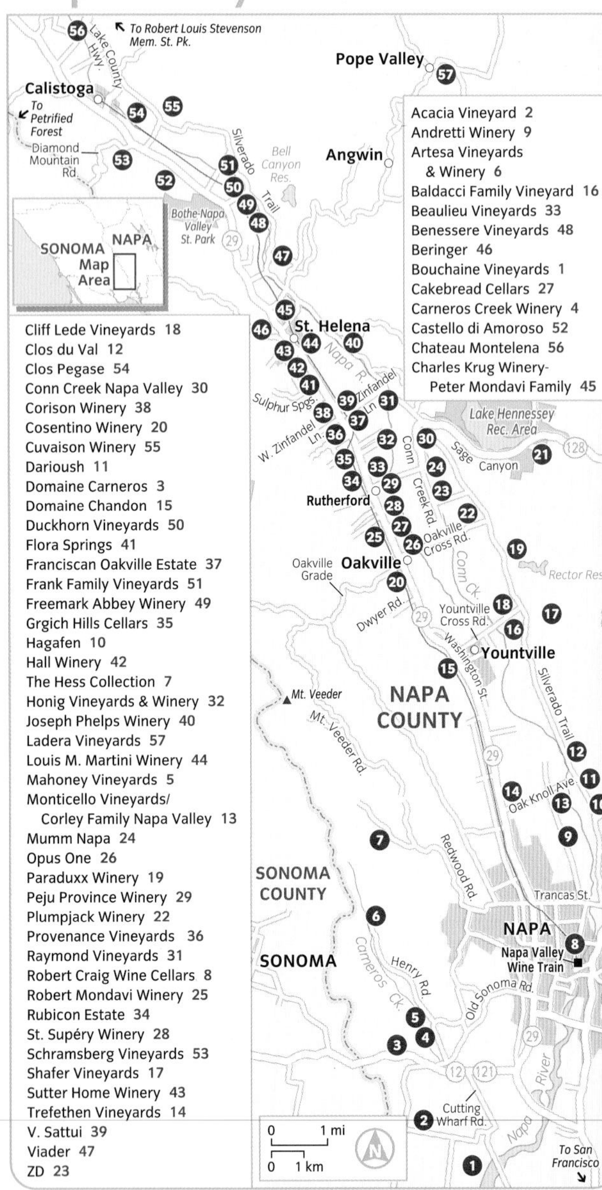

Acacia Vineyard 2
Andretti Winery 9
Artesa Vineyards & Winery 6
Baldacci Family Vineyard 16
Beaulieu Vineyards 33
Benessere Vineyards 48
Beringer 46
Bouchaine Vineyards 1
Cakebread Cellars 27
Carneros Creek Winery 4
Castello di Amoroso 52
Chateau Montelena 56
Charles Krug Winery-Peter Mondavi Family 45
Cliff Lede Vineyards 18
Clos du Val 12
Clos Pegase 54
Conn Creek Napa Valley 30
Corison Winery 38
Cosentino Winery 20
Cuvaison Winery 55
Darioush 11
Domaine Carneros 3
Domaine Chandon 15
Duckhorn Vineyards 50
Flora Springs 41
Franciscan Oakville Estate 37
Frank Family Vineyards 51
Freemark Abbey Winery 49
Grgich Hills Cellars 35
Hagafen 10
Hall Winery 42
The Hess Collection 7
Honig Vineyards & Winery 32
Joseph Phelps Winery 40
Ladera Vineyards 57
Louis M. Martini Winery 44
Mahoney Vineyards 5
Monticello Vineyards/Corley Family Napa Valley 13
Mumm Napa 24
Opus One 26
Paraduxx Winery 19
Peju Province Winery 29
Plumpjack Winery 22
Provenance Vineyards 36
Raymond Vineyards 31
Robert Craig Wine Cellars 8
Robert Mondavi Winery 25
Rubicon Estate 34
St. Supéry Winery 28
Schramsberg Vineyards 53
Shafer Vineyards 17
Sutter Home Winery 43
Trefethen Vineyards 14
V. Sattui 39
Viader 47
ZD 23

Previous page: Oak aging can be pricey. French Oak barrels cost between $500 and $1,00

Northern Sonoma Wineries

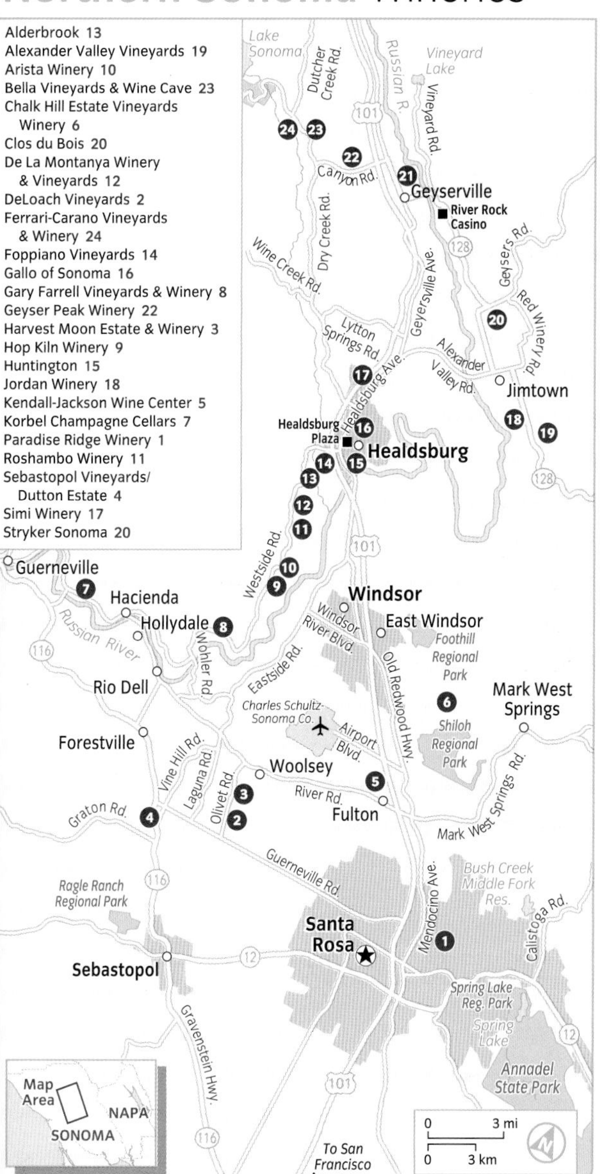

Sonoma Valley Wineries

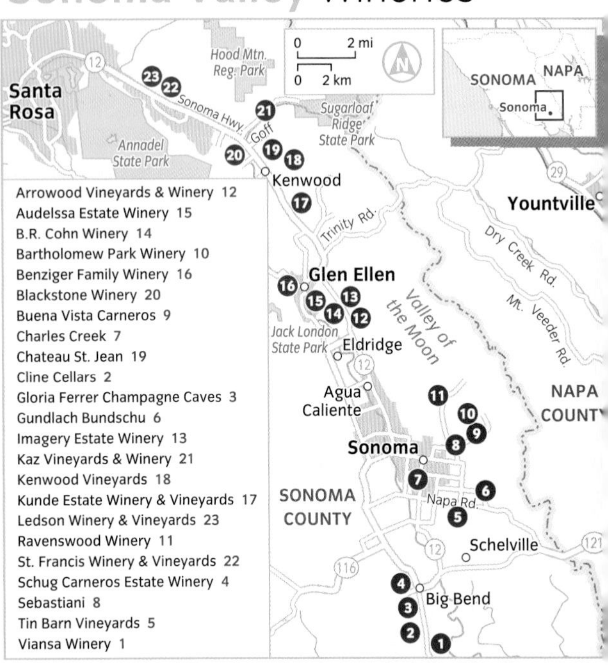

Wineries A to Z

A note about winery labels: ORG wineries use organic grapes; BIO refers to biodynamic practices; SUST indicates a winery's commitment to sustainability; and SULF wines have no added sulfites.

Acacia Vineyard NAPA Founded in 1979 in the famous Carneros region, Acacia specializes in dark pinot noir and chardonnay. Bring your camera into the tasting room: Because it's 2 miles (3.2km) from San Francisco's San Pablo Bay, you'll want to snap shots of the water views. *2750 Las Amigas Rd., Napa. ☎ 877/226-1700. www.acaciavineyard.com. By appt. Mon–Sat 10am–4pm, Sun noon–4pm. Tours ($15, including tastings) by appt. Mon–Fri 11am or 2pm. Tastings: $15 (By appt. only; last tasting at 3:30pm). North on Calif. 121, then right on Duhig Rd., left on Las Amigas Rd. Map p 130.*

Alderbrook SONOMA For a rural winery, Alderbrook is remarkably close to Healdsburg Plaza, so it's a great place for a serene wine-accented picnic away from the throngs—especially if you want a view to remember. Visitors can buy wine and specialty food items (think fruity chardonnay or dark, dry

Carignane paired with fresh French bread) in the laid-back tasting room. If it's windy out, stay in the tasting room to absorb the fireplace's heat. *2306 Magnolia Dr., Healdsburg. ☎ 800/405-5987. www.alderbrook.com. Daily 10am–5pm (closed major holidays). No tours. Tastings: free–$5, refunded with purchase. Hwy. 101 S, exit Westside, turn right. Map p 131.*

Alexander Valley Vineyards SONOMA *SUST* This estate, now owned by the Wetzel family, was once the property of Cyrus Alexander (yes, as in Alexander Valley). The Wetzels bought the land from the Alexanders and, in 1975, "AVV" was born. The winery, on the Russian River, makes for a perfect picnic spot—views of Sonoma Valley are superb from here. Try their award-winning Cyrus (a cab-dominated blend) or their zinfandels, Redemption Zin and Sin Zin; the latter was an instant sensation and is their cult wine. *8644 Hwy. 128, Healdsburg. ☎ 800/888-7209. www.avvwine.com. Daily 10am–5pm. Free tours of wine caves by appt. Tastings: free–$10 (refunded with purchase). 6 miles (9.7km) northeast of Healdsburg. Map p 131.*

Andretti Winery NAPA Andretti is a Northern Italian–style winery founded by race-car driving champion Mario Andretti in 1996. Despite the celebrity cachet, the staff here couldn't be more down-to-earth. Ask them anything about Napa; they're likely to be able to answer. Tastings take place in a Tuscan villa, adjacent to which is an outdoor patio where visitors take in views of vineyards and mountains while sipping a light, zesty chardonnay or a richer cabernet sauvignon. *4162 Big Ranch Rd., Napa. ☎ 888/460-8463. www.andrettiwinery.com. Daily 10am–5pm (closed major holidays). No tours available for groups smaller than 10 people. Tastings: $12 for 4 wines. Hwy. 29 north, then right onto Oak Knoll Rd., then right on Big Ranch Rd. Map p 130.*

Try Sin Zin, Alexander Valley Vineyards' cult wine.

Arista Winery SONOMA *BIO, SUST* Known for their small lots of pinot noir and bone-dry gewürztraminer, this family-owned boutique winery recently opened a hospitality center. There, visitors stroll through beautiful Japanese water gardens and gaze at century-old oaks while tasting wine. Picnic spots are available, and a midweek visit is best to avoid crowds. *7015 Westside Rd., Healdsburg. ☎ 707/473-0606. www.aristawinery.com. Daily 11am–5pm, Tues & Wed by appt. No tours. Tastings: free for appellation wines, $5 for single-vineyard pinot noirs (fee refunded with wine purchase). From Healdsburg, take Westside Rd. west for about 8 miles (13km). Map p 131.*

★ Arrowood Vineyards & Winery SONOMA *ORG, SUST* More than 20 years ago, a married couple founded Arrowood on a hillside overlooking Sonoma. Today,

The Lower fountain at Artesa Winery.

visitors savor samples of the handcrafted cabernets Arrowood is known for in their Hospitality House. The sun-dappled tasting room has a spacious balcony from which sippers can see Sonoma Mountain. Choose from two tours: the 40-minute overview or the in-depth 90-minute vineyard and cellar tour. Both end with tastings. *14347 Sonoma Hwy. (Hwy. 12), Glen Ellen. ☎ 800/938-5170. www.arrowoodvineyards.com. Daily 10am–4:30pm. Tours ($15–$30, including tastings) daily at 10:30am & 2:30pm, by appt. Tastings: $5–$15 (refunded with purchase). Map p 132.*

★★ Artesa Vineyards & Winery NAPA *SUST* Art and architecture strike first when encountering this winery; its modern semi-pyramid structure and stakelike sculptures impress, as do arching fountains, a water-centric courtyard, and a stark tasting room. But do the wines live up to the arresting visuals? Yes, especially the chardonnay and pinot noir. Peruse the Carneros Center, which documents the region's history, or the museum, with displays of ancient winemaking tools. *1345 Henry Rd., Napa. ☎ 707/224-1668. www.artesawinery.com. Daily 10am–5pm (last tasting 4:30pm). Tours $10 daily 11am & 2pm. Tastings: $10–$15. From Hwy. 12, turn left on Old Sonoma Rd., then left on Dealy Lane, which becomes Henry Rd. Map p 130.*

Audelssa/Navillus Birney Winery & Vineyards SONOMA This small, family-owned operation (formerly Sullivan Birney) runs a cute country-style storefront tasting room 2 miles (3.2km) from the winery. On display are artifacts documenting Glen Ellen's history and photos of authors Jack London and M. F. K. Fisher. Try the chardonnay, pinot noir, and syrah. *13647 Arnold Dr., Glen Ellen. ☎ 707/933-8514. Fri–Mon 11am–5pm. Tues–Thurs By appt. only. From Sonoma Hwy. N., turn left onto Arnold Dr. Map p 132.*

Baldacci Family Vineyards NAPA *SUST* Tom and Brenda Baldacci founded their winery in 1998 with the notion of sharing wine with friends and family; hence the reason many of their hand-farmed creations are named after relatives. Try Elizabeth, a pinot noir that shares a name with Tom's mother—but don't miss the winery's signature cabernet. *6236 Silverado Trail, Napa. ☎ 707/944-9261. www.baldaccivineyards.com. Daily 11am–4pm (by appt.). Book several weeks in advance for a tour (free with tasting). Tastings: $10 (refunded with wine purchase). Map p 130.*

Bartholomew Park Winery SONOMA *ORG* "Bart Park" is more than a winery; it's a full destination with a museum, memorial park, picnic grounds, and hiking trails. If you're here solely for tasting, you'll be satisfied with the limited-production single-vineyard wines, particularly the much-honored 2001 cabernet sauvignon (it took gold in two major competitions). If you're in a learning mood, check out Bartholomew Park Museum, which chronicles the property's whimsical history. But if you're feeling energetic, ıit the trails. All 3 miles (4.8km) of hem are well-marked and beautiful. On a clear day, you can see all the vay to San Francisco. *1000 Vineyard ane, Sonoma. ☎ 707/935-9511. vww.bartholomewparkwinery.com. aily 11am–4:30pm (closed major olidays). Tours $20 (by appt.). Tastngs: $5. From Hwy. 12, turn right on . Napa St., then left on 7th St. E., hen slight right on Castle Rd. & folow it around to the winery's gates. Map p 132.*

★★ **Beaulieu Vineyard** NAPA SUST This renowned winery was ounded in 1900 by Frenchman and apa pioneer Georges de Latour. oday, the vintage named in his onor—Georges de Latour Private eserve Cabernet—is the company's benchmark and resides in every erious collector's cellar. In the eserve Room, guests sample this nd older selections. For a more edestrian (and crowded) experince, the understated main tasting oom offers a flight of five of the inery's staple wines. ***Fun fact:*** eaulieu's wines have been served y every American president since DR. *1960 St. Helena Hwy., Rutherrd. ☎ 707/967-5233. www.bvines.com. Mon–Fri 10am–5pm losed major holidays). Tours $35 ncludes reserve tasting) 10:30am–om. Tastings: $10–$30. Hwy. 101 N. xit at Hwy. 37, then north on Calif. 21. Map p 130.*

★ **Bella Vineyards** Do yourelf a favor—call ahead for a cave our at Bella. No, not a vineyard our, a cave tour. Why? Because ou'll see mysterious arched doors uilt into the hillside when you pull o to the unassuming, barnlike tastg room. After a few sips of hearty, icy old-vine zinfandel, you'll ask e staff about the doors. They tell ou that behind the doors, flanked old olive trees, are caves housing arrels and underground function

Beaulieu Vineyard (otherwise known as B.V.).

rooms. During the tour, you'll feel cozy thanks to well-placed mood lighting and big, sturdy wood tables filling the winding caverns. You'll be so happy you stopped by this small, family-run winery (named Bella as an ode to the owners' two young daughters) in the heart of Dry Creek Valley that you'll leave plotting a way to schedule your next party underground, in these wine caves. *9711 W. Dry Creek Rd. Healdsburg. ☎ 866/572-3552 or 707/473-9171. www.bellawinery.com. Daily 11am–4:30pm. Tastings: $5–$10 Tours by appt. Map p 131.*

Benessere Vineyards NAPA SUST ***Benessere*** is the Italian word for well-being, and that's certainly the feeling one gets from being here. This 42-acre (17-hectare) country estate is known for its small lots of Italian-inspired wines, many of which come from sangiovese grapes; try Phenomenon—its makers deem it "the pinnacle of winemaking at Benessere." Visit Monday through Wednesday, when the tasting room is least crowded. *1010 Big Tree Rd., St. Helena. ☎ 707/963-5853. www.benesserevineyards.com. Daily 10am–5pm by appt. Tours ($15 including tastings) daily by appt. Tastings: $10 (refunded with wine*

Benziger's rolling hills of vines.

purchase). Hwy. 29 N., then right on Big Tree Rd. Map p 130.

★ Benziger Family Winery SONOMA BIO, SULF, SUST A highlight here is the 45-minute tractor-drawn tram tour. Sit back as a knowledgeable driver maneuvers through the estate's hilly vineyards and discusses how vines get turned into wines. Tours are first-come, first-served, so stop by in the morning to buy afternoon tickets. The winery also has a peacock aviary, rose gardens, picnic grounds, and an educational Vineyard Discovery Center. The tasting room, where visitors taste current and special releases, is in a German-style mansion. Particularly worthy of trying, if available: 2003 Sonoma Mountain Red. And, if you like dessert wines, the 2004 Port. ***1883 London Ranch Rd., Glen Ellen.*** ☎ ***888/490-2739.*** *www.benziger.com. 10am–5pm. Tram tours ($15) daily; call for schedule. Tastings: $10 (includes logo glass). Calif. 121 N. becomes Arnold Dr., then left onto London Ranch Rd. Map p 132.*

★★ Beringer Vineyards NAPA SULF Whoever knows Napa knows Beringer. Established in 1876 by German brothers Jacob and Frederick Beringer, it's Napa's oldest continually operating winery (the Beringers finagled survival during Prohibition by making sacramental

The main building at Beringer Vineyards.

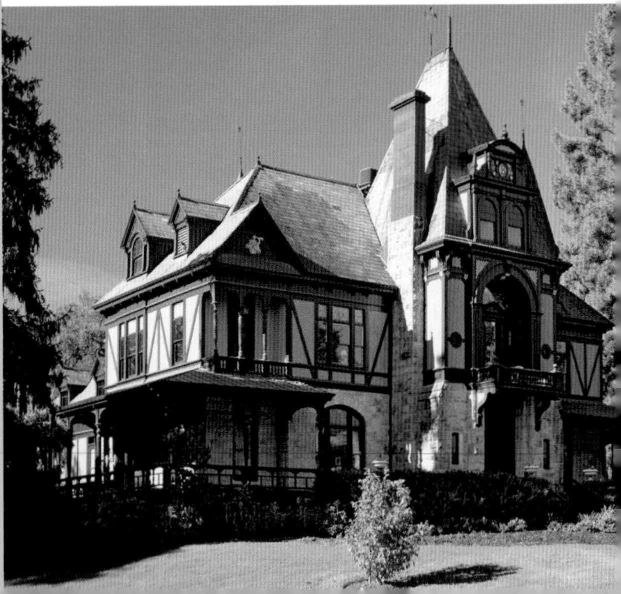

wine). That distinction earned it a spot on the National Register of Historic Places. In 1934, the brothers pioneered the idea of public winery tours and their namesake winery has since perfected their brainchild. Now there are four tour options ranging from a basic introduction to a thorough exploration of Beringer's vintage legacy. In summer, try a seasonal white, but the 2002 Knights Valley Cabernet Sauvignon is sublime in any season. ***2000 Main St., St. Helena. ☎ 707/963-7115. www.beringer.com. Daily 10am–5pm (May 30–Oct 23 until 6pm). Tours ($15–$40) daily 10:45am–3:45pm. Tastings: $10–$30. Hwy. 101 N. Hwy. 29 N. through St. Helena. Turn left into Beringer Vineyards. Map p 130.***

Blackstone Winery SONOMA
Blackstone has a charming, clean tasting room filled with lively visitors. But if the weather's nice, opt for the outdoor bar where friendly staff pour reserve wines and guests can practically reach out and touch the vines. There's also a gourmet shop where you can put together a picnic to enjoy on the grounds. For kicks, try the winery's flagship merlot—surprisingly, it's America's best-selling domestic red wine. ***8450 Sonoma Hwy. (Hwy. 12), Kenwood. ☎ 707/833-1999. www.blackstonewinery.com. Daily 10am–4:30pm. Tours $10–25; 1-week advance reservation required. Tastings: $5. Hwy. 101 N. Exit at Hwy. 37, then north on Calif. 121. Map p 132.***

Bouchaine Vineyards NAPA
SUST Carneros's oldest continuously operated winery presents tastings of its Burgundy-inspired creations in its Wine Visitor Center. Try the pinot noir and chardonnay, as well as the more exclusive wines sold only here. After tasting, step out onto the terrace, where an endless view of vineyards awaits. ***1075 Buchli Station Rd., Napa. ☎ 707/252-9065. www.bouchaine.com.***

The vines and vistas at B.R. Cohn.

Daily 10:30am–4pm (closed some Sun in winter; call to verify). Free tours by appt. Tastings: free–$5. Hwy. 101 N. Exit at Hwy. 37, then north on Calif. 121. Map p 130.

B. R. Cohn Winery SONOMA
Founded in 1984 by Bruce Cohn, this estate winery specializes in fine cabernet and merlot. And since there are olive trees all over the property, the winery also produces gourmet olive oils and vinegars. The tasting room may be small, but the flavors are big, especially if you're trying the 2001 or 2003 Sonoma Valley Merlot. Cohn, interestingly, is the Doobie Brothers' longtime band manager. His other career inspired a Doobie Red wine series, as well as many musical events at the winery (check the website for the schedule). ***15000 Sonoma Hwy. (Hwy. 12), Glen Ellen. ☎ 800/330-4064. www.brcohn.com. Daily 10am–5pm. Seasonal picnic tours ($25) by appt. Tastings: $10 (fee waived with wine purchase). Hwy. 121 N. to Hwy. 12 N., winery is 5 miles (8km) north of Sonoma Plaza. Map p 132.***

★★★ Buena Vista Carneros
SONOMA Not many wineries can boast that their tasting room is a California Historical Landmark—but then again, Buena Vista is America's

The Buena Vista Winery's tasting room is a landmark.

oldest continuously operating winery and the birthplace of California's wine industry. Founded in 1857 by Hungarian colonel Agoston Haraszthy, it still has that delightful old-world feel: ivy-covered buildings, antique fountains, and a restored 1862 press house that houses the tasting room. Try the highly rated Estate Vineyard Series, a near-perfect selection of chardonnay and pinot noir. Picnic grounds are gorgeous here. ***18000 Old Winery Rd., Sonoma. ☎ 800/926-1266. www.buenavistacarneros.com. Daily 10am–5pm (closed major holidays). Free self-guided tours all day; reservations recommended for the daily guided tours ($10–$65). Tastings: $10 & up. Calif. 121 N. to Napa St. & turn right. Take Napa St. to Old Winery Rd. Map p 132.***

Cakebread Cellars NAPA
A small, independent winery with handcrafted wines, Cakebread is known for its chardonnay and cabernet. When Jack and Dolores Cakebread founded it with $2,500 in 1973, they wanted to encourage people to incorporate wine and food into a healthy lifestyle. They've stuck to that goal and now offer a variety of wine and culinary education programs. The tasting area shares space with immense fermenting tanks. ***8300 St. Helena Hwy. (Hwy. 29), Rutherford. ☎ 800/588-0298. www.cakebread.com. Daily 10am–4pm. Tours $25, 10:30am daily (reservations required). Tastings: $10 (by appt.). Map p 130.***

Castello di Amoroso CALISTOGA
A breathtaking Tuscan-inspired castle—you'll feel like you stepped into a fairytale. The winery opened in 2007, the brainchild of well-known vintner Daryl Sattui. It offers 17 Italian-style wines including pinot noir, merlot and dessert varietals. The 121,000-square-foot (11,241sq. m) castle encompasses 107 rooms, a moat, a drawbridge, a torture chamber (!), a knight's chamber, and a chapel. A horse-drawn tour of the vineyards is available, by reservation only, for $68. ***4045 N St Helena Hwy. Entrance fee $10; tastings $10–$15 ($22–$27 with chocolate pairing). Daily 9:30am–6pm (5pm in winter). Tours Mon–Fri 9:30am–4pm (5pm in summer) $25–$37, by reservation only. ☎ 707/967-6272.***

Chalk Hill Estate Vineyards and Winery SONOMA SUST Of the estate's 1,200 acres (480 hectares), only 350 (140 hectares) support vineyards. The rest encompass winery buildings and a wilderness preserve—but that doesn't mean the wines aren't great. Selections include rich chardonnay, cabernet, merlot, sauvignon blanc, and pinot gris. Embark on the culinary tour and tasting, which turns out to be an educational ramble through chef Didier Ageorges' organic culinary garden. *10300 Chalk Hill Rd., Healdsburg. ☎ 707/838-4306. www.chalkhill.com. Daily 10am–4pm. $20 estate tour daily at various times from 10am–3pm; culinary tour $75 on Mon, Thurs & Fri. Tastings: $10. No appointment necessary. Hwy. 101 N. Exit at Shiloh, turn right. Then left on Old Redwood Hwy., right on Pleasant, left on Chalk Hill Rd. Map p 131.*

Charles Creek SONOMA Though its vineyards are scattered through wine country, the winery's tasting room is operated out of a storefront on Sonoma Plaza. Can't decide which of the handcrafted wines to taste? Charles Creek is known for its chardonnay, cabernet, and merlot. There's always local art on display and the room's *pièce de résistance*—aside from its artisan wines—is a cow sculpture made entirely of wine corks. *483 1st St. W., Sonoma. ☎ 707/935-3848. www.charlescreek.com. Daily 10am–5:30pm. From Jan 1–Apr 1, closed on Tues & Wed. No tours. Tastings: $3 (waived with purchase). Hwy. 12 to Sonoma Plaza. Map p 132.*

★ Charles Krug Winery—Peter Mondavi Family NAPA ORG One of only three Napa wineries deemed a California Historical Landmark (the others are Beringer and Schramsberg), this is the county's oldest working winery. It was founded in 1861 by Prussian immigrant Charles Krug, the first to make commercial wine in Napa. The Mondavi family bought the estate in 1943 and has operated it since. They opened the valley's first tasting room, where, over a bar made of redwood wine tanks, visitors taste the winery's signature Bordeaux varietals. There's also opportunity to try rare ports and 20-plus-year-old wines. *2800 Main St. (Hwy. 29), St. Helena. ☎ 707/967-2229. www.charleskrug.com. Daily 10:30am–5pm (closed major holidays). Tours currently unavailable during winery redevelopment. Tastings: $10–$20 (certain tastings are free for Napa County residents with ID & 4 guests). Hwy. 101 N. to Hwy. 37 E., then north on Calif. 12 to Hwy. 29 N. Map p 130.*

★ Chateau Montelena NAPA This place really is a château, complete with an immense 1882 stone castle. At the base of Mount St. Helena, it overlooks wildlife-laden Jade Lake and a Chinese garden. The entertaining tour starts with a video introduction, includes the vineyard and cellar, and ends up in the Estate Room for a vintage tasting. On the edifice's highest floor is another cavernous tasting room where non-tour visitors sample less rare wines. The chardonnay is the most acclaimed, but there's also cabernet

Peter Mondavi Sr., owner of Charles Krug Winery, takes in the aroma of a red wine.

Chateau Montalena's ivy-covered chateau.

and Riesling. *1429 Tubbs Lane, Calistoga. ☎ 707/942-5105. www. montelena.com. Daily 9:30am–4pm (except major holidays & 3rd Sat in May). Free self-guided tours. Tastings: $20–$40. Hwy. 29 to Tubbs Lane (hard to find, so call for specific directions). Map p 130.*

★ **Chateau St. Jean** SONOMA At Sugarloaf State Park's edge, these elegant grounds include European-style gardens with colorful flora and a 19th-century fountain that's a sculpture of St. John himself. There's also a gourmet food shop, picnic space, and a welcoming visitor center. Taste winemaker Margo van Staaveren's chardonnay, cabernet, and gewürztraminer before exploring the 1920 château—it's so precisely restored that it made the National Trust for Historic Preservation. If you've ever dismissed merlot as being too passé for you, this is the place at which to fall in love with it again. *8555 Sonoma Hwy. (Hwy. 12), Kenwood. ☎ 707/833-4134. www. chateaustjean.com. Daily 10am–5pm. Tours (free) daily at 11am & 3pm, or private tour & reserve tasting ($25) by appt. Tastings: $10–$15. Hwy. 101 N. Exit at Hwy. 12 E. & follow for 12 miles (19km). Map p 132.*

★ **Cliff Lede Vineyards** NAPA This art-rich winery was born when Canadian Cliff Lede bought S. Anderson Vineyard in 2002. The tasting room, in a century-old stone pump house, is where to try Lede's Bordeaux-focused varietals and the sparkling wines that still bear the S. Anderson name. Meticulously landscaped gardens are graced with rosebushes and sculptures by artists like Keith Haring. A new winemaking facility opened in 2005, and the former winery is now a modern-art gallery. Cliff Lede also offers Stags Leap District's only public lodging: the lovely Poetry Inn (p 123). *1473 Yountville Cross Rd., Yountville. ☎ 707/944-8642. www. cliffledevineyards.com. Daily 10am–4pm. Tours subject to change; call for schedules and pricing. Tastings: $20. Silverado Trail north, then left on Yountville Cross Rd. Map p 130.*

Cline Cellars SONOMA SULF This family-owned winery in the Carneros district has its tasting room in an 1850s farmhouse. With six ponds and more than 5,000 rosebushes, it's a beautiful place to sample zinfandel and Rhone-style wines, such as the Marsanne-Roussanne blend. *24737 Hwy. 121, Sonoma. ☎ 707/940-4000. www. clinecellars.com. Daily 10am–6pm (closed Christmas). Free tours daily 11am, 1 & 3pm. Tastings: free (or for*

Wannabe Winemakers

Ever dream of being a vintner? At Judd's Hill Micro-Crush (www.napamicrocrush.com; ☎ 707/255-2322), *you* get to make the wine. And not only that: you can also help with picking, sorting, and crushing—you can even choose your own label. To spend a week learning how to make your own sparkling-wine varietal, head to **Camp Schramberg** (www.schramsberg.com; ☎ 800/877-3623).

reserves, $1 per taste). Hwy. 101 N. Exit at Hwy. 37, then north on Calif. 121. Map p 132.

★ **Clos du Bois** SONOMA SUST Clos du Bois—French for "enclosure in the woods" or "vineyard of drink," depending on the translation—produces France-style varietals. On campus are pétanque courts (bocce ball for Francophiles) and a picnic area with gazebos. The educational 45-minute tour shows winemaking in progress, demonstration vineyards, and examples of Clos du Bois's sustainable-farming techniques. The best part: wine samples right from barrels. The tour ends with a reserve tasting, during which you may be lucky enough to sample the wine under the Marlstone label—though it's just Clos du Bois's fancy way of saying "meritage," these are still some of the most complex flavors around. No matter how you translate it, that's one good deal. *19410 Geyserville Ave., Geyserville. ☎ 800/222-3189. www.closdubois.com. Daily 10am–4:30pm (closed major holidays). Tours ($15, includes souvenir glass & wine tasting) daily at 11am & 2pm by appt. Tastings: $5–$10. Hwy. 101 N. Exit at Independence Lane, then left on Geyserville Ave. Map p 131.*

★ **Clos du Val** NAPA Co-founded in 1972 by a Frenchman who scoured the world for the best winery spot, Clos du Val is known for its cabernet, so try it in the rustic tasting room. A onetime fermentation chamber, it has a high, vaulted ceiling and terra-cotta walls. Double doors in the back allow guests to see steel tanks fermenting the pinot noir this

Chateau St. Jean really looks like a French château.

The tasting room at Cline Cellars.

establishment's known for (try the 2004 Carneros Pinot Noir, if you can). Outside, there's a rose garden, two picnic areas, and a pétanque court. ***5330 Silverado Trail, Napa. ☎ 707/261-5200. www.closduval.com. Daily 10am–5pm. Customized tours by 24-hour advance appointment (includes tasting). Tastings: $10 for regular tasting (waived with purchase), $20 for reserve tasting (includes souvenir glass). Map p 130.***

★★ **Clos Pegase** NAPA Book publisher Jan Shrem bought these vineyards in 1983 and named his winery after Pegasus, the mythological winged horse that created a spring that fed divine grapevines. Then, Shrem held an architects' competition. Michael Graves, the winner, designed the winery's stunning structures. They house a world-class fine-art collection, including a huge painting behind the tasting bar, where informed pourers dole out specialties like Mitsuko's Vineyard chardonnay and pinot noir. There's also a remarkable sculpture garden and a vineyard-adjacent picnic facility (call to reserve a table). ***1060 Dunaweal Lane, Calistoga. ☎ 707/942-4981. www.clospegase.com. Daily 10:30am–5pm. Tours (free) daily 11:30am & 2pm. Tastings: $15. Hwy. 101 N. Exit at Hwy. 37, then north on Calif. 121. Left on Hwy. 29 N., then right on Dunaweal Lane. Map p 130.***

Conn Creek Napa Valley NAPA This winery focuses on limited-production cabernets and Bordeaux blends. Also try the sauvignon blanc—it's only available here. Taking its name from the stream running alongside the vineyard, Conn Creek has a Mediterranean-style building with a pleasant garden. It's just below Rutherford Hill, in the shadow of the renowned Auberge du Soleil resort and spa (p 118). ***8711 Silverado Trail, St. Helena. ☎ 707/963-9100. www.conncreek.com. Daily 11am–4pm (from 10am on Sat). Tastings: $10–25, including reserve tasting (waived if you join the winery's mailing list or refunded with purchase). Hwy. 29 N., turn right on Oakville Cross Rd., then left on Silverado Trail. Map p 130.***

Corison Winery NAPA ORG Tastings here are conducted the old-fashioned way: in the barrel cellar. Winemaker Cathy Corison specializes in handcrafted cabernets and her labels bear ancient symbols. One depicts rain; the other, a sprouting seed. Tours include a visit to the winery's organically farmed Kronos Vineyard. ***987 St. Helena***

Hwy. (Hwy. 29), St. Helena. ☎ 707/963-0826. www.corison.com. Daily 10am–5pm. Free tours daily by appt. Tastings: $10 (deducted from purchase). Map p 130.

Cosentino Winery NAPA Founder and winemaker Mitch Cosentino offers more than 30 hand-harvested, small-lot wines, including some rich, sweet ones, like the romantically named Francesca d'Amore Vin Santo. Though this is fine and artistic wine, the staff is friendly. ***7415 St. Helena Hwy. (Hwy. 29), Yountville.** ☎ 707/944-1220. www.cosentinowinery.com. Daily 10am–5:30pm. Tastings: $15–$30. Map p 130.*

Cuvaison Winery NAPA This mission-style winery on the Silverado Trail was founded in 1969 by Silicon Valley techies. Since then, Cuvaison, a French word roughly meaning "fermentation of grape skins," has proved that its wines are award-worthy—praise has been especially heaped on the 2003 and 2004 Estate Selection chardonnays, so try them if possible. From the tasting room site, there are great views of northern Napa. Picnic grounds are noteworthy for their 350-year-old oak trees. ***4550 Silverado Trail, Calistoga.** ☎ 707/942-2468. www.cuvaison.com. Daily 10am–5pm. Tours ($15) by appt. Tastings: $10–$15 (includes souvenir glass). Map p 130.*

Clos du Val is a Napa favorite.

★★ **Darioush** NAPA "Impressive" is hardly an adequate word to describe this new winery. Inspired by the ancient Persian city of Persepolis, Darioush Khaledi, a native of Iran's Shiraz region, founded this epic complex in 1997. Rows of Greco columns and scalloped rooflines greet visitors outside. Inside, a blend of modern and ancient decor commingles with the effects of the strong Bordeaux-style wines Darioush is known for. To splurge, try the "Private Tasting with Cheese Pairing Experience." In addition to a private tour of the visitor center and amphitheatre, a personal host leads you to the classy six-seat Barrel Chai

The sculptures and architecture at Clos Pegase are one-of-a-kind.

If you visit Napa and Sonoma during the fall harvest, you'll see plenty of heavy vines, like these pristine cabernet grapes in Napa Valley.

(say "shay") Private Tasting Room, where flights of Darioush's finest wines are expertly paired with local cheeses. *4240 Silverado Trail, Napa.* ☎ *707/257-2345. www.darioush.com. Daily 10:30am–5pm. Current-release tasting available for walk-ins ($25). Private tasting & cheese pairing tours ($50) daily 2pm by appt. Map p 130.*

De La Montanya Winery and Vineyards SONOMA This upbeat country-style winery has a tasting room surrounded by beauty: Apple orchards, golden poppies, and Felta Creek. Most days, owner Dennis De La Montanya is behind the counter pouring. Best to try are the primitivo, pinot noir, Viognier, and zinfandel. Book the short walking tour of the small winery; you'll see the vineyards and the barrel room. Bring lunch—there's a vineyard patio on which visitors can eat *al fresco.* And if you want to stay overnight, know that the winery's cozy Little Yellow Cottage sleeps four people. *999 Foreman Lane, Healdsburg.* ☎ *707/433-3711. www.dlmwine.com. Fri–Sun 11am–4:30pm, Mon–Thurs by appt. Tours (free) by appt. Tastings: free. Hwy. 101 N. to central Healdsburg exit. Left on Mill St., which turns into Westside Rd. Right onto Felta Rd. & go under the bridge. Map p 131.*

DeLoach Vineyards SONOMA BIO Guided tours at this Russian River winery include the biodynamic garden and wine samples straight from the barrel. In DLV's tasting room, remodeled by sought-after local architect Howard Backen, sample single-vineyard pinot noir, chardonnay, and zinfandel. Fresh bread is served with the wine to appease the moderately hungry. For a bigger meal, bring lunch and savor it in the outdoor courtyard with a refreshing bottle of, say, the winery's 2004 O.F.S. Sauvignon Blanc. Afterward, toss a game of horseshoes. *1791 Olivet Rd., Santa Rosa.* ☎ *707/526-9111. www.deloachvineyards.com. Daily 10am–5pm. Tours (free with $10 tasting) daily, by appt. Tastings: $10 (fee waived with wine purchase). Hwy. 101 N. Exit at River Rd., then left on Olivet Rd. Map p 131.*

★ **Domaine Carneros** NAPA Owned by French champagne magnate Claude Taittinger, this is the only sparkling-wine producer to use only Carneros grapes. Domaine Carneros also offers a sophisticated welcome: Visitors ascend to the imposing Louis XV–style château via a grand staircase flanked by vineyards. In the tasting room and on the sunny veranda, sampler courses pair with cheese, and tastings come with free hors d'oeuvres. Try a light wine called Le Reve—it's a dream. Come at twilight, since hours here are later than at other wineries. *1240 Duhig Rd., Napa.* ☎ *707/257-0101, ext.108. www.domainecarneros.com. Daily 10am–6pm. Tours (free–$30) daily 11am–4pm. Tastings: $6.75–$15 by the glass; $15 for flights. Hwy. 12 N. to Duhig Rd. Map p 130.*

★ **Domaine Chandon** NAPA French champagne house Moët et

The grounds of Domaine Carneros are fit for a queen.

Chandon founded this prominent winery in 1973. Enjoy bubbly-and-food pairing—the Chandon Blanc de Noirs is highly recommended—while taking in fine art and even better views. Domaine Chandon also has an exceptional fine-dining restaurant. *1 California Dr. (at Hwy. 29), Yountville. ☎ 707/944-2280. www.chandon.com. Daily 10am–6pm. Tours ($12–$30) daily. Tastings: $16.* *Map p 130.*

Duckhorn Vineyards NAPA At Duckhorn's high-end Estate House, taste smooth Bordeaux varietals, like the 2002 Estate Grown Napa Valley Cabernet Sauvignon, at the O-shaped bar. Prior to the 1pm estate tasting (make reservations), take the intimate winery tour and be sure to see the waterfowl art collection and the handsome gardens. Owners Dan and Margaret Duckhorn are known for their hospitality. *1000 Lodi Lane, St. Helena. ☎ 888/354-8885. www.duckhornvineyards.com. Daily 10am–4pm. Tours $35 at 11am and 2pm. Tastings: $15–$25. Hwy. 29 N., then right on Lodi Lane.* *Map p 130.*

★★ **Ferrari-Carano Vineyards and Winery** SONOMA Ferrari-Carano is one of wine country's most beautiful wineries. Villa Fiore, its Tuscan-style hospitality center, has a tasting bar overlooking the estate's impressive fountains. Limited releases are seasonally available, but the winery's classics, like the Italian-influenced 2003 Siena, are more likely to be behind the bar. On the tour, experience behind-the-scenes winemaking, an underground cellar, and an eye-popping ramble through 5 acres (2 hectares) of verdant gardens laced with streams and waterfalls. *8761 Dry Creek Rd., Healdsburg. ☎ 800/831-0381. www.ferrari-carano.com. Daily 10am–5pm (closed major holidays). Tours (free) daily at 10am (reservations required). Tastings: $5 (refundable with $25 wine purchase). Hwy. 101 N. Exit & left on Dry Creek Rd.* *Map p 131.*

Flora Springs Winery NAPA Forsake the crowds and get off the beaten path at this small, tucked-away estate in the Rutherford appellation. The Komes family specializes in bold reds, so try the Meritage blend and the cabernet—but don't miss the smooth sauvignon blanc, either. Tours include hillside caves and barrel samples of not-yet-released wines. Flora Springs also has a tasting room at 677 Hwy. 29, next to Dean & Deluca. *677 S. St. Helena Hwy., St. Helena. ☎ 707/967-8032. www.florasprings.com. Daily*

Steel tanks at Domaine Chandon.

10am–5pm. Tours ($20) Mon–Fri 10am & 2pm by appt. Tastings: $15 by appt. On Hwy. 29 just south of St. Helena. Map p 130.

Foppiano Vineyards SONOMA SUST The self-guided tour is a highlight at Sonoma County's oldest continually owned family winery (founded 1896); visitors can walk through the petite sirah, chardonnay, cabernet, and merlot vines and learn about the recycled pumice pile (a sustainable way to feed vines). This low-key winery also has picnic tables, so bring lunch. ***12707 Old Redwood Hwy., Healdsburg. ☎ 707/433-7272. www.foppiano.com. Daily 10am–4:30pm. Self-guided tours (free) all day. Tastings: free. Hwy. 101 S., exit Old Redwood Hwy. Map p 131.***

★ Franciscan Oakville Estate NAPA This high-end property, with sunny patios and a visitor center offering a range of tastings, is known for its merlot and cabernet, though its best wine is the Magnificat, a deep, round blend named after Bach's music. Also interesting is the Cuvée Sauvage, a chardonnay made from fermented wild yeast. To try blending your own wine, book "Mastering Magnificat," one of the estate's educational seminars. ***1178 Galleron Rd., Rutherford. ☎ 707/967-3993. www.franciscan.com. Daily 10am–5pm (closed major holidays). No tours. Tastings: $5–$50 (personalized tastings require reservations). At Hwy. 29. Map p 130.***

Frank Family Vineyards NAPA Originally known for its sparking wine, this winery now specializes in still ones: cabernet and chardonnay in particular (try the smoky 2002 Rutherford Reserve Cabernet Sauvignon). But it maintains a separate tasting space for its five versions of ***méthode champenoise*** bubbly—festive Champagne Rouge is worth trying. The winery's staff is known for its friendliness, and the entertaining tour includes all the lore that comes with being old enough for the National Register of Historic Places (it was built in 1884). Outside, a picnic area with vineyard views and centuries-old oak trees awaits. ***1091 Larkmead Lane, Calistoga. ☎ 800/574-9463. www.frankfamilyvineyards.com. Daily 10am–4pm. No tours. Tastings: free. Hwy. 29 N., then right on Larkmead Lane. Map p 130.***

Freemark Abbey Winery NAPA Established in 1886, Freemark Abbey was founded by California's first female winery owner, Josephine Tychson. In 1939, the estate got its name from three partners who bought it: **Charles Freeman, Mark Foster,** and **Abbey Ahern.** The tour goes to a century-old cellar, the crushing area, and an adjacent vineyard. The tasting room, once a candle factory, has a fireplace and live piano music on weekends. Winemaker Tim Bell's Cabernet Bosché is a must-try, as is the limited-production dessert Riesling. ***3022 St. Helena Hwy. (Hwy. 29), St. Helena. ☎ 800/963-9698. www.freemarkabbey.com. Daily 10am–5pm. Tours by appt. Tastings: $10–$25. Map p 130.***

Gallo of Sonoma SONOMA Gallo has a new tasting room on

Healdsburg Square with a country atmosphere. Try the pinot gris or pinot noir for free, or splurge and try the chardonnay or cabernet. Shell out a bit more money (provided you've made reservations), and you'll be whisked away to Barrelli Creek Vineyard in northwestern Alexander Valley for an educational vineyard-farming experience. Then, by a lake, you'll sample wines and local cheeses. ***320 Center St., Healdsburg.*** ☎ ***707/433-2458. www.galloofsonoma.com. Daily 10am–6pm. Tours ($45, includes transportation to vineyard & tasting; reservations required) daily 10:45am. Tastings: $8–$15. Hwy. 101 N. Exit at Central Healdsburg, left on Plaza St., right on Center St. Map p 131.***

Gary Farrell Vineyards & Winery SONOMA At this boutique producer of premium Russian River Valley pinot noir, sauvignon blanc, and chardonnay, there's a great view from the hilltop tasting room. The tour shows off the state-of-the-art winemaking facility and includes four wine tastes. ***10701 Westside Rd., Healdsburg.*** ☎ ***707/473-2900. www.garyfarrellwines.com. Daily 11am–4pm. Tour and tasting $20 daily 10am, 11am, 2pm (reservations required). Tastings: $10–15. Hwy. 101 N. Exit & left at River Rd., then right on Wohler Rd., then left on Westside Rd. Map p 131.***

Geyser Peak Winery SONOMA Two levels of wine tasting occur here: The sunlit downstairs tasting offers free tastes of 10 popular wines (sauvignon blanc stands out). Upstairs, the classy Reserve Tasting Room offers table service for those who pay the nominal fee for reserve wines (don't miss the unusual sparkling shiraz) while viewing the barrel cellar below. Both rooms are stocked with knowledgeable, welcoming staff. Bring a picnic to enjoy on the flagstone patio; in summer, there's live music on Saturday afternoons. ***22281 Chianti Rd., Geyserville.*** ☎ ***707/857-2500. www.geyserpeakwinery.com. Daily 10am–5pm (closed major holidays). No tours. Tastings: $5–$10. Hwy. 101 N. Exit & left at Canyon Rd. Exit, then right on Chianti Rd. Map p 131.***

★ **Gloria Ferrer Champagne Caves** SONOMA The so-called "first lady of Sonoma," Gloria Ferrer is the culmination of seven generations of winemaking. The winery is known for its sparklers, though it also makes chardonnay, pinot noir,

The Ferrari-Carano estate comes with a grand pool.

The champagne caves at Gloria Ferrer.

merlot, and syrah. Its large hacienda-style tasting room, where wine is served with spiced almonds, opens onto an outdoor terrace overlooking the vineyards. Take the free tour of the fermenting tanks, bottling line, and underground aging caves. *23555 Carneros Hwy. (Calif. 121), Sonoma. ☎ 707/996-7256. www.gloriaferrer.com. Daily 10am–5pm. Daily guided underground cave tours ($10, including tasting) 11am, 1pm, 3pm. Tastings: $10. Hwy. 101 N. Exit at Hwy. 37, then north on Calif. 121. Map p 132.*

Grgich Hills Cellar NAPA BIO, SUST Ever since Croatian immigrant Miljenko "Mike" Grgich founded **Grgich Hills** in 1977, his winery has won acclaim. The new Hospitality Center begins serving wine earlier than most tasting rooms, so if you want an early start, come here. At the dark-wood bar, taste handcrafted cabernets and chardonnays made from sustainably farmed organic grapes. On Friday afternoons, the $5 tasting fee includes barrel tasting—a before-the-bottle preview of new releases. *1829 St. Helena Hwy. (Hwy. 29), Rutherford. ☎ 800/532-3057. www.grgich.com. Daily 9:30am–4:30pm. Tours ($10) daily 11am & 2pm (walk-ins OK). Tastings: $10 Map p 130.*

★★ Gundlach Bundschu Winery SONOMA SUST Outdoorsy as opposed to stuffy, Gundlach Bundschu's cavernous tasting room is built right into the hillside. In it, winemaker Linda Trotta's creations—mostly red wines—are poured for eager guests as they enjoy light snacks. If it's available, try the Kleinberger; it's the only one made in America. An informative tour includes the caves and vineyard, and colorful tales about the winery's illustrious past; it's been around since 1858, after all, and is America's oldest family-owned winery. A variety of excellent picnic grounds overlook the valley. *2000 Denmark St., Sonoma. ☎ 707/938-5277. www.gunbun.com. Daily 11am–4:30pm (closed major holidays). Free tours on weekends at 2pm; weekdays by appt. Tastings: $20. Hwy. 101 N. Exit at Hwy. 37, then north on Calif. 121. Right on Napa St., then right on 8th St. Left on Denmark St. Map p 132.*

Hagafen Cellars NAPA In Hebrew, **hagafen** means "the vine," and there are plenty of them at this small kosher winery—Napa's only one. Banish thoughts of Manischewitz, though. Sure, Hagafen's wines might be made according to Jewish law and blessed by an in-house rabbi, but these wines are as premium and flavorful as any other on the Silverado Trail—the award party on the tasting room wall attests to that. The most bedecked vintage offered is the white Riesling, so don't decline a taste. Hagafen wines have even been served at the White House. *4160 Silverado Trail, Napa. ☎ 707/252-0781. www.hagafen.com. Daily 10am–5pm. Free tour daily 11am by appt. Tastings: $5–$10. Map p 130.*

★ Hall Winery NAPA Hall Winery is actually two wineries: one in St. Helena and one in Rutherford. They're both owned by Kathryn Hall, the former U.S. Ambassador to Austria, and Craig Hall, her husband. The

St. Helena location dates back to 1885—though Frank O. Gehry is in the process of modernizing the architecture. The courtyard works well for picnics, and tours include the original 1885 building. At the smaller, newer Rutherford location in the eastern hills, visitors see underground caves and modern art—plus, they're treated like VIPs as they taste premium cabernet in the chandeliered tasting room. *ST. HELENA: 401 St. Helena Hwy. (Hwy. 29), St. Helena. ☎ 707/967-2620. Daily 10am–5:30pm. Tours by appt. only. Tastings: $30. RUTHERFORD: 56 Auberge Rd., Rutherford. ☎ 707/967-0700. www.hallwines.com. Tours & tasting ($30) daily 10am–5pm by appt. Silverado Trail north, left on Rutherford Hill Rd., left on Auberge Rd. Map p 130.*

Harvest Moon Estate & Winery SONOMA Harvest Moon is a little family-owned winery with welcoming servers in the small but nice tasting room. Though they focus on zinfandel, the gewürztraminer is more tasteworthy. *2192 Olivet Rd., Santa Rosa. ☎ 707/573-8711. www.harvestmoonwinery.com. Daily 10:30am–5pm. Tours daily by appt. Tastings: $5. Hwy. 101 N. Exit at River Rd. & go west, then left on Olivet. Map p 131.*

★★★ **The Hess Collection Winery** NAPA SUST This winery might be remote, but the drive up Mt. Veeder is an attraction unto itself. Inside, design is contemporary to match Donald Hess' museum-quality art collection on the upper levels of the 1903 stone winery (formerly Christian Brothers). Downstairs is a dramatic tasting room with a maple bar, over which patrons taste internationally influenced wines, like the ones in the New World collection, produced with sustainable farming methods. In the wine store, French oak barrels line the walls. The concierge room provides tourist info and a phone for reservations. *4411 Redwood Rd., Napa. ☎ 877/707-4377. www.hesscollection.com. Daily 10am–5:30pm (closed major holidays). Free self-guided art tours all day. Tastings: $5–$20. Hwy. 101 N. to Hwy. 29 N. Exit Trancas St./Redwood Rd. Map p 130.*

Honig Vineyard & Winery NAPA SUST In addition to its normal winery tours, Honig hosts educational eco-walks through the vineyard to see the winery's sustainable agriculture methods: bat boxes, beehives, row management, and so on. Guides talk about trellising, pruning, growth cycles, and

The tasting room counter at Hess Collection Winery.

Spring mustard blooms in the vineyard at Joseph Phelps.

organic pest prevention. It's followed by wine tasting in the tasting room or on the patio. This midsize, family-run winery's award-winning sauvignon blanc and cabernet are handcrafted and blended. ***850 Rutherford Rd., Rutherford. ☎ 707/963-5618. www.honigwine.com. Daily 10am–5pm. No tours. Tastings: $10 by appt. Hwy. 29 N., turn right on Rutherford Rd. Map p 130.***

★★ Hop Kiln Winery SONOMA The distinctive and old-fashioned Hop Kiln structure is a California Historical Landmark. Built by Italians in 1905 as a hop-drying barn, its three stone kilns point skyward, making this winery unmistakable. Its ranch-like Western feel permeates the grounds, whether you're savoring free tastings in the rustic tasting room or picnicking at Old Fig Garden or Duck Pond. Notable vintages include the 2005 Thousand Flowers (a citrus-flavored blend) and the 2004 Big Red (a lush confluence of cabernet sauvignon, pinot noir, and Valdiguié). ***6050 Westside Rd., Healdsburg. ☎ 707/433-6491. www.hopkilnwinery.com. Daily 10am–5pm. No tours. Tastings: free. Hwy. 101 N. Exit at Central Healdsburg, then left on Mill St./Westside Rd. Map p 131.***

Huntington SONOMA One of Healdsburg's newer tasting rooms, Huntington isn't far from the town plaza. Over its wooden bar in a historic building, whites and reds go glass to mouth. Try the gold-winning 2001 Russian River Valley Chardonnay. ***53 Front St., Healdsburg. ☎ 707/433-5215. www.huntingtonwine.com. Thurs–Sun 11am–5pm. No Tours. Tastings: free. Hwy. 101 N. Exit & right on Healdsburg Ave., then right on Front St. Map p 131.***

★ Imagery Estate Winery & Art Gallery SONOMA This is a winery for art lovers; each bottle label is a tiny version of an original painting, commissioned specifically for the wine it hugs. Each must somehow include Benziger Estate's Parthenon replica (Imagery is Benziger's sister winery and its winemaker is Joe Benziger). A curated collection of more than 175 artworks hangs in Imagery's gallery, a testament to the variety of small, uncommon lots (like malbec, petite sirah, and Viognier) produced here. There's a patio, a picnic lawn, and a bocce ball court. ***14335 Hwy. 12, Glen Ellen. ☎ 707/935-4515. www.imagerywinery.com. Daily 10am–5pm (weekends & Memorial Day to Labor Day open until 5:30pm). No tours. Tastings: $10–$15. Map p 132.***

★ Jordan Vineyard & Winery SONOMA For the ultimate in classic, refined opulence—with a serious and stately tour and tasting to match—visit Jordan's stunning estate. Inspired by southwestern France's grand châteaux, owner and oil magnate Tom Jordan's vine-covered winery was founded in 1972 and spans more than 1,500 acres (600 hectares). It's committed to cabernet sauvignon, merlot, and chardonnay. During the free tour, you'll see that every detail is attended to—from the winery construction to the way the beautiful stainless-steel tanks line the fermentation room, to the seating under the patio's great oak trees, to the manicured grounds. The tour ends with a tasting in the formal library. *1474 Alexander Valley Rd., Healdsburg. ☎ 800/654-1213 or 707/431-5250. www.jordanwinery.com. Mon–Fri 8am–5pm, Sat 9am–4pm (reservations required for tours). From Hwy. 101, take Dry Creek Rd. exit & turn left at 2nd traffic light onto Healdsburg Ave.; go 2 miles and turn right onto Alexander Valley Rd.; go 1[bf]1⁄2 miles, then turn right to enter the estate. Map p 131.*

Joseph Phelps Vineyards NAPA *BIO* This state-of-the-art winery is a favorite stop for serious wine lovers. Tastings and seminars include blending, smelling, or a wine-themed history lesson. For a quicker experience, taste the fabulous flagship wine, Insignia, on the terrace. *200 Taplin Rd. (off the Silverado Trail), St. Helena. ☎ 800/707-5789. www.jpvwines.com. Tastings & seminars by appt. only. Mon–Fri 9am–5pm; Sat–Sun 10am–4pm. Map p 130.*

Kaz Vineyard & Winery SONOMA The philosophy at quirky Kaz is "no harm in experimenting"—and that venturesome spirit pays off in the form of some innovative wines: Sangiofranc, for example, is a blend of sangiovese and cabernet franc. One of Sonoma's smallest wineries, Kaz is exceedingly family-friendly. Its pumpkin patch, coloring books, koi pond, barn-like building, and croquet lawn ensure that kids will have fun while parents relax. The Little House is the winery's cozy on-site lodging (a stay guarantees free wine). *233 Adobe Canyon Rd., Kenwood. ☎ 877/833-2536. www.kazwinery.com. Daily 11am–5pm. Tastings: $5. From Sonoma Hwy. N, turn right on Adobe Canyon Rd. Map p 132.*

★ **Kendall-Jackson Wine Center** SONOMA There are two Kendall-Jackson hotspots: the Wine Center in Santa Rosa and a tasting room on Healdsburg Square. The Wine Center's picture-perfect manor is surrounded by gardens, including a culinary and sensory garden and a demonstration vineyard. Picnic grounds are in a 100-year-old walnut grove, but if you're hungry, consider the food-and-wine reserve tasting. At the recently remodeled Healdsburg tasting room, visitors can try any Kendall-Jackson offering, including their best: the Stature and Estate wines. *WINE CENTER: 5007 Fulton Rd., Santa Rosa. ☎ 800/769-3649. www.kj.com. Daily 10am–5pm. Garden tours (free) daily 11am, 1 & 3pm. Tastings: $5–$18. Hwy. 101 N. West on River Rd., right on Fulton Rd. TASTING ROOM: 337 Healdsburg Ave., Healdsburg. ☎ 707/433-7102. Daily 10am–5pm. Tastings: $2–$10. Hwy. 101 N. Exit Central Healdsburg. Map p 131.*

★ **Kenwood Vineyards** SONOMA *SULF, SUST* Though known for its reds, tastings at Kenwood include an array of varietals; the 2002 Russian River Valley Reserve Chardonnay is one of its better whites. The tasting room is in one of the winery's original 1906 structures—a farmhouse,

Kendall Jackson is one of many wineries switching to synthetic corks.

actually. The interior, of course, has been re-done; it's now cozy and welcoming. *9592 Sonoma Hwy. (Hwy. 12), Kenwood. ☎ 707/833-5891. www.kenwoodvineyards.com. Daily 10am–4:30pm. Tours by appt. only. Tastings: start at $5. Hwy. 101 N. Exit at Hwy. 37, then north on Calif. 121. Map p 132.*

★★ Korbel Champagne Cellars SONOMA To see the very pretty grounds of America's oldest méthode champenoise champagne producer, take the tour. It starts at an old railroad station and includes the cellars and History Museum. There's also a rose garden tour, during which you'll see more than 1,000 flower varieties. The tasting room is humongous, and the sandwiches from the fancy deli are amazing. Of the wines to taste, the brut is the most popular, but the pinot grigio, a zesty cuvée, is more exclusive. Korbel is on the way to Armstrong Redwoods State Reserve, so the winery is surrounded by ancient redwoods. *13250 River Rd., Guerneville. ☎ 707/824-7000. www.korbel.com. Daily 10am–4:30pm (May–Sept open until 5pm). Tours by reservation only; call for schedule). Tastings: free. Hwy. 101 N. Exit & left on River Rd. Map p 131.*

The tower at Korbel Champagne Cellars.

★ Kunde Estate Winery & Vineyards SONOMA SUST Owned and run by fourth-generation Kundes, this winery produces estate-grown wines; a surefire bottle to take home is the 2002 Reserve Cabernet Sauvignon. The wide tasting room, in a cow-barn replica, overlooks a reflecting pool with a fountain and nicely displays the winery's century-long history on the wall behind the bar. Available to buy are Kunde's popular cabernet chocolate cherries, which are a great dessert after picnicking on the oak-surrounded grounds. *10155 Sonoma Hwy. (Hwy. 12), Kenwood. ☎ 707/833-5501. www.kunde.com. Daily 10:30am–4:30pm. Tours (free) all day Fri–Sun. Tastings: $10 (refunded with purchase). Map p 132.*

Ladera Vineyards NAPA This off-the-beaten-path winery, built in 1898 on Howell Mountain, was restored as a gravity-flow facility. Owner Anne Stotesbery treats visitors like personal guests and leads tours that begin in the gardens and end with tastes in the fermentation room. Ask to try the low-yield, high-quality malbec, which is tapered by a small quantity of cabernet sauvignon. *150 White Cottage Rd., Angwin. ☎ 707/965-2445. www.laderavineyards.com. Tours & tastings ($25; reservations required) Mon–Sat 10am, noon & 2pm. Call for directions. Map p 130.*

★ Ledson Winery & Vineyards SONOMA Known to locals as "The Castle," Ledson is memorable for its fairy-tale-like architecture, complete with regal gates and a hyper-pruned fountain courtyard. In the Gothic Normandy–style behemoth of a structure, taste handcrafted wines made from a wide range of small varietal lots at one of multiple bars.

Its library and reserve wines are available only at the winery, so tote home the much-praised 1997 Estate Merlot Reserve (if you can afford it, that is: A 1.5-liter bottle sets you back $425). Hungry? There's picnic space and a gourmet market. *2355 7335 Sonoma Hwy. (Hwy. 12), Kenwood. ☎ 707/537-3810. www.ledson.com. Daily 10am–5pm. Tours (free) given upon request. Tastings: $5–$10. Hwy. 101 N. Exit at Hwy. 37, then north on Calif. 121. Map p 132.*

★ **Louis M. Martini Winery** NAPA The winery's circa-1933 name notwithstanding, the drink it's best known for is cabernet sauvignon. Its whites, too, have made a name for themselves and you're likely to find gewürztraminer, pinot gris, and chardonnay among the options. Operated by third-generation Martinis (though it's now owned by Gallo), this tasting room was recently redesigned. Be sure to cap your tasting flight with the winery's 55-year-old tawny port. *254 St. Helena Hwy. (Hwy. 29), St. Helena. ☎ 800/321-9463. www.louismartini.com. Daily 10am–6pm (closed major holidays). Tours daily at 11am and 2pm, $30; book 3 days in advance. Tastings: $10–$20. Map p 130.*

★ **Monticello Vineyards/ Corley Family Napa Valley** NAPA For a just-off-the-beaten-path experience, choose Monticello. In its grand colonial-style Jefferson House (inspired by oenophile Thomas Jefferson), the Corley family hosts comparative seminars and private tastings featuring wines that have been served in the White House. This limited-production winery is known for its cabernet, chardonnay, pinot noir, and merlot. The sheltered picnic grove is a perfect lunch spot. *4242 Big Ranch Rd., Napa. ☎ 707/253-2802. www.monticellovineyards.com. Daily 10am–4:30pm. Tastings: from $15.*

Ledson Winery is the perfect place to pull up at in your stretch limo.

Hwy. 29 to Oak Knoll Ave., then south on Big Ranch Rd. Map p 130.

★★ **Mumm Napa** NAPA Known for its sparkling wines, Mumm's glass-enclosed tasting room and its terrace are the places to sample Brut Prestige, Blanc de Noirs, or Santana DVX (developed with Carlos Santana) while soaking in expansive valley views. Mumm's photography gallery includes many dramatic Ansel Adams works and rotating exhibits in long, Spanish-style hallways. Tours visit the demonstration vineyard and winery, where guides demystify méthode champenoise. *8445 Silverado Trail, Rutherford. ☎ 800/686-6272. www.mummnapa.com. Daily 10am–5pm. Tours (free) 10am–3pm. Tastings: $7–$25. Hwy. 101 N. Exit at Hwy. 37, then north on Calif. 121. Map p 130.*

★★ **Opus One** NAPA *BIO* Opus One is synonymous with sheer luxury—not surprising, given that two huge names founded it: Robert Mondavi and Baron Philip de Rothschild (d. 1988). Today, Baroness Philippine de Rothschild (Philip's daughter) and Robert Mondavi run the place—and what a place. Striking architecture blends Californian and European influences, the salon is plush and opulent, and views from the rooftop deck are unsurpassed. Though the tasting fee is

Take a break on the terrace at Mumm Napa.

steep, it comes into context when you learn that in 1981, a single case sold for $24,000. Always accessible to the average visitor is the current vintage, usually a preponderance of ripe cabernet sauvignon blended with smaller quantities of merlot, malbec, petit verdot, and cabernet franc. ***7900 St. Helena Hwy., Oakville. ☎ 707/944-9442. www.opusone winery.com. Daily 10am–4pm (closed major holidays). Tours ($35, reservations required) daily 10:30am and 1:30pm. Tastings: $30. Hwy. 29 N. becomes Main St., then St. Helena Hwy. Map p 130.***

Paradise Ridge Winery SONOMA This family-owned boutique winery on a hill devotes itself to art almost as ardently as it does to wine (small lots of cabernet, sauvignon blanc, and chardonnay). Among the oaks is a sculpture grove with abstract metal works. The champagne cellar houses a tribute to Kanaye Nagasawa, who produced the majority of Sonoma County wine in the late 1800s. Come for the spectacular view—you can see Point Reyes from here. ***4545 Thomas Lake Harris Dr., Santa Rosa. ☎ 707/528-9463. www.paradiseridgewinery.com. Daily 11am–5pm. Self-guided tours only. Tastings: $5 (refunded with purchase). Hwy. 101 N. Exit at Bicentennial Way, then merge onto Fountaingrove Pkwy. Turn left on Thomas Lake Harris Dr. Map p 131.***

★ Paraduxx Winery NAPA *SUST* This brand-new winery (opened Sept 2005) has a sunny, chic sit-down tasting room where personable wine educators pour red wine (a zinfandel-cabernet blend) into stemless glasses. Also provided: local artisan foods to pair with the wine. ***7257 Silverado Trail, Yountville. ☎ 707/945-0890. www.paraduxx.com. Daily 10am–4pm. No tours. Tastings: $20–$30 by appt. Map p 130.***

Peju Province Winery NAPA *ORG* Beautiful gardens and unique architecture are a big draw here; sculptures and fountains are featured throughout the lush grounds, while a 50-foot (15m) tower houses the tasting room. Ask the musically inclined tasting-room staff to pour samples of Peju's artisan red wines, like the summery Carignane, or opt for the food-and-wine pairing, offered only on weekdays. Though this winery stays open later than most, it gets crowded in the late afternoon, especially on weekends. ***8466 St. Helena Hwy. (Hwy. 29), Rutherford. ☎ 707/963-3600. www.peju.com. Daily 10am–6pm (closed major holidays). Self-guided tours only. Tastings: $10 (refunded with wine purchase). Map p 130.***

★ PlumpJack Winery NAPA This hip winery, founded in a partnership between oil heir Gordon Getty and Gavin Newsom (San Francisco's mayor), has always been progressive in its approach to winemaking: It pretty much started the trend of using screw caps instead of corks on cabernet. The full-bodied, berry-tinged 2003 PlumpJack Estate Cabernet Sauvignon is proof that the system works. The best part? PlumpJack offers reasonably priced bottles to take home. *620 Oakville Cross Rd., Oakville. ☎ 707/945-1220. www.plumpjack.com. Daily 10am–4pm. No tours. Tastings: $10. Hwy. 101 N. Exit at Hwy. 37, then north on Calif. 121. Right on Oakville Cross Rd. Map p 130.*

Provenance Vineyards NAPA Provenance's deep-red building matches the wines it's known for (though winemaker Tom Rinaldi does make one white, a heck of a sauvignon blanc). The well-lit, cleanly designed tasting room opened in late 2003. Be sure to look down while sipping these hand-crafted wines—the floor is made entirely of recycled oak barrels. Tours include the cellar and vineyard. *1695 St. Helena Hwy. (Hwy. 29), Rutherford. ☎ 707/968-3633. www.provenancevineyards.com. Daily 10am–4:30pm (closed major holidays). Tours ($10, including tasting) by appt. Tastings: $10–$15. Map p 130.*

★ Ravenswood Winery

SONOMA This family-owned winery's "no wimpy wines" slogan holds true—these bold zins pack a punch. The tasting room is less than a mile from Sonoma Plaza and tours include up-close views of the vines and barrel tasting in the cellar. *18701 Gehricke Rd., Sonoma. ☎ 707/933-2332. www.ravenswood-wine.com. Daily 10am–5pm. Tours ($15) daily at 10:30am. Tastings: $10–$15 (including a keepsake glass). Hwy. 101 N. Exit at Hwy. 37, then north on Calif. 121. Map p 132.*

Raymond Vineyards NAPA *SUST* The Raymonds are fifth-generation winemakers with lineage tracing them to Jacob Beringer. They founded this estate in 1971 between Rutherford and St. Helena. Taste current releases and library vintages of the winery's cabernet, zinfandel, merlot, and chardonnay. *849 Zinfandel Lane, St. Helena. ☎ 800/525-2659. www.raymondvineyards.com. Daily 10am–4pm. Tours ($15) daily at 11am (24-hr. advance reservation required). Tastings: $10–$15. Just off Hwy. 29. Map p 130.*

Robert Craig Wine Cellars

NAPA Though Robert Craig's winery isn't open to the public, fans of his upscale mountain cabernet can visit the tasting room in downtown Napa. Call ahead to schedule a personalized sit-down tasting and get ready for wines served in restaurants of French Laundry caliber. The 2002 Mt. Veeder Cabernet Sauvignon, with its enveloping mahogany essence, promises to age uncommonly well. Weekend open houses with barrel tastings happen whenever new vintages are released. *880 Vallejo St., Napa. ☎ 707/252-2250. TASTING ROOM: 625 Imperial Way. www.robertcraigwine.com. Mon–Sat 10am–4pm by appt. No tours. Tastings: $15 (credited toward wine purchase). Hwy. 29 N. Right on Lincoln, then right on Soscol, then right on Vallejo St. Map p 130.*

★★ Robert Mondavi Winery

NAPA Robert Mondavi is Napa's most powerful winery in terms of sheer size and strength, perhaps because the man himself (Mondavi, that is) pioneered the concept of

The distinctive red at Provenance Vineyards.

The Robert Mondavi Winery fountain.

public tastings; everyone else followed. Still devoted to wine education, this mission-style complex has three tasting rooms and an array of tours, from one focusing on flavor profiling to another ending with a gourmet three-course meal. Try the fumé blanc (Mondavi coined the term) and the reserve cabernet, then enjoy the rotating art exhibit or, if it's summer, a music concert (check website for schedule). ***7801 St. Helena Hwy. (Hwy. 29), Oakville.*** ☎ ***707/226-1395. www.robertmondaviwinery.com. Daily 10am–5pm (closed major holidays).Call for tour schedule ($25; reservations required). Tastings: $15–$20. Map p 130.***

★★ **Roshambo Winery + Gallery** SONOMA Roshambo's über-cool tasting lounge has glass walls and great Russian River Valley views. There's also a smooth wooden ceiling and a serious modern-art collection. Roshambo was founded in 1999 by Naomi Brilliant, a photographer who inherited her grandfather's vineyards. Named after the Japanese rock-paper-scissors game—they actually hold invitational tournaments—there's no denying the playful spirit here. Other silly events include Willy Wonka costume parties and Drag Brunches. With all the edgy hipness, it's easy to forget this is a winery—but don't: The inspired artisanal creations here, with names like "The Obvious" and "Imago," are definitely taste-worthy. ***3000 Westside Rd., Healdsburg.*** ☎ ***888/525-WINE. www.roshambowinery.com. Daily 10am–5pm. No tours. Tastings: $5–$15. Hwy. 101 N. Exit at Central Healdsburg, then left on Mill St. (turns into Westside Rd.). Map p 131***

Autumn oak trees along the Silverado Trail in Napa Valley.

★★★ **Rubicon Estate** NAPA ORG, SULF Formerly Niebaum-Coppola, this eminent estate is still owned by the Coppola family of filmmaking fame. Every over-21 visitor pays a $25 admission fee (unless they're Napa residents), but that includes wine tasting within original 1882 sandstone walls, access to the gardens and ivy-covered château, and entry to the Centennial Museum, a historical tribute to wine and film. Founded in 1887 by Finnish seaman Gustave Niebaum, this remarkable winery offers five different tours, all of which highlight the property's understated glitziness. Try the winery's classics, like Blancaneaux, a Viognier-Roussanne-Marsanne blend, or Rubicon, a cabernet sauvignon–dominated claret. ***1991 St. Helena Hwy., Rutherford.*** ☎ ***707/968-1100. www.rubiconestate.com. Daily 10am–5pm. Tours free–$45 (call for schedule). Tastings included in $25*** entrance fee. Hwy. 29 N. becomes St. Helena Hwy. Map p 130.

St. Clement Vineyards SONOMA This winery, once owned by Charles Krug and now part of the Beringer Wine Estates, uses fruit from independent growers to make its reds and whites. The 2002 Howell Mountain Cabernet Sauvignon is among the winery's more exceptional selections, but the less pricey 2004 Carneros Chardonnay isn't bad, either. Imbibe at the hospitality center in the New England–style Rosenbaum House, built in 1878. Relax afterward on the veranda or at picnic tables. *2867 St. Helena Hwy. (Hwy. 29), St. Helena. ☎ 800/331-8266. www.stclement.com. Daily 10am–4pm (closed major holidays). Tours by appt. available daily at 10:30am, 12:30 & 2:30pm. Tastings: $10–$25.*

★ St. Francis Winery & Vineyards SONOMA At the foot of Hood Mountain, this mission-style winery offers views as enjoyable as its wine. "The House of Big Reds," as it's known, offers three tasting experiences, the most expensive of which pairs reserve zins, merlots, and cabernets with chef Todd Muir's gourmet hors d'oeuvres. *100 Pythian Rd., Santa Rosa. ☎ 800/543-7713, ext. 242. www.stfranciswinery.com. Daily 10am–5pm (closed major holidays). No tours. Tastings: $10–$15. Hwy. 12 W., then left on Pythian Rd. Map p 132.*

St. Supéry Winery NAPA Known for its Meritage whites and reds, the emphasis at St. Supéry, besides wine production, is educating visitors. Don't be put off by the Atkinson House's somewhat nondescript exterior; inside is a beautiful art gallery and informative displays (one sprays out smells of different grape varieties). Near the house, there's a demonstration vineyard and family-friendly picnic grounds. *8440 St. Helena Hwy. (Hwy. 29), Rutherford. ☎ 800/942-0809. www.stsupery.com. Daily 10am–5pm (6pm Oct–Apr; closed major holidays). Guided winemaker's tour Mon–Thurs ($45; self-guided tours are free). Tastings: $10–$15. Map p 130.*

★★ Schramsberg Vineyards NAPA California Historical Landmark No. 561 earned the distinction for its founding date (1862) plus its rich history: Robert Louis Stevenson was so inspired by his 1880 visit that he included Schramsberg in "Silverado Squatters." Today, the sparkling wines are so venerable that U.S. presidents present them to foreign dignitaries. Tours feature hand-carved champagne caves housing 2 million bottles and culminate at a round table in the wood-paneled tasting room, where seated visitors may try Brut Rosé, J. Schram, or other vintages. *Schramsberg Rd., Calistoga. ☎ 707/942-2414. www.schramsberg.com. Daily 10am–4pm. Guided tour & tasting ($35) daily by appt. End of Schramsberg Rd. on Hwy. 29. Map p 130.*

★ Schug Carneros Estate Winery SONOMA Founded in 1980, this family-owned winery's specialty is French-style pinot noir and chardonnay. Try them in the small tasting room, which is in a German-style timber-frame building. Afterward, picnic at tables near an herb garden, visit the duck pond, or merely take in the view; if it's clear, try to spot Mt. Diablo in the distance. *602 Bonneau Rd., Sonoma. ☎ 800/966-9365. www.schugwinery.com. Daily 10am–5pm. Tours available by appt. Tastings: $5. Hwy. 101 N. Exit at Hwy. 37, then north on Calif. 121. Left on Bonneau Rd. Map p 132.*

★★ Sebastiani Vineyards & Winery SONOMA Sonoma's oldest family-owned winery was founded in 1904 by Samuele

You are now at the House of Sebastiani.

Sebastiani, though the vineyards have been here since 1825. At the large tasting room, try the winery's specialties: cabernet, merlot, and barbera. The grounds display examples of antique winemaking equipment, including the winery's original press. Cuneo Cottage is the estate's homey vacation rental. ***Tip:*** Sebastiani is 4 blocks from Sonoma Plaza, so park at the winery and walk into town, since parking can be difficult during high season. *389 4th St. E., Sonoma. ☎ 707/933-3230. www.sebastiani.com. Daily 10am–5pm. Trolley tours in summer at noon and 2pm ($15 for adults, $10 for kids); free tours at 11am, 1pm, and 3pm. Tastings: $10. From Broadway/Calif. 12 N., turn right on E. Napa St., then left on 4th St. E. Map p 132.*

Sebastopol Vineyards/Dutton Estates SONOMA Taste Sebastopol Vineyards' Russian River Valley chardonnay, pinot noir, and syrah in the Spanish-style hospitality center surrounded by palm trees. Picnic grounds available. *8757 Green Valley Rd. (at Hwy. 116), Sebastopol. ☎ 707/829-9463. www.sebastopolvineyards.com. Daily 10am–5pm. No tours. Tastings: $10–$15. Map p 131.*

★ **Shafer Vineyards** NAPA SUST Though you have to make reservations 4 to 6 weeks in advance for this 90-minute visit, it's worth it to see Shafer's cellar, cave, barrel room, and sustainably farmed vineyards and to try six Shafer wines, including the stunning Hillside Select. The bright, intimate tasting room has a fireplace and serene vineyard views. *6154 Silverado Trail, Napa. ☎ 707/944-2877. www.shafervineyards.com. Mon–Fri 9am–4pm. Tours & tasting ($45) 10am & 2pm by reservation only. Map p 130.*

★ **Simi Winery** SONOMA After encountering a UC Davis enology professor at a wine festival, Steve Reeder transferred colleges to learn how to make wine. His creations (chardonnay, cabernet, and sauvignon blanc) are the focal point of Simi's redwood-paneled tasting room. Tours include stone cellars and discussions on how Italian brothers Giuseppe and Pietro founded Simi in 1876—they'd come for the Gold Rush but discovered another California treasure: grapes. For picnics, there's a grove with 70-year-old redwoods. *6275 Healdsburg Ave., Healdsburg. ☎ 800/746-4880. www.simiwinery.com. Daily 10am–5pm. Tours ($10 adults; $5 children, includes tasting) daily 11am & 2pm. Tastings: $10 (refunded with purchase). Hwy. 101 N. Exit & right at Dry Creek Rd., then left on Healdsburg Ave. Map p 131.*

★★ **Sterling Vineyards** SONOMA The most distinctive part of this winery is the aerial gondola that takes you there, providing far-reaching views of Napa Valley. Just this alone is worth the $20 to get in ($15 if it's a winter weekday, $10 if you're younger than 21). Admission also includes a self-guided tour that includes wine-related art and artifacts (videos and placards provide info) and sit-down wine sampling in the impressive tasting facility. A reserve tour and tasting is $45 and includes samples of wines like the SVR (a Bordeaux blend) and reserve merlot, cabernet sauvignon, and chardonnay. *1111 Dunaweal Lane, Calistoga. ☎ 707/942-3300. www.sterlingvineyards.com. Daily 10:30am–4:30pm (closed major holidays). Between Hwy. 29 & Silverado Trail.*

★ Stryker Sonoma SONOMA
Stryker Sonoma has attitude. A friendly, young attitude. It's an extension of founders Pat Stryker and Craig and Karen McDonald. You'll feel it when you arrive at this boutique winery's slatted-wood walkway, march up to the sleek and polished curved bar, gaze up at the lofted wood ceiling, order a taste of zin, and gaze out at the vines through floor-to-ceiling windows. If you tire from the view, cross the mahogany-stained cement floor and peer through the windows overlooking the barrel room below. ***Note:*** Stryker only sells out of its tasting room, online, and, per winemaker Tim Hardin, "to a few local restaurants we like." Like many vineyards in the Alexander Valley, you won't pay a tasting fee here. Cheers to that. *5110 Hwy. 128, Geyserville. ☎ 707/433-1944. Fax 707/433-1948. www.strykersonoma.com. Daily 10:30am–5pm. Tastings: free–$15. Tours by appt. Map p 131.*

★ Sutter Home Winery NAPA
Built in 1874 and founded as a winery in 1890, Sutter Home was bought in 1947 by the Trinchero family, who claim to have invented white zinfandel in 1973. Today, similar blush-colored wines characterize the winery's specialties. The tasting room is in the original 1874 building. The organic White Zinfandel garden, with its handsome gazebo, nurtures 125 rose species, and century-old palm trees flank the manor. *277 St. Helena Hwy. (Hwy. 29), St. Helena. ☎ 707/963-3104, ext. 4208. www.sutterhome.com. Daily 10am–5pm. Free self-guided garden tours all day. Tastings: free. Map p 130.*

The striking white buildings at Sterling Vineyards.

Tin Barn Vineyards SONOMA
Adding to the trend toward wineries self-contained in warehouses is Tin Barn, which is family-owned and eager to show off its facility. Book the hands-on tour with winemaker Michael Lancaster, who guides visitors above massive fermenting tanks and lets them sample wines from the barrel. The no-frills, tin-topped tasting room has a metal-and-wood tasting bar, over which small-lot zinfandel, cabernet, syrah, and sauvignon blanc are paired with local cheeses. *21692 8th St. No. 340, Sonoma. ☎ 707/938-5430. www.tinbarnvineyards.com. Sat–Sun 11am–4pm, Mon–Fri by appt. Tastings: $6 (waived with purchase). Hwy. 101 N. Exit at Hwy. 37, then north on Calif. 121 to 8th St. E. Map p 132.*

Fluffy, white clouds frame a sea of Sonoma vines.

A blanket of fog rests over the vineyards in Napa Valley.

★ **Trefethen Vineyards** NAPA Trefethen was designed and built in 1886 by Scottish seaman Hamden McIntyre, who also designed Far Niente, Rubicon Estate, and the Culinary Institute of America. An old-fashioned wooden gravity-flow winery helped the winery qualify for the National Register of Historic Places. In the tasting room, try Riesling, Viognier, and chardonnay. *1160 Oak Knoll Ave., Napa. ☎ 707/255-7700. www.trefethen.com. Daily 10am–4:30pm. Free tours by appt. Tastings: $10–$20. Hwy. 37 W., then right on Hwy. 29, then right on Oak Knoll Ave. Map p 130.*

★★ **V. Sattui Winery** NAPA In 1885, Vittorio Sattui established his winery in San Francisco. When Prohibition was enacted, he said, "I'll do nothing against the law" and shut the operation down. In 1976, his descendents reopened the winery in St. Helena. In the large, festive tasting room, a fourth-generation Sattui is likely to pour your wine. V. Sattui's wines aren't sold in shops or restaurants, so stock up here on vintages like the 2005 Rosato, an interestingly dry rosé. If you buy food at the gourmet deli (lots of free nibbles to try), you can use the picnic grounds, where giant oaks provide shade and beauty. *1111 White Lane, St. Helena. ☎ 707/963-7774. www.vsattui.com. Daily 9am–6pm (5pm Nov–Feb). Free self-guided tours all day. Tastings: $5–$10. Just off Hwy. 29. Map p 130.*

Viader Vineyards and Winery NAPA *BIO* On 1,300-foot-high (390m) Howell Mountain, Delia Viader's winery affords stunning valley views from its terrace. The tasting fee includes all five of her high-end wines, including hard-to-find "V," a blend of Petit Verdot and cabernet. *1120 Deer Park Rd., St. Helena. ☎ 707/963-3816. www.viader.com. Daily 10am–4pm. Tastings: $35 (by appt.). From the Silverado Trail, turn east on Deer Park Rd. Map p 130.*

★★ **Viansa Winery** SONOMA Founded in 1989 by Vicki and Sam Sebastiani (the winery's moniker is an amalgam of their first names), this Tuscan-style hilltop estate houses a branch of the Sonoma Valley Visitors Bureau. It also has an Italian deli that sells excellent focaccia sandwiches and tours into Viansa's underground cellars. An old-world marketplace offers comprehensive wine tastings and plenty of food samples made fresh in the cucina. Plus, you can buy their Italy-inspired varieties like the berry-flavored 2003 Lorenzo and the Sempre Avanti, a blend of four types of red grapes. *25200 Arnold Dr. (Hwy. 121), Sonoma. ☎ 800/995-4740. www.viansa.com. Daily 10am–5pm. Tours ($5) daily 11am & 2pm, 3:30pm. Tastings: $5–$10. Map p 132.*

ZD Wines NAPA *ORG* Try Abacus, the winery's best cabernet, at the wood-paneled tasting bar. Weekends bring specialized tasting experiences: On Saturdays, ZD presents a wine-and-cheese seminar, while Sundays are reserved for sensory-component tastings. Be sure to reserve both of these in advance. *8383 Silverado Trail, Rutherford. ☎ 800/487-7757. www.zdwines.com. Daily 10am–4:30pm. Tours and tastings $20–$25 by appt. Tastings: $5–$25. Map p 130.*

8 San Francisco

The Best of SF in One Day

Previous page: San Francisco icons: trolleys, bridges, hills, and sun.

San Francisco has rightly earned its reputation as America's most beautiful city. This first full-day tour introduces you to its best-known neighborhoods: Union Square, Fisherman's Wharf, North Beach, and Chinatown. After arriving at Fisherman's Wharf, you can do the rest on foot—but public transportation options are listed just in case. **START: BART/Muni: Powell or Montgomery. Bus: 2, 3, 4, or 38 to Powell St.; 30 or 45 to Geary St. Cable car: Powell lines.**

1 ★★ **Union Square.** Start your tour at this hub of San Francisco. The square (named for a series of uproarious pro-Union mass demonstrations staged here on the eve of the Civil War) reopened in 2002 after a $25-million restoration that replaced stretches of lawn with a 245-foot-long (74m) granite floor and scattered greenery, which turned it into a welcoming and memorable plaza. All that remains from the old square is the 90-foot (27m) Victory tower, dedicated by Theodore Roosevelt after the Spanish-American War. During the holidays, the square gets decked out with thousands of twinkling adornments, including a colossal Christmas tree. ◷ *30 min.; best before 9am. Between Post, Geary, Stockton & Powell sts. BART: Powell or Montgomery. Bus: 2, 3, 4, or 38 to Powell St.; 30 or 45 to Geary St. Cable car: Powell lines.*

2 ★ kids **Ride the Powell-Hyde Cable Car.** Head to the cable-car turnaround at Powell and Market streets and await the Powell-Hyde line. The first of these engineless, open-air cars started running in 1873. As the cable car takes you over Russian Hill, pay attention as you crest Hyde Street at Greenwich Street—you'll catch your first breathtaking glimpse of the San Francisco Bay and Alcatraz Island. ◷ *30 min.; best before 9:30am. Powell & Market sts. $6 per ride.*

3 ★ **Lombard Street.** "The crookedest street in the world" is in fact not even the crookedest street in San Francisco (Vermont St. between 20th and 22nd sts. in Potrero Hill is curvier). Zigzags were added in the 1920s because the street's 27-degree pitch was too steep for automobiles. Cars are permitted only to descend, but pedestrians can take the stairs up or down on either side. The street is loveliest in spring, when the hydrangeas are in bloom. ◷ *30 min.; best weekday mornings. Lombard St. (between Hyde & Leavenworth sts.). Cable car: Powell-Hyde line.*

4 ★★ **Fisherman's Wharf.** San Francisco's most visited attraction has history and lots to do. Although much of the wharf is rife with tacky souvenir shops and overpriced

Riding a cable car is one of San Francisco's most distinctive activities.

restaurants, this is still a must-see. Consider the following mini-tour; it highlights the wharf's most scenic spots and keeps time near the throngs to a minimum. *Hyde & Beach sts. www.fishermanswharf.org. Cable car: Powell-Hyde line to Fisherman's Wharf, Powell-Mason line to Taylor & Bay sts.; F streetcar to Jones & Beach sts. Bus 10, 30, or 47 to Van Ness Ave. & N. Point St.; 19 to Polk & Beach sts.*

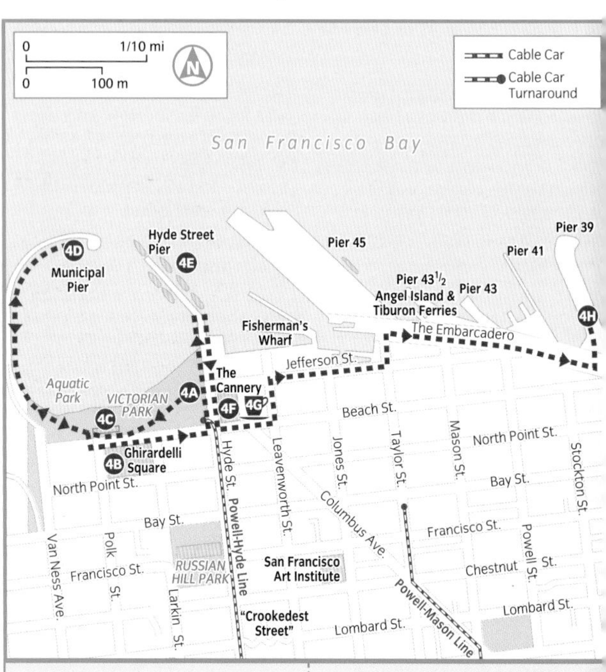

4A Victorian Park. is where you'll alight from the cable car. You'll see arts and crafts for sale as you walk toward **4B Ghirardelli Square,** built in 1893 as Domingo Ghirardelli's chocolate factory. When the factory relocated in the 1960s, the building became a National Historic Landmark and now houses a shopping center and eateries. **4C The recently renovated Maritime Museum,** a three-story Art Deco structure shaped like an ocean liner, offers a free look at the city's seafaring past. A walk along **4D Municipal Pier** affords views of the Golden Gate Bridge. **4E Hyde Street Pier** berths refurbished antique ships, including a 19th-century square-rigger. **4F The Cannery,** once a fruit-canning facility, now houses shops, restaurants, and the National Maritime Visitors Center. **4G Order a crepe** from the cart in the Cannery courtyard. Now fortified, you can brave the happy crowds at **4H Pier 39.** The vocal sea lions at the end of the pier are a sight to behold. *2–3 hr.; go in the morning to beat the crowds.*

Pier 39's sea lions bathe, bark, and splash about.

❺ **Coit Tower.** The 210-foot (63m) landmark atop Telegraph Hill was erected in 1933 with $125,000 bequeathed by local character Lillie Hitchcock Coit, who wished to add **beauty** to the city. Inside the tower's base are murals by several artists, many of whom studied under Diego Rivera. Commissioned as part of the New Deal's WPA, the murals have a pro-worker motif that caused a stir in their day. The fee to ascend the tower is worth it: A 360-degree city view awaits. While on Telegraph Hill, try to spot the flock of wild, green parrots; no one's sure how they got there. *45 min. From Fisherman's Wharf, walk or take bus 39 to Coit Tower. ☎ 415/362-0808. Admission to the top $4.50, $3.50 seniors, $2 kids 6–12. Daily 10am–5pm.*

❻ ★★ **North Beach.** Immigrants from Genoa and Sicily who founded the Bay Area's fishing industry settled here in the 1870s, establishing a variety of Italian restaurants, cafes, bakeries, and bars. In the 1950s, these spots became havens for some of the era's most influential writers and artists. Today, the neighborhood exudes a combination of Mediterranean warmth and bohemian spirit. Don't miss the famous ❼ **City Lights Booksellers & Publishers** (at 261 Columbus Ave.), an intimate tribute to Beat literature. *1–2 hr. Walk from Coit Tower, or take bus 39 to Washington Sq. Best Mon–Sat from 11am–4pm. Shops are closed Sun and early mornings.*

❽ **Mario's Bohemian Cigar Store Café.** Pick up sandwiches here and enjoy them in ❾ **Washington Square Park** across the street. *566 Columbus Ave. (at Union St.). ☎ 415/362-0536. $.*

❿ ★ **Chinatown.** San Francisco's most densely populated neighborhood is home to more than 14,000 people. Walk down Grant Street to find shops filled with eclectic knickknacks. Chinatown locals shop on Stockton Street, which teems with grocery stores, herb shops, and vendors of ceremonial items.

At 56 Ross Alley (between Washington and Jackson sts.) is 11 ★★ **Golden Gate Fortune Cookie Factory,** a hidden treasure in which you can sample and buy prophetic confections.

Coit Tower crowns Telegraph Hill.

The Best of SF in Two Days

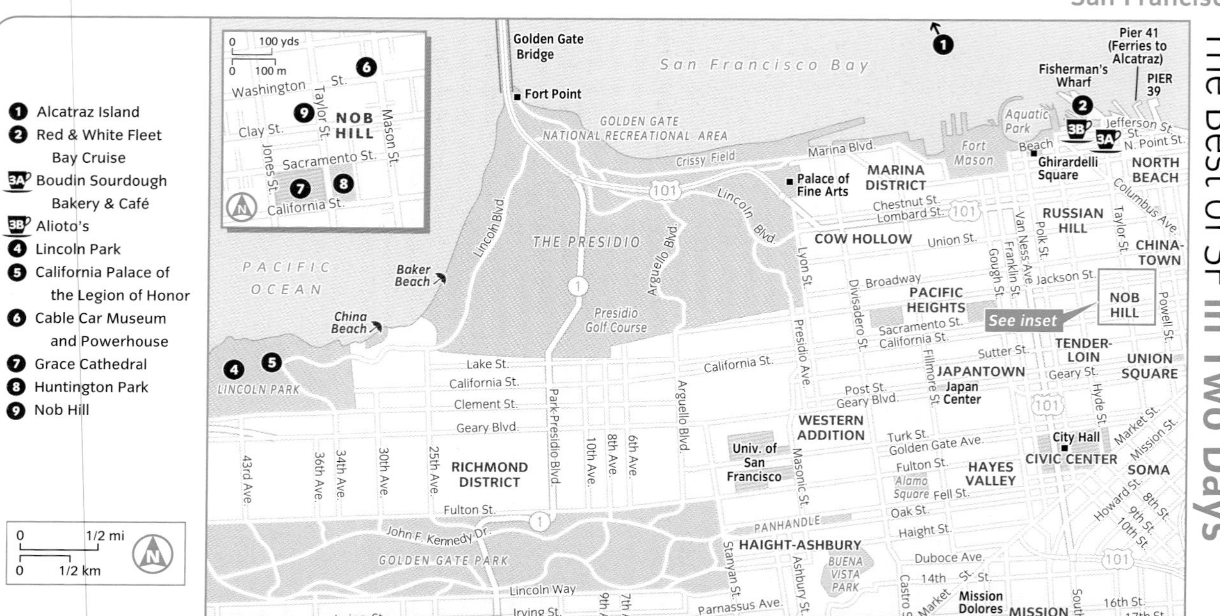

If you have 2 days, plan your first day as detailed on p 162. For your second day, start with a major highlight—a visit to Alcatraz. Pre-reserved tickets are required, but if you didn't plan ahead, an alternative bay cruise is listed below. After Alcatraz (or the cruise), visit Lincoln Park, a less visited but still striking corner of San Francisco, and experience 19th-century San Francisco on Nob Hill. START: **Pier 41, Fisherman's Wharf. Cable car: Powell-Mason. Bus: 30. Streetcar: F.**

Alcatraz Island is in the middle of San Francisco Bay.

1 ★★★ **Alcatraz Island.** Spanish for "pelican," Alcatraz was so named in 1775 by Juan Manuel Ayala for the birds nesting on its rocky shores. From the 1850s to 1933, the U.S. military used Alcatraz as a fort to protect the bay and its shoreline. In 1934, the government converted the island to a maximum-security prison for the country's most hardened criminals, including Al Capone, "Machine Gun" Kelly, and Robert "The Birdman" Stroud. Given its sheer cliffs, frigid waters, and treacherous currents, Alcatraz was considered inescapable. However, the prison's upkeep cost a fortune; all supplies had to come by boat. After three convicted bank robbers (Frank Lee Morris and brothers Clarence and John Anglin) escaped in 1962 using sharpened spoons and a makeshift raft, the prison closed. The island remained unoccupied until 1969, when Native Americans took it over, bringing their civil-rights issues to the forefront. They were removed in 1971, but not before Congress passed more than 50 legislative proposals supporting tribal self-rule. Today, the National Park Service manages Alcatraz. Once there, you'll receive a headset that plays an audio tour that includes riveting tales from former guards and inmates. From October to mid-February, you can tour the island on a walking path. For an eerie evening experience, take the "Alcatraz After Hours" tour. *2–3 hr., including ferry ride. Take the 1st ferry of the day, if possible. Wear a jacket & walking shoes; it's an uphill walk from the ferry landing to the cellblock (motorized carts carry visitors with disabilities). The ferry sells snacks, but there's no food on the island. Pier 41, Fisherman's Wharf.* ☎ *415/773-1188 for information, or 415/705-5555 to* *reserve tickets. www.nps.gov/alcatraz.* ***Tip:*** *Buy a ticket that includes the audio tour. Admission (ferry & audio tour): $26, $25 seniors 62+, $16 kids 5–11. Without audio tour: $12, $9.75 seniors, $8.25 kids 5–11. Winter daily 9:30am–2:15pm; summer daily 9am–3:55pm. Ferries run every half-hour. Arrive 30 min. before departure in summer (45 min. in winter). After-hours tours depart at 6:10 & 6:45pm in summer; 4:20 & 5:10pm in winter. Bus: 30. Cable car: Powell-Mason line. Streetcar: F.*

2 kids ★ Red & White Fleet Bay Cruise. If you were unable to pre-reserve Alcatraz tickets, take this 1-hour bay cruise (named after Stanford University's school colors) with audio narration. You'll travel under the Golden Gate Bridge and around Alcatraz. *1 hr. Pier 43½. ☎ 415/673-2900. www.redandwhite.com. Ferry ride & audio tour: $22, youth 5–17, $16, children younger than 5 free. Check the website for discount fares. Transport: see bullet 1.*

No SF visit is complete without trying the city's famous bread; taste it at 3A ★ kids **Boudin Sourdough Bakery & Café.** *160 Jefferson St. ☎ 415/928-1849. $.* For a sit-down meal with a view, opt for 3B **Alioto's.** *No. 8 Fisherman's Wharf at Taylor St. ☎ 415/673-0183. $$.*

4 Lincoln Park. This lovely park in the city's northwest corner boasts expansive lawns, eucalyptus trees, an 18-hole golf course, and gorgeous views. Walk north to the Land's End trail head for a closer look at the Marin Headlands and a western profile of the Golden Gate Bridge. *30 min.; best in the afternoon, when the fog has burned off & the sun makes the Marin hills appear golden. Clement Ave. & 33rd Ave.*

Fresh Dungeness crab at Fisherman's Wharf.

Powell-Hyde cable car to Geary St., transfer to bus 38 to Geary Blvd. & 33rd Ave.; then walk or take bus 18 to Legion of Honor.

5 ★★ California Palace of the Legion of Honor. Adding to Lincoln Park's splendor is this neoclassical memorial to Californian soldiers who died in World War I. This exact replica of Paris's Legion of Honor Palace opened on Armistice Day in 1924. Its fine-art collection spans 4,000 years and includes paintings by Monet and Rembrandt, plus international tapestries, prints, and drawings. There's also an excellent collection of Rodin sculptures, including an original cast of *The Thinker*. *1 hr. Clement St. & 34th Ave. ☎ 415/863-3330. www.thinker.org. Admission $10, $7 seniors 65+, $6 youths 13–17, free for kids 12 and younger, free to all first Tues of each month. Tues–Sun 9:30am–5:15pm. Transport: see bullet 4.*

6 kids Cable Car Museum and Powerhouse. When British-born engineer Andrew Hallidie saw a horse and its heavy carriage fall backward down a steep San Francisco hill, he vowed to create a mechanical transportation device for the city. By 1873, the first cable car had traversed Clay Street. Cable cars have no engines; instead, they're attached to an electrically powered cable that runs at a constant 9½-mph (15kph) rate through an underground rail. When it's time to stop, the car's conductor, or "gripper," pulls a lever to release the car's grip on the cable. Inside this free, fascinating museum, you'll see the cables that carry the cars. Though it once ran more than 600 cars, today's system operates only three lines. *20 minutes. 1201 Mason St. (at Washington St.). 415/474-1887. www.cablecarmuseum.com. Free admission. Daily 10am–5pm; until 6pm Apr–Oct. Closed major holidays. Cable car: Powell lines.*

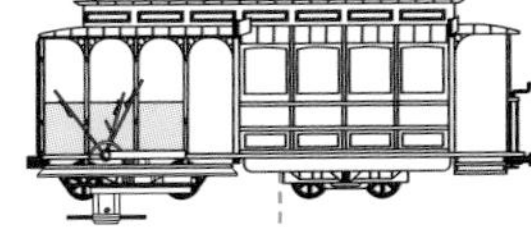

Learn how a cable car actually works at the Cable Car Museum.

7 ★★ **Grace Cathedral.** After the Crocker mansion was destroyed by the 1906 earthquake and fires, the Crockers donated its site to the Episcopal Church; in 1964, Grace Cathedral was complete. Pay special attention to the main doors—stunning replicas of Ghiberti's bronze Doors of Paradise on the Baptistery of Florence—and the Singing Tower to the right of the main entrance, which has a 44-bell carillon. The cathedral's exterior is made of reinforced concrete beaten to achieve a stonelike effect. Inside, note the 1840 organ and the impressive stained-glass windows, some of which depict modern figures like Justice Thurgood Marshall, poet Robert Frost (a San Francisco native), and Albert Einstein. *25 min. 1100 California St. (at Taylor St.). www.gracecathedral.org. 415/749-6300. Free admission. Mon–Fri 7am–6pm, Sat 8am–6pm, Sun 7am–7pm. Bus: 1. Cable car: All lines.*

8 **kids** **Huntington Park.** David Colton, who helped build the Southern Pacific Railroad, had his mansion here until he sold it to Collis Huntington in 1892. The mansion burned as a result of the 1906 quake, and the lot lay empty for 9 years until Huntington donated it to the city. Today, the park is a lovely oasis in an urban section of town. It's still framed by the granite walls that were part of the Colton estate. *15 min. Taylor & California sts. Bus: 1. Cable car: All lines.*

9 **Nob Hill.** This famous hillcrest neighborhood is named for its wealthy former residents, or "nabobs," as San Francisco elites were then known. The "Big Four" railroad barons of the Southern Pacific Railroad—Leland Stanford, Mark Hopkins, Charles Crocker, and Collis Huntington—built ostentatious mansions here in the late 1870s, all doomed for destruction by the fires following the 1906 quake. Today, some of the city's most prestigious hotels occupy Nob Hill. *20 min. Taylor & Sacramento sts. Bus: 1 from Clement St. & 33rd Ave. to Taylor & Sacramento sts. Visit during daylight hours, though the view from the Top of the Mark (p 191), a fancy penthouse lounge, is magnificent at night.*

A view of the Transamerica building from atop Nob Hill.

The Best of SF **in Three Days**

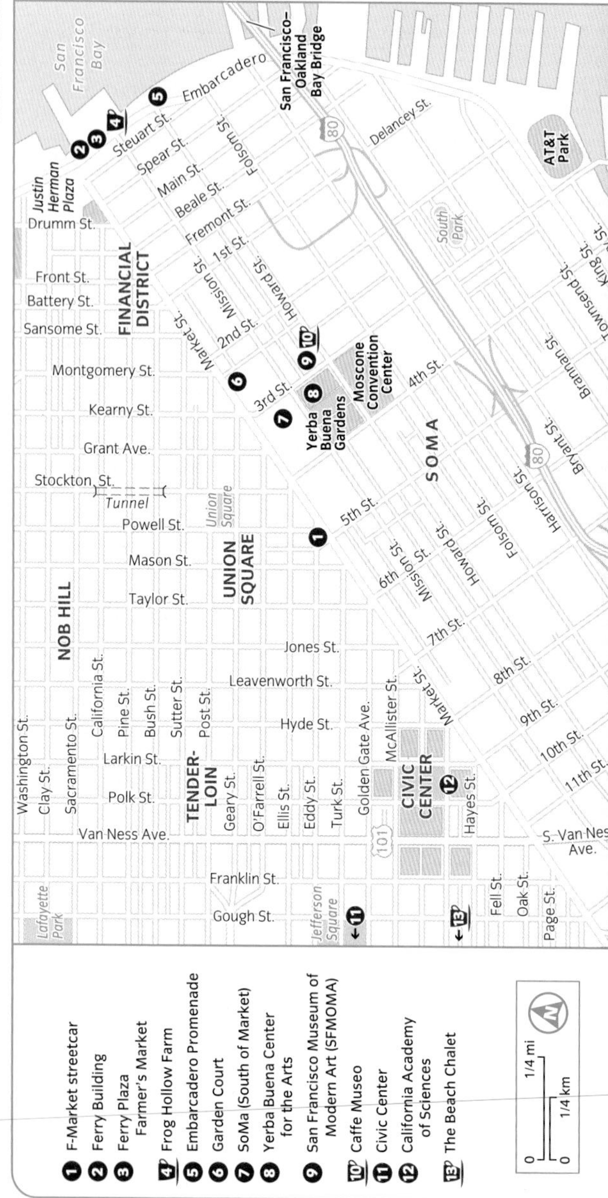
1 F-Market streetcar
2 Ferry Building
3 Ferry Plaza Farmer's Market
4 Frog Hollow Farm
5 Embarcadero Promenade
6 Garden Court
7 SoMa (South of Market)
8 Yerba Buena Center for the Arts
9 San Francisco Museum of Modern Art (SFMOMA)
10 Caffe Museo
11 Civic Center
12 California Academy of Sciences
13 The Beach Chalet
0
1/4 mi
0
1/4 km
San Francisco Bay
Embarcadero
San Francisco–Oakland Bay Bridge
Justin Herman Plaza
Drumm St.
Steuart St.
Spear St.
Main St.
Beale St.
Fremont St.
Folsom St.
1st St.
Mission St.
Howard St.
2nd St.
Market St.
3rd St.
4th St.
5th St.
6th St.
7th St.
8th St.
9th St.
10th St.
11th St.
Delancey St.
AT&T Park
South Park
King St.
Townsend St.
Brannan St.
Bryant St.
Harrison St.
Folsom St.
Howard St.
Mission St.
Moscone Convention Center
Yerba Buena Gardens
SOMA
FINANCIAL DISTRICT
Front St.
Battery St.
Sansome St.
Montgomery St.
Kearny St.
Grant Ave.
Stockton St.
Tunnel
Powell St.
Mason St.
Taylor St.
Union Square
UNION SQUARE
NOB HILL
Jones St.
Leavenworth St.
Hyde St.
Larkin St.
Polk St.
Van Ness Ave.
Franklin St.
Gough St.
Washington St.
Clay St.
Sacramento St.
California St.
Pine St.
Bush St.
Sutter St.
Post St.
TENDER-LOIN
Geary St.
O'Farrell St.
Ellis St.
Eddy St.
Turk St.
Golden Gate Ave.
McAllister St.
CIVIC CENTER
Hayes St.
Fell St.
Oak St.
Page St.
S. Van Ness Ave.
Lafayette Park
Jefferson Square
80
101

If you've already made your way through "The Best in Two Days," you'll find that this third full-day tour gives you a taste of the city's epicurean underpinnings, as well as its rich artistic and cultural life. Devote an entire day for this tour. It can be done on foot, though the antique F-Market streetcars are attractions unto themselves. ***Note:*** Though the Civic Center is just a few blocks from SoMa, the east–west blocks are quite long. START: **From Union Sq., hop on the F-Market streetcar at the Powell St. station; exit at the Ferry Terminal loop.**

1 kids ★ F-Market streetcar. Several streetcar lines travel along Market Street, but the F line also heads along the scenic waterfront. Its streetcars were imported from around the world, including vintage cars from Europe and turn-of-the-20th-century trolleys from other U.S. cities. *15 min. From Union Sq., enter at the Powell St. station; exit at the Ferry Terminal loop. Fare $1.50, 50¢ seniors & kids 5–17. Free for kids younger than 5. Avoid rush hour (Mon–Fri, before 9:30am & 4:30–6:30pm).*

2 ★★ Ferry Building. This 1898 building reopened in 2003 after a 4-year, multimillion-dollar renovation. Outside is a 240-foot (72m) clock tower. Inside, a collection of restaurants and gourmet stores sell an impressive array of specialty foods. Make your way to the back of the building for a view of the Bay Bridge. Try to visit on a Farmer's Market day (see bullet 3 and p 20). *1 hr. 1 Ferry Building (at the Embarcadero & Market St.). Minimum hours: Mon–Fri 10am–6pm; Sat 9am–6pm; Sun 11am–5pm (hours for individual businesses may vary). www.ferrybuildingmarketplace.com. F or any Market St. streetcar to the Ferry Bldg. or Embarcadero; bus 2, 7, 14, 21, 66, or 71 to Steuart & Market sts. Also see p 187.*

Take a ride on a vintage F-market streetcar.

3 ★★★ Ferry Plaza Farmers Market. Tuesdays and Saturdays (and from spring to fall, Thurs and Sun too), local food producers set up booths around the Ferry Building. Saturday mornings are busiest, as locals make their regular trek to stock up on fruits and vegetables, fresh-baked goods, and other gustatory delights. Saturdays also feature trailer cars out back, from which city restaurants serve gourmet breakfasts. Given the penchant for using local, organic, and naturally grown produce at many San Francisco restaurants—not to mention homes—this market is a hallmark of city life. *1 hr. 1 Ferry Building (at the Embarcadero & Market St.). 415/291-3276. Tues & Sun 10am–2pm; Sat 8am–2pm; Thurs 4–8pm. Also see p 20.*

4 Frog Hollow Farm. Grab coffee and a fruit-filled pastry here before strolling the scenic waterfront. *Ferry Building Marketplace. 415/445-0990. $.*

5 ★ Embarcadero Promenade. The 1989 Loma Prieta earthquake encouraged city leaders to decommission the ugly elevated freeway that once obscured this lovely stretch of waterfront that extends from AT&T Park to Fisherman's Wharf. The wide sidewalk and scenic views make this a favored destination for pedestrians and joggers. Notice the Embarcadero Ribbon, a 2½-mile (4km) continuous line of glass encased in concrete. The 13-foot-tall (3.9m) metal pylons and bronze plaques embedded in the sidewalk are imprinted with photographs, drawings, poetry, and historical facts. *30 min.–1 hr.; a walk in either direction is pleasant at any time of day, but avoid the traffic on weekday afternoons 4–6pm. Return to Market St. to catch the F-Market streetcar to the Montgomery St. station, or walk there.*

6 Garden Court. The extravagant Palace Hotel astounded San Franciscans and bankrupted its owner, who allegedly committed suicide a day before the 1875 grand opening. Three decades later, the hotel was ravaged by one of the many fires following the 1906 earthquake. The hotel was restored and reopened in 1909, along with the magnificent Garden Court. This impressive atrium's domed ceiling is made from 80,000 glass panes and houses the Garden Court Restaurant (p 181). After absorbing Garden Court's grandeur, step into the Pied Piper Bar to glimpse the $2.5-million Maxfield Parrish painting of the same name. *20 min. 2 New Montgomery St. (at Market St.). ☎ 415/546-5089. Daily 6:30am–2pm; tea Sat 1–3pm. BART/Muni: Powell or Montgomery.*

7 ★★ SoMa (South of Market). This former industrial area south of Market Street has become a major center for museums, galleries, and major-league baseball. *2–4 hr. to stroll through the neighborhood; visit during daylight hours. Note: SFMOMA (see bullet 9) is closed Wed.*

8 ★ kids Yerba Buena Center for the Arts is SoMa's cultural anchor. It serves as a major arts-and-entertainment center, with cultural programs, oasis-like gardens, and recreational facilities. Pay tribute at the Martin Luther King Jr. Memorial and its 50-foot (15m) waterfall, or catch a flick at the Sony Metreon Entertainment Center. *Best time: daylight hours.* *1 hr. 101 4th*

The ceiling of the Garden Court is a glittering masterpiece of glass.

St. ☎ 415/978-2787. *www.ybca.org.* 🕘 *1–3 hr. Between 3rd, 4th, Mission & Folsom sts.*

9 ★★ **San Francisco Museum of Modern Art (SFMOMA).** In 1995, SFMOMA moved into its $62-million home designed by architect Mario Botta. Its permanent collection includes more than 15,000 works by the likes of Henri Matisse, Jackson Pollock, and Georgia O'Keeffe. The first major museum to have recognized photography as an art form, SFMOMA also exhibits the works of Ansel Adams, Man Ray, and other luminaries. Not enough of the permanent collection is on display at any one time, but temporary exhibits are usually superb. 🕘 *1½ hr. 151 3rd St. (between Mission & Howard sts.).* ☎ *415/357-4000. www.sfmoma.org. Admission $13, $8 seniors 62+, $7 students with ID, free for kids younger than 13. Half price Thurs 6–8:45pm. Free to all 1st Tues of the month. Thurs 11am–8:45pm; Fri–Tues 11am–5:45pm. Closed Wed & major holidays. Opens at 10am in summer. Bus: 15, 30, 45. BART/Muni: Montgomery St. Best time: weekdays.*

10 **Caffe Museo.** SFMOMA's on-site cafe has excellent soups, sandwiches, and salads. *151 3rd St.* ☎ *415/357-4500. $.*

11 ★ **Civic Center.** Less than a decade after the 1906 earthquake destroyed SF's original City Hall, architect Arthur Brown erected a lavish Beaux Arts–style administrative and cultural center to take its place. Buildings here include extravagant City Hall itself, topped with a 308-foot-tall (92m) dome; the 376,000-square-foot (35,000-sq.-m) main public library; the Asian Art Museum, recently transformed by the architect who did France's Musée d'Orsay; and the War

SFMOMA's skylight is just one of the museum's architectural highlights.

Memorial Opera House, where the 1951 U.S.-Japan peace accord was signed. 🕘 *1 hr. Most Civic Center buildings are bordered by Hayes, Franklin & Hyde sts. & Golden Gate Ave. Best time: weekdays during daylight hours.*

12 ★★★ kids **California Academy of Sciences.** This newly reopened science museum in Golden Gate Park is an expansive, interactive world of discovery that mesmerizes everyone who visits. Highlights include captivating planetarium shows, an aquarium, and a four-story rainforest, complete with critters—all under one "living roof". 🕘 *2–4 hrs, weekday afternoons are best, as mornings are full with school tours. 55 Music Concourse Dr.* ☎ *415/379-8000. www.calacademy.org. Admission $25, $20 seniors & kids 12–17, $15 for students & kids 7–11, free for kids younger than 7, free for all the 1st Wed of the month. Mon–Sat 9:30am–5pm, Sun 11am–5pm. Bus: 44, 74X.*

13 **The Beach Chalet.** Dinner at this airy Golden Gate Park restaurant and brewery near the ocean is a lively affair made better by good-quality American food. Don't miss the 1930s-era fresco murals in the adjoining Golden Gate Park Visitor's Center. *1000 Great Highway at Ocean Beach.* ☎ *415/386-8439. $$. Bus: 5.*

San Francisco Lodging & Dinin

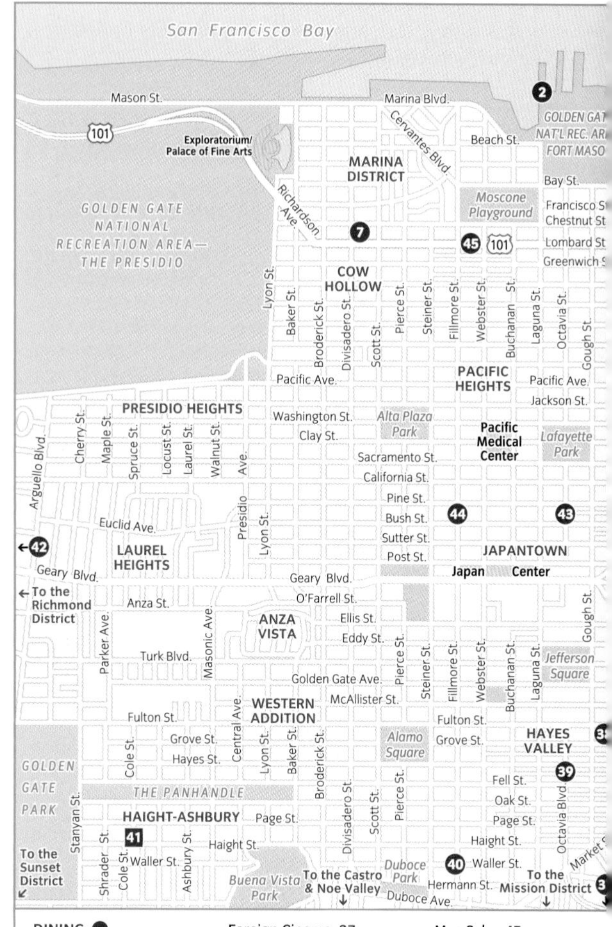

DINING ●

A16 7
Aqua 16
Boogaloos 37
Boulevard 13
Carnelian 9
Chez Papa 36
Cliff House 42
Dottie's True Blue Café 30
Fifth Floor 32
Fleur de Lys 27
Florio Bar & Cafe 44
Foreign Cinema 37
Garden Court Restaurant 34
Gary Danko 6
Ghirardelli Soda Fountain & Chocolate Shop 5
Greens 2
Hawthorne Lane 35
Indian Oven 40
Jardiniere 38
Kokkari 10
L'Osteria del Forno 8
Mas Sake 45
Michael Mina 25
Millennium 29
Mitchell's Ice Cream 37
One Market 13
Postrio 28
Quince 43
The Slanted Door 11
Suppenküche 39
Tacqueria Pancho Villa 37

BERKELEY INSET

Chez Panisse 1

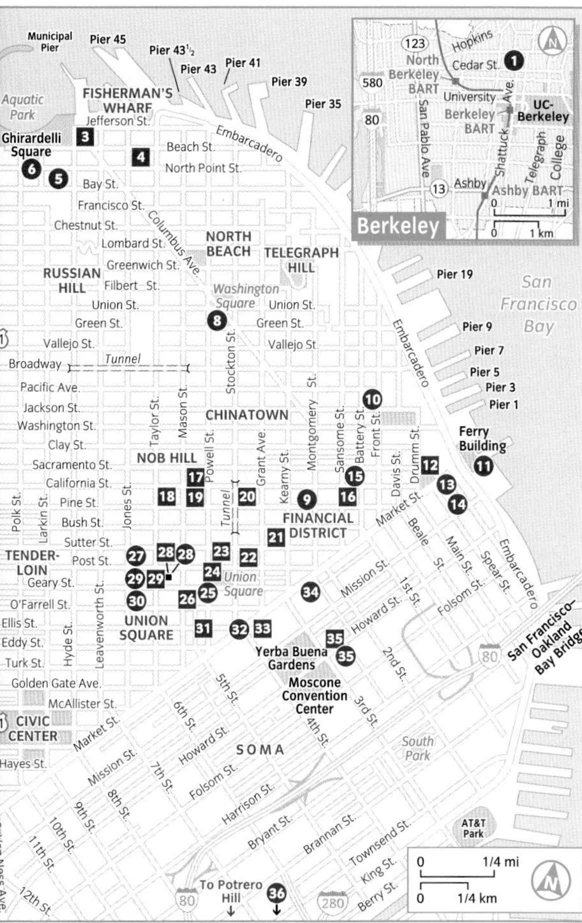

LODGING ■

Adagio 29
The Argonaut 3
Campton Place Hotel 22
Clift Hotel 28
Fairmont Hotel 17
Four Seasons 33
The Huntington Hotel 18
Hotel Abri 31
Hyatt at Fisherman's Wharf 4
Hyatt Regency San Francisco 12
InterContinental Mark Hopkins 19
King George Hotel 26
Mandarin Oriental 16
The Palace Hotel 24
Red Victorian 41
Ritz-Carlton 20
Sir Francis Drake 23
Hotel Triton 21
W San Francisco 35
Westin St. Francis 24

Lodging A to Z

★ **Adagio** UNION SQUARE Sleek charm for a good price. Double queen rooms are a great deal for families. The in-house Cortez restaurant shines. ***550 Geary St. (between Jones & Taylor sts.). ☎ 800/228-8830 or 415/775-5000. www.thehoteladagio.com. 173 units. Doubles $139–179. AE, DC, DISC, MC, V. Bus: 2, 3, 4, 38. BART/Muni: Powell St. Map p 175.***

★★ kids **The Argonaut** FISHERMAN'S WHARF The beautifully restored 1907 building in the Maritime National Historical Park has nautical-themed decor, a great location, and some bay views. Best choice at the wharf. ***495 Jefferson St. (corner of Jefferson & Hyde sts.). ☎ 866/415-0704. www.argonauthotel.com. 252 units. Doubles $179–$329. AE, DC, MC, V. Bus: 10, 30. Cable car: Powell-Hyde. Map p 175.***

★★ **Campton Place Hotel** UNION SQUARE The epitome of refined opulence and exclusivity. Bathrooms, with Portuguese limestone and deep soaking tubs, are a dream. ***340 Stockton St. (between Post & Sutter sts.). ☎ 866/234-4300 or 415/781-5555. www.camptonplace.com. 110 units. Doubles $350. AE, DC, DISC, MC, V. Bus: 2, 3, 4. BART/Muni: Montgomery St. Cable car: Powell lines. Map p 175.***

Muted, pale colors infuse a tranquil vibe at the trendy Clift Hotel.

★ **Clift Hotel** UNION SQUARE Hotelier Ian Schrager and designer Philippe Starck created this überhip hotel with modern furnishings. Most rooms scream minimalism, and bathrooms are stylish but small. The stunning Redwood Room is a hopping lounge (p 190). ***495 Geary St. (at Taylor St.). ☎ 800/652-5438 or 415/775-4700. www.clifthotel.com. 389 units. Doubles $150–$355. AE, DC, DISC, MC, V. Bus: 2, 3, 4, 27, 38. Map p 175.***

★★★ **The Fairmont** NOB HILL This 1907 landmark's exterior makes an immediate impression. A recent $85-million restoration recaptured architect Julia Morgan's (of Hearst Castle fame) original design. The Fairmont is where U.S. presidents stay, and where the UN charter was drafted in 1945. For great views, opt for the Tower Building. ***950 Mason St. (at California St.). ☎ 800/441-1414 or 415/772-5000. www.fairmont.com. 591 units. Doubles $229–$509. AE, DC, DISC, MC, V. Bus: 1. Cable car: All. Map p 175.***

★★★ **Four Seasons** SOMA This divinely luxurious hotel has plush furnishings and large marble bathrooms. Impeccable service and access to the massive Sports Club/LA add to the wonders. ***757 Market St. (at 3rd St.). ☎ 415/633-3000. www.fourseasons.com. 277 units. Doubles begin at $395. AE, DC, DISC, MC, V. BART/Muni: Montgomery St. Map p 175.***

★★ **Hotel Majestic** PACIFIC HEIGHTS Ornately furnished with

European antiques, the Majestic is an escape from the rough edges of modern living. *1500 Sutter St. (between Octavia & Gough sts.). ☎ 800/869-8966 or 415/441-1100. www.thehotelmajestic.com. 58 units. Doubles $100–150 w/breakfast. AE, DISC, MC, V. Bus: 2, 3, 4.*

★ Hotel Triton UNION SQUARE A rock-themed hotel with Wi-Fi-equipped suites designed by famous musicians, eco-friendly floors, and free Friday-night wine parties with tarot-card readings and chair massages. Rooms are tiny. *342 Grant Ave. (at Bush St.). ☎ 800/433-6611 or 415/394-0500. www.hoteltriton.com. 140 units. Doubles $129–$189. AE, DC, DISC, MC, V. Bus: 2, 3, 4, 15, 30. BART/Muni: Montgomery St. Map p 175.*

★★★ The Huntington Hotel & Nob Hill Spa NOB HILL A discreet but very upscale Nob Hill choice. Rooms are sizable and seven suites have kitchens. The hotel's spa is magnificent. *1075 California St. (at Powell St.). ☎ 800/227-4683 or 415/474-5400. www.huntingtonhotel.com. 135 units. Doubles $225 & up. AE, DC, MC, V. Bus: 1. Cable car: All. Map p 175.*

kids Hyatt at Fisherman's Wharf FISHERMAN'S WHARF Best of the wharf chain hotels. All rooms were recently renovated to create a clean, contemporary look. There are new luxury beds, an outdoor pool, and a sports-bar-like restaurant. *555 N. Point St. (between Jones & Taylor sts.). ☎ 415/563-1234. www.fishermanswharf.hyatt.com. 313 units. Doubles $162–198. AE, DC, DISC, MC, V. Bus: 10, 30. Streetcar: F. Map p 175.*

★ Hyatt Regency San Francisco FINANCIAL DISTRICT This hulking, corporate hotel has a 17-story atrium, spacious rooms, some fine views, the Embarcadero Center next door, and the Ferry Building across the street. *5 Embarcadero Center (at Market St. by The Embarcadero). ☎ 800/233-1234 or 415/788-1234. www.sanfranciscoregency.hyatt.com. 802 units. Doubles $112–159. AE, DC, DISC, MC, V. BART/Muni: Embarcadero. Map p 175.*

The ultrahip Hotel Triton comes with Friday-night freebies like wine parties and chair massages.

★★★ InterContinental Mark Hopkins NOB HILL Plush rooms have stellar views and the Top of Mark sky-lounge is a stunning place

The Mark Hopkins Hotel (above) sits on the site of the former mansion (destroyed in the 1906 earthquake) of Mark Hopkins, a founder of the Southern Pacific Railroad.

to dine. An extra $50 per day grants access to the club lounge and its food. *1 Nob Hill (at Mason & California sts.). ☎ 800/327-0200 or 415/392-3434. www.san-francisco.intercontinental.com. 380 units. Doubles $119–379. AE, DC, DISC, MC, V. Bus: 1. Cable car: All. Map p 175.*

King George Hotel UNION SQUARE Popular with European tourists, this 1912 hotel offers modern amenities and handsome, albeit petite, rooms. On weekends and holidays, English afternoon tea is served in the hotel's Windsor Tea Room. *334 Mason St. (between Geary & O'Farrell sts.). ☎ 800/288-6005 or 415/781-5050. www.kinggeorge.com. 163 units. Doubles $109–$179. AE, DC, DISC, MC, V. Bus: 2, 3, 4, 38. Cable car: Powell lines. BART/Muni: Powell St. Map p 175.*

★★★ **Mandarin Oriental** FINANCIAL DISTRICT Atop SF's third-tallest building, the Mandarin affords jaw-dropping views. Every room has international flavor and an oversized bed. Regal service impresses. *222 Sansome St. (between Pine & California sts.). ☎ 800/622-0404. www.mandarinoriental.com. 158 units. Doubles $505–$735. AE, DC, DISC, MC, V. BART/Muni: Montgomery St. Cable car: California. Map p 175.*

★★ **The Palace Hotel** SOMA Over-the-top decor encompasses the landmark Garden Court Restaurant (p 181). Large rooms are graced with 14-foot (4.2m) ceilings and marble bathrooms. *2 New Montgomery St. (at Market St.). ☎ 415/512-1111. www.sfpalace.com. 553 units. Doubles $239–489. AE, DC, DISC, MC, V. BART/Muni: Montgomery St. Map p 175.*

Red Victorian HAIGHT There should be a sign in front of this eccentric Haight-Ashbury B&B that reads, "WELCOME BACK TO 1967." Each guest-room has its own flowery theme. *1665 Haight St. (at Belvedere St.). ☎ 415/864-1978. www.redvic.com. 18 units (6 w/private bath). Doubles $89–$229. AE, DISC, MC, V. Bus: 6, 7, 43, 66, 71. Muni: Carl & Cole. Map p 175.*

★★★ **The Ritz-Carlton** NOB HILL At this expensive, palatial property, modern features—Wi-Fi, flat LCD TVs, 400-thread-count linens, Bvlgari toiletries—don't detract from classic ones: regal decor, 18th-century antiques, a spa and fitness center, and the exceptional Dining Room. Above all, this 1909 landmark maintains excellent service. *600 Stockton St. (at California St.). ☎ 800/241-3333 or 415/296-7465. www.ritzcarlton.com. 336 units. Doubles $489 & up. AE, DC, DISC, MC, V. Cable car: All. Map p 175.*

Sir Francis Drake UNION SQUARE Despite the grandiose lobby and beefeater-clad doormen, stay here only if you get a great deal. The tiny rooms aren't as well-maintained as the lobby. It's always a party, though, at 21st-floor **Harry Denton's Starlight Lounge** (p 190). *450 Powell St. (at Sutter St.). ☎ 415/392-7755. www.sirfrancisdrake.com. 417 units. Doubles $239–$259. AE, DC, DISC, MC, V. Bus: 2, 3, 4. BART/Muni: Powell St. Cable car: Powell lines. Map p 175.*

★★ **W San Francisco** SOMA This ultrahip hotel adjacent to SFMOMA is home to sleek rooms, great views, 24-hour concierge service, the aptly named Bliss Spa, free poolside yoga, and XYZ restaurant. *181 3rd St. (at Howard St.). ☎ 415/777-5300. www.whotels.com. 408 units. Doubles $579–$609. AE, DC, DISC, MC, V. Bus: 15, 30, 45. BART/Muni: Montgomery St. Map p 175.*

★★ kids **Westin St. Francis** UNION SQUARE The historic "grand dame" of SF hotels, this Westin couldn't be better located; it's right on Union Square. Whichever foreign flag hangs outside the hotel represents the nationality of a dignitary currently inside on a given day. *335 Powell St. (at Geary St.).* ☎ *415/397-7000. www.westin.com. 1,195 units. Doubles $275–$479. AE, DC, DISC, MC, V. Bus: 2, 3, 4, 30, 45. BART/Muni: Powell St. Cable car: Powell lines. Map p 175.*

Dining A to Z

★★ **A16** MARINA *ITALIAN* A chic crowd comes for wood-fired pizza and an exciting wine list. *2355 Chestnut St. (between Scott & Divisadero sts.).* ☎ *415/771-2216. Entrees $9–$25. AE, DC, MC, V. Lunch Wed–Fri. Dinner daily. Bus: 30. Map p 174.*

★★★ **Aqua** FINANCIAL DISTRICT *SEAFOOD* Resplendent dishes stunningly presented against an opulent backdrop. *252 California St. (between Battery & Front sts.).* ☎ *415/956-9662. Entrees $19–$25. AE, DC, DISC, MC, V. Lunch Mon–Fri. Dinner nightly. BART/Muni: Embarcadero. Map p 174.*

★★ **Boogaloos** MISSION *LATIN* A well-loved brunch cafe with funky mosaic decor and a long wait. *3296 22nd St. (at Valencia St.).* ☎ *415/824-4088. Entrees $4.50–$10. DISC, MC, V. Breakfast & lunch daily. BART: 24th St. Mission Station. Map p 174.*

★★★ **Boulevard** SOMA *AMERICAN* A seasonal globally influenced menu and industrial Belle Epoque decor. *1 Mission St. (at Steuart St.).* ☎ *415/543-6084. Entrees $15–$40. AE, DC, DISC, MC, V. Lunch Mon–Fri. Dinner daily. Bus: 12. BART/Muni: Embarcadero. Map p 174.*

Carnelian Room FINANCIAL DISTRICT *GLOBAL* For a breathtaking panoramic view, dine on the 52nd floor of the corporate high-rise formerly known as the Bank of America Building. *555 California St. (at Montgomery).* ☎ *415/433-7500. AE, MC, V. Dinner Mon–Sat. Bus: 1, 10, 20, 30, 41, 45. Bart/Muni to Montgomery.*

Chez Panisse BERKELEY *CALIFORNIA* Alice Waters's famous restaurant still delivers an ever-changing

Alice Waters, the queen of California cuisine and chef of Chez Panisse (above), in her garden.

The Cliff House may be pricey, but it's more than worth it for its view of the Pacific Ocean.

menu that epitomizes California cuisine (see box p 182). *1517 Shattuck Ave. (between Cedar & Vine sts.). ☎ 510/548-5525. Entrees $60–$95 (prix-fixe). AE, DC, DISC, MC, V. Dinner Mon–Sat. BART: Downtown Berkeley. Map p 174.*

★★ **Cliff House** SUNSET *AMERICAN* Truly breathtaking ocean views and charming early-20th-century decor make the whole experience here—food is almost an afterthought. *1090 Point Lobos Ave. (just west of 48th Ave. Geary Blvd. turns into Point Lobos Ave. after 43rd Ave.). ☎ 415/386-3330. Entrees $16–$28. AE, DC, DISC, MC, V. Breakfast, lunch & dinner daily. Bus: 18, 38. Map p 174.*

★ kids **Dottie's True Blue Café** UNION SQUARE *TENDERLOIN AMERICAN* Ample portions of cornmeal pancakes and eggs. Lunch features salads and burgers. Kitschy decor. *522 Jones St. (between Geary & O'Farrell sts.). ☎ 415/885-2767. Entrees $5.75–$11. DISC, MC, V. Breakfast & lunch Wed–Mon. Bus: 2, 3, 4, 27, 38. Map p 174.*

★★ **Fifth Floor** SOMA *FRENCH* An acclaimed restaurant serving well-executed meals in a swank space. Try to meet Emily Wines, one of the few female master sommeliers in the world, and a Remi Krug Cup winner. *12 4th St. (in the Hotel Palomar, at Market St.). ☎ 415/348-1555. Entrees $24–$36. AE, DC, DISC, MC, V. Dinner Mon–Sat. Bus: 30, 45. Map p 174.*

★★★ **Fleur de Lys** UNION SQUARE *FRENCH* This epitome of luxury dining is the city's most classic French affair. *777 Sutter St. (between Jones & Taylor sts.). ☎ 415/673-7779. Prix-fixe from $70. AE, DC, MC, V. Dinner Mon–Sat. Bus 2, 3, 4, 27. Map p 174.*

Catch a flick with dinner at Foreign Cinema's alfresco tables.

I've written a song. Do you
want to hear it?

★★ Foreign Cinema MISSION *CALIFORNIA/ MEDITERRANEAN* Eat on this fancy restaurant's patio and watch foreign films while sampling interesting dishes. *2534 Mission St. (between 21st & 22nd sts.). ☎ 415/648-7600. Entrees $16–$30. AE, DISC, MC, V. Dinner daily, brunch Sat–Sun. Bus: 14, 49. BART: 24th St. Map p 174.*

★ Garden Court Restaurant SOMA *AMERICAN* Elegant service in a lovely historic setting. *Palace Hotel, 2 New Montgomery St. (at Market St.). ☎ 415/546-5089. Entrees $12–$28. AE, DC, DISC, MC, V. Breakfast & lunch daily. BART/Muni: Montgomery St. Map p 174.*

★★★ Gary Danko FISHERMAN'S WHARF *CALIFORNIA* SF's best restaurant boasts flawless service, outstanding wines, and a superlative menu that changes daily. Reserve 4 weeks ahead or try your luck at the bar. *800 N. Point St. (at Hyde St.). ☎ 415/749-2060. Prix-fixe menu from $66. DC, DISC, MC, V. Dinner daily. Bus: 10, 30. Cable car: Powell-Hyde. Map p 174.*

★ kids Ghirardelli Soda Fountain & Chocolate Shop FISHERMAN'S WHARF *ICE CREAM* The ever-present line attests to consistently great sundaes—all chocolate-topped, of course. *Ghirardelli Sq., 900 N. Point St. (at Larkin St.). ☎ 415/474-3938. Desserts $5–$20. AE, DC, DISC, MC, V. Mon–Thurs 10am–11pm; Fri–Sat 10am–midnight. Bus: 10, 30. Cable car: Powell-Hyde. Map p 174.*

★ Gordon Biersch SOMA *AMERICAN* A social place for a house-made brew and a hearty bite to eat, Gordon Biersch is a local favorite near the ballpark. *2 Harrison St. (at Embarcadero). ☎ 415/243-8246. Entrees $9.50–$26. AE, DC, DISC, MC, V. Sun–Thurs 11:30am–midnight; Fri–Sat 11:30am–2am. Bus: 32.*

Gary Danko won the James Beard Foundation's "Best New Restaurant" award in 2000; today, it still lives up to its acclaim.

★★ Greens MARINA *VEGETARIAN* Fabulous flavors and stunning views impress even dedicated carnivores. *Building A, Fort Mason Center (by Buchanan & Marina sts.). ☎ 415/771-6222. Entrees $8–$23; Sat prix-fixe $48. AE, DISC, MC, V. Lunch Tues–Sun. Dinner daily. Bus: 28, 30. Map p 174.*

★ Indian Oven HAIGHT *INDIAN* The city's best Indian restaurant. *233 Fillmore St. (between Haight & Waller sts.). ☎ 415/626-1628. Entrees $8–$19. AE, DC, DISC, MC, V. Dinner daily. Bus: 6, 7, 22, 66, 71. Map p 174.*

★ Jardiniere HAYES VALLEY *FRENCH* Symphony and opera patrons begin (or complete) a night with dinner at this upscale Civic Center staple. *300 Grove St. (at Franklin St.). ☎ 415/861-5555. Entrees $29–$45. AE, DC, DISC, MC, V. Dinner daily. Bus: 21. Map p 174.*

★★ Kokkari FINANCIAL DISTRICT *GREEK* Greek classics in a warm, upscale setting. *200 Jackson St. (at Front St.). ☎ 415/981-0983. Entrees $15–$39. AE, DC, DISC, MC, V. Lunch Mon–Fri. Dinner Mon–Sat. Bus: 10. Map p 174.*

★★ L'Osteria del Forno NORTH BEACH *ITALIAN* A small, romantic dining room with a small, quintessentially Italian menu. *519 Columbus Ave. (between Union & Green sts.).*

California Cuisine

What is California cuisine? The birth of California cuisine can be traced to chef Alice Waters, owner of Berkeley's Chez Panisse (p 179), which has been hailed as one of America's best restaurants. Waters revolutionized American cuisine by championing the use of fresh, seasonal, local ingredients. Her culinary revelation came during a year spent in France, where she lived next to a market street teeming with vendors selling fresh, high-quality produce.

The fact that Waters's grand vision came while she was overseas highlights California cuisine's multicultural, transnational character. It draws from the entire world, and, as such, it's always evolving. While Waters was inspired by France's food, other California chefs have drawn from Italy, the Middle East, Asia, and South America. But the thread that unites all California cuisine is this: a strong preference for uncomplicated dishes with superior ingredients that change with the seasons.

The Bay Area's location and immigrant history were central to the development of this epicurean style. Today there are still a good number of family farms (many organic) and ranches (specializing in naturally raised meats and poultry) surrounding San Francisco. Add the Pacific's bounty of fresh seafood, and the city's treasure trove of ethnic influences, and you've got a perfect city in which to sample California cuisine.

☎ *415/982-1124. Entrees $5–$15. No credit cards. Lunch & dinner Wed–Mon. Bus: 15, 30, 41. Cable car: Powell-Mason. Map p 174.*

★★ Mas Sake Freestyle Sushi MARINA *JAPANESE/MEXICAN* If you're young, stylish, and appreciate good service and quality ingredients crafted into unique culinary creations, this is your spot to see and be seen. There's often a DJ spinning the latest tunes and a bevy of beautiful people swaying to the beat. *2030 Lombard St. (between Webster & Fillmore sts.)* ☎ *415/440-1505. Entrees less than $30. AE, DC, MC, V. Dinner daily. Bus: 22. Map p 174.*

★★★ Michael Mina UNION SQUARE *CALIFORNIA* A remarkably elegant dining room with expert waitstaff, world-class sommeliers, and startlingly vibrant flavors. *335 Powell St. (in the Westin St. Francis Hotel, at Geary St.).* ☎ *415/397-9222. Prix-fixe $105. AE, DC, DISC, MC, V. Dinner daily. Cable car: Powell line. Map p 174.*

★★ Millennium UNION SQUARE *VEGETARIAN* Nothing at this upscale restaurant is made with animal products, and everything tastes amazing, proving that an ethical menu doesn't have to sacrifice taste. *580 Geary St. (at Jones St.).* ☎ *415/345-3900. Entrees $20–$24. AE, DC, DISC, MC, V. Dinner daily. Bus: 2, 3, 4, 27, 38. Map p 174.*

★ kids Mitchell's Ice Cream MISSION *ICE CREAM* Try unexpected flavors like avocado, ginger, and sweet corn. *688 San Jose Ave. (at 29th St., just south of where Guerrero St. turns into San Jose*

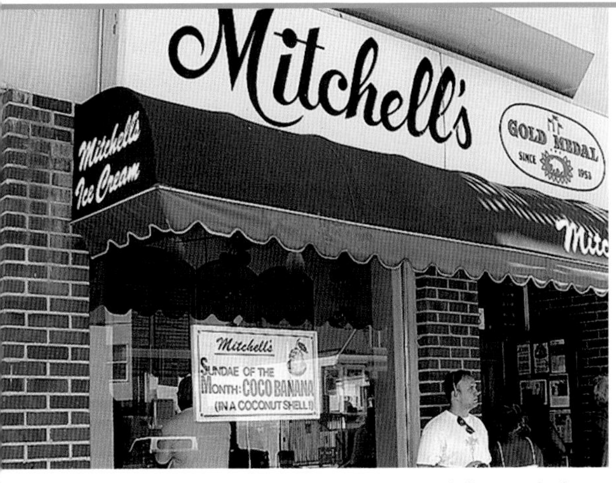

Open since 1953, Mitchell's Ice Cream's original owner Larry Mitchell imports fresh fruit from the Philippines to make his tropical flavors.

Ave.). ☎ 415/648-2300. $3–$6. No credit cards. Daily 11am–11pm. Bus: 14, 49. Muni: Church & 30th St. Map p 174.

★★ **One Market** FINANCIAL DISTRICT *CALIFORNIA* Bradley Ogden's SF outlet, across from the Ferry Building, is larger than life. *1 Market St. (at Steuart St.). ☎ 415/777-5577. Entrees $15–$33. AE, DC, DISC, MC, V. Lunch Mon–Fri. Dinner Mon–Sat. BART/Muni: Embarcadero. Map p 174.*

★ **Postrio** UNION SQUARE *CALIFORNIA* Wolfgang Puck's creation remains a lovely (and celebrity-studded) place to dine. *545 Post St. (in the Prescott Hotel, between Taylor & Mason sts.). ☎ 415/776-7825. Entrees $16–$39. AE, DC, DISC, MC, V. Lunch & dinner daily. Bus 2, 3, 4. Map p 174.*

★★ **Quince** PACIFIC HEIGHTS *ITALIAN* Seasonal dishes in an elegant, discreet setting. *1701 Octavia St. (at Bush St.). ☎ 415/775-8500. Prix-fixe $68. AE, MC, V. Dinner daily. Bus: 2, 3, 4. Map p 174.*

★★★ **The Slanted Door** FINANCIAL DISTRICT *VIETNAMESE* A perpetual crowd awaits Charles Phan's upscale Vietnamese cooking and his modern restaurant's Embarcadero view. Call ahead. *Ferry Bldg., 1 Ferry Plaza (at The Embarcadero & Market St.). ☎ 415/861-8032. Entrees $11–$33. AE, MC, V. Lunch & dinner daily. BART/Muni: Embarcadero. Map p 174.*

★ **kids** **Taqueria Pancho Villa** MISSION *MEXICAN* This humble standby is one of SF's best taquerias. *3071 16th St. (between Mission & Valencia sts.). ☎ 415/864-8840. Entrees $1.35–$10. AE, MC, V. Lunch & dinner daily. Bus: 14, 22, 49. BART: 16th St. Map p 174.*

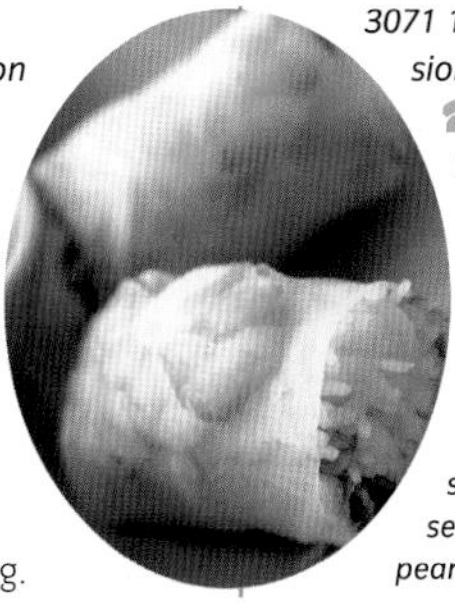

The Slanted Door's spring rolls, stuffed with shrimp, pork, and mint, are served with a Vietnamese peanut sauce.

SF Shopping, Nightlife & Arts

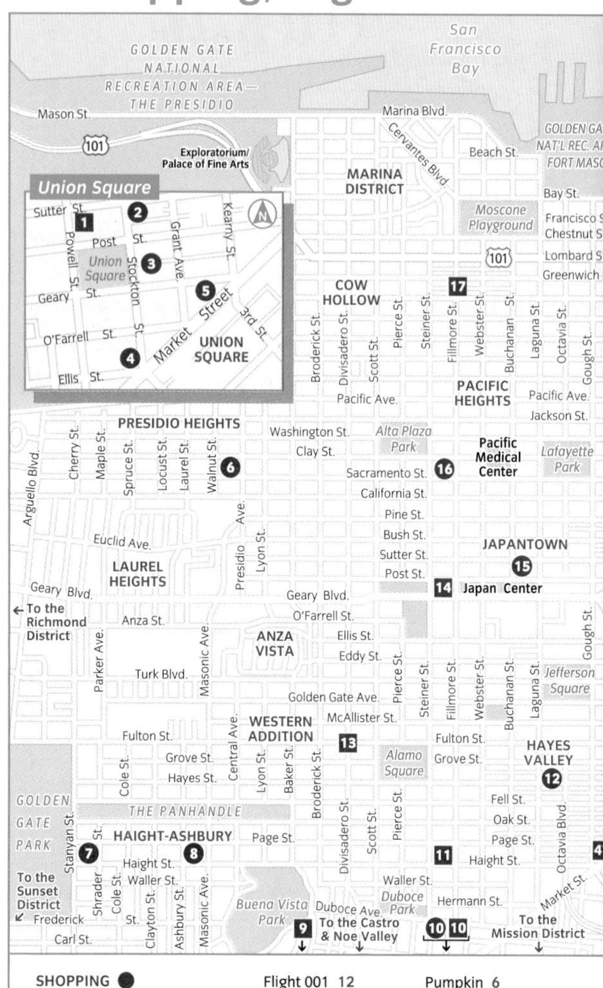

SHOPPING ●

49 Geary 5
Ambassador Toys 31
Amoeba Music 7
Apple Store San Francisco 4
Barnes & Noble 21
Canton Bazaar 33
Chinatown Kite Shop 15
City Lights Bookstore 27
Ferry Building Marketplace 32
Flight 001 12
Ghirardelli Square 18
Golden Gate Fortune Cookies Co. 34
Good Vibrations 10, 35
Maiden Lane 3
Nordstrom 41
Patagonia 20
Piedmont 8
Pumpkin 6
Rainbow Grocery 10
Ruby's Artist Coop. 22
SF Antique & Design Mall 45
SF Shopping Centre 41
Shabby Chic 16
Soko Hardware 15
Wilkes Bashford 2
Wine Club San Francisco 4

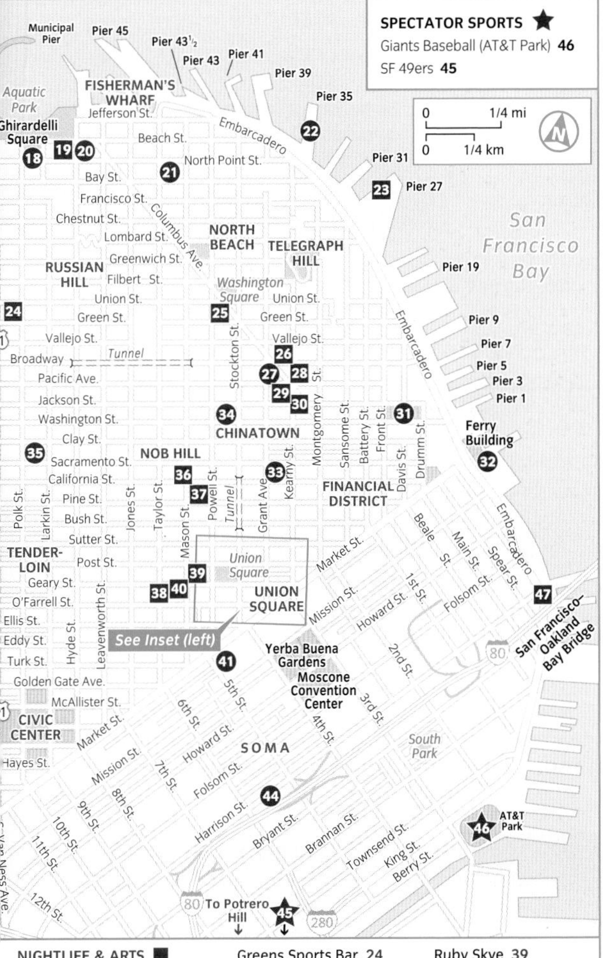

NIGHTLIFE & ARTS ■

Beach Blanket Babylon 25
Boom Boom Room 14
Buena Vista Café 19
Curran Theatre 40
Dalva 10
Elbo Room 10
Enrico's Sidewalk Café 26
Fly Bar 13
The Fillmore 14
Gordon Biersch 47
Greens Sports Bar 24
Harry Denton's Starlight Lounge 1
Hotel Biron 47
Laszlo 10
La Rondalla 10
Mad Dog in the Fog 11
Matrix Fillmore 17
The Mint 10
Moby Dick 9
Redwood Room 38
Ruby Skye 39
SF Brewing Co. 28
SF Opera 42
SF Symphony 43
Teatro Zinzanni 23
The Tonga Room & Hurricane Bar 37
The Top of the Mark 36
Tosca 30
Vesuvio 29

Shopping A to Z

Art

★★ **49 Geary Street** UNION SQUARE You'll find several top galleries here. *49 Geary St. (between Grant Ave. & Kearny St.). Streetcar: F. Most galleries closed Sun–Mon. Bus: 16, 17, 50. BART/Muni: Powell St. Map p 184.*

Books

★ kids **Barnes & Noble** FISHERMAN'S WHARF A superstore of the popular chain. *2550 Taylor St. (between Bay & N. Point sts.). ☎ 415/292-6792. AE, DISC, MC, V. Cable car: Powell/Hyde line. Map p 184.*

★★ **City Lights** NORTH BEACH Founded by Beat poet Lawrence Ferlinghetti in 1953, this landmark shop still stocks avant-garde and alternative lit. *261 Columbus Ave. (at Broadway St.). ☎ 415/362-8193. www.citylights.com. AE, DISC, MC, V. Bus: 15, 30, 41. Map p 184.*

Department Store

★ **Nordstrom** UNION SQUARE Quality clothes for the whole family and an excellent shoe department. *865 Market St. (at 5th St.). ☎ 415/243-8500. www.nordstrom.com. AE, DC, DISC, MC, V. Bus: 27, 30, 38, 45. Streetcar: F. Map p 184.*

Electronics

★★ **Apple Store** UNION SQUARE This beautiful store houses trendy gear. *1 Stockton St. (at Market St.). ☎ 415/392-0202. www.apple.com. AE, DC, DISC, MC, V. Bus: 30, 38, 45. Streetcar: F. Map p 184.*

Fashion

★★ **Maiden Lane** UNION SQUARE Top designers like Marc Jacobs have boutiques on this pedestrian alley. Louis Vuitton, Kate Spade, and others are nearby. *Maiden Lane, off Stockton St. Bus: 30, 38, 45. Map p 184.*

★ **Patagonia** FISHERMAN'S WHARF An excellent source for high-quality outerwear and a staple in most locals' closets. *770 N. Point St. (between Hyde & Leavenworth sts.). ☎ 415/771-2050. www.patagonia.com. AE, DC, DISC, MC, V. Bus: 10, 30. Cable car: Powell-Hyde. Map p 184.*

City Lights contains an impressive selection of art, poetry, and political paperbacks.

★ **Piedmont** HAIGHT Absolutely outrageous vintage women's garments—sold mostly to men. The giant fishnet legs over the entrance epitomize The Haight. *1452 Haight St. (at Ashbury). ☎ 415/864-8075. AE, MC, V. Closed Mon. Bus: 21. Map p 184.*

★★★ **Wilkes Bashford** UNION SQUARE SF's best-known men's clothing store, selling fine European fashions. *375 Sutter St. (at Stockton St.). ☎ 415/986-4380. www.wilkes bashford.com. AE, DC, DISC, MC, V. Bus: 2, 3, 4, 30, 45. Map p 184.*

Gifts & Souvenirs

★★ **Canton Bazaar** CHINATOWN This complex carries Chinese porcelain, jade, antiques, and hand-carved furniture. *616 Grant Ave. (between California & Sacramento sts.). ☎ 415/362-5750. AE, DISC, MC, V. Bus: 1, 15, 30, 45. Map p 184.*

Good Vibrations MISSION AND NOB HILL The first and probably best pro-woman erotic shop. If you're not shy, the employees give great advice. *603 Valencia St. (at 17th St.). ☎ 415/522-5460. Bus: 22, 26. Bart to 16th St. 1620 Polk St. (at Sacramento St.). ☎ 415/345-0400. www.goodvibes.com. Bus: 1, 19. Cable car: California line. AE, DISC, MC, V. Map p 184.*

Housewares & Furnishings

★ **Soko Hardware** JAPANTOWN A great selection of ceramic plates, tea sets, sake cups, and more at bargain prices. *1698 Post St. (at Buchanan St.). ☎ 415/931-5510. MC, V. Bus: 2, 3, 4, 38. Map p 184.*

Jewelry

★★ **Ruby's Artist Cooperative** MISSION Local jewelers' one-of-a-kind creations. *3602 20th St. (at Valencia St.). ☎ 415/550-8052. www.rubygallery.com. MC, V. Bus: 12, 27. Streetcar: J. BART to 16th or 24th St. Map p 184.*

The famous red-heeled legs looming over the entrance to Piedmont.

Music

★★ **Amoeba** HAIGHT The planet's biggest and best independent music store has listening booths and frequent free live performances. Ask staffers for advice, but only about something adequately obscure. *1855 Haight St. (between Shrader & Stanyan sts.). ☎ 415/831-1200. www.amoebamusic.com. DISC, MC, V. Bus: 6, 7, 66, 71. Map p 184.*

Shopping Centers

★ **San Francisco Antique & Design Mall** POTRERO HILL More than 200 antiques specialists in a huge warehouse. *701 Bayshore Blvd. ☎ 415/656-3530. www.sf antique.com. AE, DISC, MC, V. Bus: 9. Map p 184.*

San Francisco Shopping Centre SOMA Anchored by Nordstrom and Bloomingdale's, this attractive mall has some interesting chains like Kenneth Cole, Calvin Klein, and Hugo Boss. *865 Market St. (at 5th St.). ☎ 415/512 6776. www.westfield.com/sanfrancisco. Bus: 27, 30, 38, 45. Streetcar: F. Map p 184.*

★★★ **Ferry Building Marketplace** FINANCIAL DISTRICT All sorts of food-specific shops and minirestaurants. Don't miss Cowgirl

Amoeba Music carries CDs plus a massive selection of classic LPs.

Creamery's Artisan Cheese Shop, Scharffen Berger Chocolates, Recchiuti Confections, or Book Passage. Go on Saturday or Tuesday, when the farmers' market takes center stage. *The Embarcadero (at Market St.). ☎ 415/983-8000. www.ferrybuildingmarketplace.com. Streetcar: F. Map p 184.*

★★ kids **Ghirardelli Square** FISHERMAN'S WHARF A former chocolate factory with a priceless view and quaint shops. Ghirardelli's flagship store (p 184) is right here. *900 N. Point St. (at Larkin St.). ☎ 415/775-5500. www.ghirardellisq.com. Bus: 10, 30. Streetcar: F. Map p 184.*

The SF Shopping Center (p 187) is a mall to explore on a damp, foggy afternoon.

Specialty Foods & Wines

For Ghirardelli chocolate and the Ferry Building Farmers' Market, see above.

★★ kids **Golden Gate Fortune Cookies Factory** CHINATOWN Buy fortune cookies hot off the press at this tiny Chinatown shop in an alley. Bring your own message and watch it get folded in. *56 Ross Alley (between Washington & Jackson sts.). ☎ 415/781-3956. No credit cards. Bus: 30, 45. Cable car: Powell-Mason. Map p 184.*

★★ **Rainbow Grocery** MISSION A gargantuan health-food co-op where you can browse through virtually any kind of health food that exists and a mind-boggling selection of bulk spices and teas. *1745 Folsom St. (at 13th St.). ☎ 415/863-0620. www.rainbowgrocery.org. AE, DISC, MC, V. Bus: 12. Map p 184.*

Wine Club San Francisco SOMA The West's largest wine merchant; surprisingly affordable. *953 Harrison St. (between 5th & 6th sts.). ☎ 415/512-9086. www.thewineclub.com. AE, MC, V. Bus: 12, 19, 27. Map p 184.*

Toys

★ kids Ambassador Toys FINANCIAL DISTRICT European dolls, wooden toys, and clever games are among the whimsical playthings. *2 Embarcadero Center (at Sacramento St., between Front & Davis sts.). ☎ 415/345-8697. AE, DISC, MC, V. Bus: 1. Cable car: California line. Map p 184.*

Travel Goods

Flight 001 HAYES VALLEY Hip travel accessories like sleek luggage, "security-friendly" manicure sets, and other midair must-haves. *525 Hayes St. (between Laguna & Octavia sts.). ☎ 415/487-1001. www.flight001.com. AE, DISC, MC, V. Bus: 21. Map p 184.*

Your child will be mesmerized by the traditional toys on sale at Ambassador Toys.

Nightlife & Arts A to Z

Bars, Lounges, Pubs & Clubs

★★ The Boom Boom Room WESTERN ADDITION This dark, steamy joint hosts some of America's best blues bands. *1601 Fillmore St. (at Geary Blvd.). ☎ 415/673-8000. Cover free–$22. Bus: 22, 38. Map p 185.*

★ The Buena Vista COW HOLLOW It's served more Irish coffees than any other bar in the world. A SF tradition. *2765 Hyde St. (at Beach St.). ☎ 415/474-5044. Bus: 10, 30. Map p 185.*

★★ Dalva MISSION A dark, intimate cocktail lounge with an eclectic crowd and excellent sangria. *3121 16th St. (between Valencia and Albion sts.). ☎ 415/252-7740. Bus: 26, 49. BART: 16th St. (before dark). Map p 185.*

★★ Elbo Room MISSION Chill out by the inviting bar or head upstairs for excellent live music

Boogie down to the blues at the Boom Boom Room.

(separate cover up to $10). *647 Valencia St. (between Clarion Alley and Sycamore St.). ☎ 415/552-7788. Bus: 26, 49. BART: 16th St. (before dark). Map p 185.*

★ Enrico's Sidewalk Café NORTH BEACH Sit on the front patio for people-watching and jazz. *504 Broadway (at Kearny St.). ☎ 415/982-6223. Bus: 12, 15, 41. Map p 185.*

★★ Fly Bar PANHANDLE A neighborhood lounge with interesting soju and sake drinks, great pizzas, and rotating art. *762 Divisadero*

St. (at Fulton St.). ☎ 415/931-4359. Bus: 5, 21, 22, 24. Map p 185.

★ **Gordon Biersch** SOMA SF's largest brewery restaurant serves tasty German-style beers and garlic fries within view of the waterfront. *2 Harrison St. (at The Embarcadero). ☎ 415/243-8246. Bus: 12. Map p 185.*

★ **Greens Sports Bar** RUSSIAN HILL SF's best sports bar boasts 15 TVs and 18 on-tap beers. *2239 Polk St. (at Green St.). ☎ 415/775-4287. Bus: 19. Cable car: Powell-Hyde. Map p 185.*

★ **Harry Denton's Starlight Lounge** UNION SQUARE A 1930s-style gathering place with dancing, stellar views, a long appetizer menu, and, on weekends, an orchestra. *Sir Francis Drake Hotel, 450 Powell St. (between Sutter & Post sts.). ☎ 415/395-8595. Cover varies; call ahead. Bus: 2, 3, 4. Map p 185.*

Hotel Biron HAYES VALLEY This little gem of a wine bar is tucked away in an alley right behind Market Street. They have an excellent wine menu and an appetizing selection of cheeses. Open daily till 2am. *45 Rose St (at Gough). Bus: 21. Muni to Van Ness. Bus: 21. ☎ 415/703-0403.*

Beautiful people dominate the Redwood Room.

★★ **Laszlo** MISSION This industrial-chic bar serves funky cocktails. *2534 Mission St. (between 21st & 22nd sts.). ☎ 415/401-0810. Bus: 14, 49. BART to 24th St. Map p 185.*

Mad Dog in the Fog HAIGHT This quirky British pub is where to watch European soccer. *530 Haight St. (between Steiner & Fillmore sts.). ☎ 415/626-7279. Bus: 22, 67. Map p 185.*

Matrix Fillmore COW HOLLOW The center of SF's singles' scene. *3138 Fillmore St. (between Greenwich & Filbert sts.). ☎ 415/563-4180. Bus: 22, 30. Map p 185.*

★ **The Mint Karaoke Lounge** MISSION This once-gay song spot now draws patrons of all orientations, who, after a potent cocktail, take to the stage. *1942 Market St. (between Guerrero & Dolores sts.). ☎ 415/626-4726. No cover, but a 2-drink minimum. Drinks $4.75–$10. Bus: 22. Streetcar: F, J, N. Map p 185.*

★ **Moby Dick** CASTRO This gay bar is a 25-year-old Castro institution. *4049 18th St. (between Castro & Noe sts.). ☎ 415/861-1199. Bus: 33. Streetcar: F. Map p 185.*

★ **Redwood Room** UNION SQUARE A historic lounge with famous decor. *Clift Hotel, 495 Geary St. (at Taylor St.). ☎ 415/929-2372. Bus: 2, 3, 4, 27, 38. Map p 185.*

Ruby Skye UNION SQUARE This former Victorian movie house is SF's biggest dance club. *420 Mason St. (between Post & Geary sts.). ☎ 415/693-0777. Cover free–$35. Bus: 2, 3, 4, 38. Map p 185.*

★ **San Francisco Brewing Co.** NORTH BEACH This old-time saloon with stained-glass windows and a mahogany bar serves homemade brews to a usually packed house. *155 Columbus Ave. (between Jackson St.*

Vesuvio, City Lights Bookstore's neighbor and Jack Kerouac's old haunt, attracts an eclectic clientele.

& Pacific Ave.). ☎ 415/434-3344. Bus: 12, 14, 15. Map p 185.

★ **The Tonga Room & Hurricane Bar** NOB HILL Umbrella drinks and faux thunderstorms, plus a $7 all-you-can-eat happy hour. *Fairmont Hotel, 950 Mason St. (at California St.). ☎ 415/772-5278. Bus: 1. Cable car: All. Map p 185.*

★★★ **The Top of the Mark** NOB HILL A historic venue with the best view in town and a 100-martini menu. Occasional live entertainment. *InterContinental Mark Hopkins, 1 Nob Hill (at Mason & California sts.). ☎ 415/616-6916. Cover $5–$10. Bus: 1. Cable car: All. Map p 185.*

★★ **Tosca** NORTH BEACH This traditional old North Beach institution draws local politicos and celebs. With a dark-wood bar and a jukebox playing only opera, it's a classic. *242 Columbus Ave. (between Broadway St. & Pacific Ave.). ☎ 415/986-9651. Bus: 12, 15, 41. Map p 185.*

★ **Vesuvio** NORTH BEACH Once the favored beatnik watering hole, famous Vesuvio still draws an artsy crowd. *225 Columbus Ave. (at Pacific Ave.). ☎ 415/362-3370. Bus: 12, 15, 41. Map p 185.*

Live Entertainment

★★★ **Beach Blanket Babylon** NORTH BEACH For more than 30 years, BBB's outrageously hatted comedians have spoofed pop culture. *Club Fugazi, 678 Green St. (at Columbus Ave.). ☎ 415/421-4222. Tickets $25–$80. Bus: 15, 30, 45. Cable car: Powell-Mason. Map p 185.*

★ **Curran Theatre** UNION SQUARE Established in 1922 to host European and East Coast productions. Along with the ★ **Orpheum Theater** *(1192 Market St.; ☎ 415/551-2000)* and the **Golden Gate Theater** *(1 Taylor St.; ☎ 415/551-2000),* its "Best of Broadway" series brings NY hits to SF. *445 Geary St. (between Mason & Taylor sts.). ☎ 415/551-2000. Tickets $25–$99. Bus: 2, 3, 4, 38. BART/Muni: Powell St. Map p 185.*

★★★ **The Fillmore** WESTERN ADDITION The venue that presented bands like Jefferson Airplane and the Grateful Dead is SF's best rock venue. *1805 Geary Blvd. (at Fillmore St.). ☎ 415/346-6000. Tickets $20–$40. Bus: 22, 38. Map p 185.*

★★ **San Francisco Opera** CIVIC CENTER North America's second-largest opera company is outstanding. ***Tip:*** $10 standing-room tickets

Expect the unexpected at Beach Blanket Babylon.

Two SF ballet dancers leaping during a performance of Tomasson's Criss-Cross.

are sold on the day of the show (cash only; one per person). The season runs from September to December and June to July. The top-notch San Francisco Ballet also performs here. *War Memorial Opera House, 301 Van Ness Ave. (at Grove St.). ☎ 415/864-3330. Tickets $25–$250. Bus: 5, 21. BART/Muni: Civic Center. Map p 185.*

★★ San Francisco Symphony CIVIC CENTER Founded in 1911 and conducted by internationally acclaimed Michael Tilson Thomas. *Davies Symphony Hall, 201 Van Ness Ave. (between Grove & Hayes sts.). ☎ 415/864-6000. Tickets $3.50–$107. Bus: 5, 21. BART/Muni: Civic Center. Map p 185.*

★★ Teatro Zinzanni EMBARCADERO Circus artists and a five-course meal come together for a 3-hour dinner extravaganza. *Pier 29, The Embarcadero (at Battery St.). ☎ 415/438-2668. Tickets $110–$186. Bus: 10. Streetcar: F. Map p 185.*

Spectator Sports

★★★ kids Giants Baseball SOMA AT&T Park is arguably the world's best baseball stadium. Dramatic bay views, lots of kids' amenities, excellent food, and a compellingly entertaining team make a visit here time well spent. *24 Willie Mays Plaza (King & 2nd sts.). ☎ 415/972-2000. Tickets $5–$85. Bus: 10, 15, 30, 45. Muni: N. Map p 185.*

San Francisco 49ers CANDLESTICK POINT SF's pro football team. Because there are so many season-ticket holders, single tickets are hard to come by. Check Ticketmaster or Craigslist. *Monster Park, Candlestick Point. ☎ 415/656-4900. Tickets $59–$94. Map p 185.* ●

A game at AT&T Park comes with an unobstructed view of San Francisco Bay.

The
Savvy Traveler

Before You Go

Tourist Offices

Napa Valley Conference and Visitors' Bureau, 1310 Napa Town Center, Napa, CA 94559 (☎ 707/226-7459; www.napavalley.com).

Yountville Chamber of Commerce, 6484 Washington St. (☎ 707/944-0904; www.yountville.com).

Santa Rosa Convention & Visitors' Bureau, 9 4th St., Santa Rosa (☎ 800/404-7673 or 707/577-8674; www.visitsantarosa.com).

Healdsburg Chamber of Commerce and Visitors Bureau 217 Healdsburg Ave., Healdsburg (☎ 707/433-6935; www.healdsburg.org).

Sonoma Valley Visitors Bureau 453 1st St. E., Sonoma (☎ 707/996-1090; www.sonomavalley.com).

Sonoma County Tourism Bureau (☎ 800/5-SONOMA or 707/576-6662; www.sonomacounty.com).

When to Go

Wine country's beauty is striking at any time of year, but it's most memorable during the September and October harvest months, when wineries are in full gear and the landscape is swept with rich autumnal colors. Spring is also gorgeous; mustard flowers bloom profusely, and since this is when tourist season just begins, there'll be less traffic, thinner crowds, and better deals. Though winter boasts the best rates and fewest people, there's a reason: The days are often chilly and rainy, while miles of bare vines lay dormant. The summer months bring hot weather and lots of traffic.

The Weather

Though the valleys claim a year-round average temperature of 70°F (21°C), if you come with a suitcase packed with T-shirts and shorts during the winter holiday season, you're likely to shiver your way to the nearest department store to stock up on warm clothes and possibly an umbrella. In summer, if you rent a car without air-conditioning, you're liable to want to stop at every hotel swimming pool you pass. And don't let that morning fog and those early cool temperatures fool you; on most days, come noon, the hot sun sends down plenty of rays. Dress in layers and remember that the temperature can drop dramatically at night.

Festivals & Special Events

SPRING: A favorite Sonoma Valley festival is the **Barrel Tasting Weekend,** held on March's third full weekend. The event, which gives the public a glimpse of Sonoma Valley's finest future releases and raises money for the American Heart Association, is a 2-day celebration that includes demonstrations, pairings, hors d'oeuvres—and all the world-class wine you can drink. Tickets are about $30; buy them well in advance. For details, call the St. Francis Winery. ☎ *800/543-7713. www.heartofsonomavalley.com*. Early April brings the **Sonoma Valley Film Festival,** a 5-day extravaganza screening more than 75 new independent films, including features, documentaries, and shorts. Day passes are $75 each, and basic passes to the whole festival are $225, but patrons can buy travel packages costing upward of $3,600. *www.cinemaepicuria.org.* ☎ *707/933-2600.*

Previous page: See Napa from above with Bonaventura Balloon Co. (p 65).

AVERAGE SEASONAL TEMPERATURES IN WINE COUNTRY

	SPRING (MAR–MAY)	SUMMER (JUNE–AUG)	FALL (SEPT–NOV)	WINTER (DEC–FEB)
Average highs (in °F)	78	92	85	72
Average highs (in °C)	26	33	29	22
Average lows (in °F)	64	81	74	61
Average lows (in °C)	18	27	23	16

AVERAGE MONTHLY TEMPERATURES IN SAN FRANCISCO

	JAN	FEB	MAR	APR	MAY	JUNE
High F/°C	56/13	59/15	60/16	61/16	63/17	64/18
Low F/°C	46/8	48/19	49/9	49/9	51/11	53/12

	JULY	AUG	SEPT	OCT	NOV	DEC
High F/°C	64/18	65/18	69/21	68/20	63/17	57/14
Low F/°C	53/12	54/12	56/13	55/13	52/11	47/8

In late April, the annual **Vineyard to Vintner (V2V)** day includes seminars, blind tastings, and open houses at many wineries. In the evening, Stags' Leap Winery and Manor House hosts barrel tastings, alfresco dining, and live music. It's $285 for the whole day including a fancy soiree, $135 for the open houses only. *www.stagsleapdistrict.com.* ☎ *707/255-1720.* Calistoga's **Cinco de Mayo Parade & Festival** happens the first weekend of May. It's the valley's largest celebration and features Mexican culture at its best: mariachis in traditional costumes, *charros* performing equestrian feats, elaborate parade floats, and lots of music, dancing, and food. Admission is $5, and proceeds fund scholarships for disadvantaged students. *www.napavalleycincodemayo.com.* ☎ *707/942-6333.*

SUMMER: The **Napa Valley Wine Auction,** held each June, is the area's most renowned—and exclusive—event. The annual charity affair brings about 2,000 deep-pocketed wine aficionados to Napa Valley to schmooze and spend serious cash. Tickets are $2,500 per couple, and they sell out every year. ☎ *707/963-3388.* Another big June attraction is the 10-day **Healdsburg Jazz Festival.** Venues range from vineyards to restaurants to intimate theaters, and headliners sell out quickly. Admission prices vary, and tickets are available via the website or at the venue. *www.healdsburgjazzfestival.com.* ☎ *707/433-4644.* Summer is also time for the **Napa Sonoma Wine Country Film Festival,** a month-long celebration of cinema, cuisine, and wine. Open-air venues screen flicks while film buffs sip, nibble, and socialize. Other activities include symposia, celebrity receptions, and chef demonstrations. Tickets are $10 to $25 per movie. *www.winecountryfilmfest.com.* ☎ *707/935-FILM (3456).*

AUTUMN: The annual **Napa Valley Harvest Festival and Art Exhibition** takes place in September in a garden setting at Charles Krug Winery. Hundreds of Napa residents and tourists come to check out art, the products of more than 20 wineries, the cuisine of more than 15 restaurants, and constant live music. A large silent auction means you can try to buy any of the art you see. Advance tickets are $50; at the door, they're $60. ☎ *800/550-6260.* Another major Sonoma event is the **Vintage Festival,** held the last weekend in September at Sonoma's historic plaza. This is a real party, complete with live music, dancing, parades, art displays, and, of course, copious wine tasting. *www.sonomavinfest.org.* ☎ *707/996-2109.*

WINTER: February's **Napa Valley Mustard Festival** kicks off tourist season with a celebration of the mustard blossoms that speckle the valley. Its 6 weeks' worth of activities range from a formal gourmet gala at CIA Greystone featuring local restaurants, wineries, artists, a wine auction, golf benefit, recipe and photography competition, and plenty of food and wine celebrations, including **A Taste of Yountville** in mid-March. ☎ *707/938-1133. www.mustardfestival.org.* Right before heavy tourist season kicks off, Healdsburg holds a barrel-tasting weekend at nearly 100 wineries along the **Russian River Wine Road.** If you fall in love with a wine you've sampled, secure your share of bottles—at discounted prices—long before they even hit the stores, never mind sell out. (It's called buying futures.) ***Tip:*** It's free if you bring your own wine glass, $5 if you need to purchase one to tote from winery to winery. *www.wineroad.com.* ☎ *800/723-6336.*

Useful Websites

- **www.napachamber.com**
- **www.napadowntown.com**
- **www.napavalleyreservations.com**
- **www.napavintners.com**
- **www.silveradotrail.com**
- **www.sonomavalley.com**
- **www.sonoma.com**
- **www.sonomavalleywine.com**
- **www.staysonoma.com**
- **www.winecountry.com**

Cell (Mobile) Phones

One good wireless rental company is InTouch USA (☎ 800/872-7626). Though Napa and Sonoma don't have stores that rent cell phones, sometimes hotels' business centers, like the one at Vintners Inn (☎ 707/575-7350), will. A store in downtown San Francisco: Triptel Mobile Rental Phones (☎ 415/474-3330; 1525 Van Ness Ave., between California and Pine sts.) rents cellular phones for $3 per day, or $15 per week. Airtime rates are 95¢ per minute for domestic calls, with an additional $2.50 per minute for international calls. Triptel also sells SIM cards for foreign travelers bringing their own phones. International travelers will be happy to know that cell phones (mobiles) with triband GSM capabilities work in the U.S. Also remember that you'll be charged for calls received on a U.K. mobile used abroad. U.K. visitors can rent a U.S. phone before leaving home. Contact Cellhire (☎ 877/244-7242 or, from London, 44 20 7490 7799. www.cellhire.co.uk).

Car Rentals

When booking rental cars online, the best deals are usually listed on rental-car company websites. Major car-rental companies operating in wine country include Enterprise (☎ 800/325-8007 or 707/253-8000; www.enterprise.com); Budget (☎ 800/527-0700 or 707/224-7846; www.budget.com); and Hertz (800/654-3131 or 707/226-2037; www.hertz.com). U.K. visitors should check HolidayAutos (online only; www.holidayautos.co.uk). San Francisco International Airport (SFO) and Oakland International Airport (OAK) both have car-rental centers at which the above companies are represented. Rates vary depending on season and other factors, but generally, compact cars run about $200 to $350 per week, including taxes and other charges. Most rentals in the U.S. are automatics.

Getting **There**

By Plane

Wine country is easily accessed by the Bay Area's two major airports: San Francisco International (SFO) and Oakland International (OAK), across the Bay Bridge. San Francisco International Airport (☎ 650/821-8211; www.flysfo.com) is a 2-hour drive from wine country. Oakland International Airport (☎ 510/577-4000; www.oaklandairport.com) is less crowded than SFO and more accessible, but offers fewer carriers. It's a bit more than a 1-hour drive from downtown Napa.

Getting To & From the Airport

Rent a car and drive to wine country (see "Car Rentals," above, for companies and "By Car," below, for driving directions). Since there's no useful public transportation in either valley, it's almost impossible to explore the region without wheels, so you might as well rent right at the airport. If you need to, though, for $29, you can ride to Napa Valley from SFO with Evans Transportation (☎ 707/255-1559), and the Sonoma Airporter (☎ 707/938-4246) offers door-to-door service six times daily from SFO to hotels and inns in most areas of Sonoma ($50 for home pickup, $45 for standard downtown pickup locations).

By Car

All these routes to wine country are well marked.

To Napa Valley

FROM SAN FRANCISCO Cross the Golden Gate Bridge and go north on U.S. 101; turn east on Highway 37 (toward Vallejo), then north on Highway 29, the main road through Napa Valley. You can also take Highway 121/12 from Highway 37 and follow the signs.

FROM OAKLAND Head eastbound on I-80 toward Sacramento; a few miles past the Carquinez Bridge ($4 toll) and the city of Vallejo, exit on Highway 12 west, which, after a few miles, intersects with Highway 29 and leads directly into Napa.

To Sonoma Valley

FROM SAN FRANCISCO Cross the Golden Gate Bridge and stay on U.S. 101 north. Exit at Highway 37; after 10 miles, turn north onto Highway 121. After another 10 miles, turn north onto Highway 12 (Broadway), which will take you directly into the town of Sonoma.

FROM OAKLAND Head eastbound on I-80 toward Sacramento. A few miles past the city of Vallejo (and after paying a $4 toll to cross the Carquinez Bridge), exit on Highway 12, which, after a few miles, intersects with Highway 29 at the south end of Napa Valley. Just before entering the town of Napa, you'll come to a major intersection, where Highway 29 meets Highway 12/121. Turn left onto Highway 12/121, which will take you directly into Sonoma Valley.

To Northern Sonoma

FROM SAN FRANCISCO Cross the Golden Gate Bridge and stay on U.S. 101 north. Exit anywhere from Santa Rosa to Healdsburg, depending on your final destination.

FROM OAKLAND Head eastbound on I-80 toward Sacramento. A few miles past the city of Vallejo (and after paying a $4 toll to cross the Carquinez Bridge), exit on Highway 12, which, after a few miles, intersects with Highway 29 at the south end of Napa Valley. Just before entering the town of Napa, you'll come to a major intersection, where Highway 29 meets Highway 12/121. Turn left onto Highway 12/121, then turn right onto California 116/Arnold Drive. When the road forks, veer right onto Adobe Road. Turn left on East Washington Street, merge onto U.S. 101 north when you see the on-ramp, and exit at the town of your choice.

By Train & Bus

Amtrak (☎ 800/872-7245 or 800/USA-RAIL; www.amtrak.com) doesn't stop in Sonoma, but maintains two stops in Napa. One is at the Napa Wine Train stop (1275 McKinstry St.), but is only for Amtrak Thruway connecting bus service. The other is at 1151 Pearl St. Wine country's only Greyhound (☎ 800/231-2222 or 707/545-6495; www.greyhound.com) terminal is located at 435 Santa Rosa Ave. in Santa Rosa and is open daily (except holidays) from 10 to 11:30am and 1:30 to 5pm.

Getting **Around**

With hundreds of wineries scattered amidst Napa and Sonoma's tens of thousands of acres of vineyards, it's understandably difficult to explore wine country without wheels. See "Getting There," above, for details on renting a car.

By Car

Driving in wine country is relatively straightforward and enjoyable. All the streets and highways are well-marked and most of them are strikingly beautiful, even when there's traffic. As you drive, keep in mind that one of the preeminent dangers of driving through wine country is that it's an area highly focused on alcohol consumption. The importance of avoiding drinking and driving can't be stressed strongly enough. Refrain from driving if you feel even a little tipsy (see "By Cab," below, in case you feel too inebriated). And beware of others on the road who might have consumed too much in the tasting room.

The only other bungling factor is that some wine-country highways have many different names. For example, Highway 12 is also Highway 121 is also Carneros Highway is also Sonoma-Napa Highway. You'll see examples of this kind of multiple street-naming throughout wine country and it may throw you off; if you get confused, pull over and look at a map (or ask your passenger to guide you). A great online resource for getting directions is MapQuest: www.mapquest.com.

By Cab

(No, not cabernet.) You have to call for a taxi in wine country unless you are boarding one from your hotel. Companies: Napa Valley Cab (☎ 707/257-6444); Yellow Cab (☎ 707/226-3731); Black Tie Taxi (☎ 707/-259-1000 or 888/544-8294); and Wine Valley Taxi (☎ 707/251-9463). In Sonoma, your best bet is Vern's Taxi Service (☎ 707/938-8885) and, in Northern Sonoma, Healdsburg Taxi Cab (☎ 707/433-7099). Rates hover at $2.85 for the first mile and $2.70 for each mile thereafter.

On Foot

Many of wine country's treasures within towns can be seen on foot, though you can't easily walk from town to town. See chapter 4 for the area's best walking tours. Though most of these tours traverse flat surfaces, wear comfortable shoes: You'll likely be standing up for a long time, especially if you shop and visit tasting rooms.

Crossing from County to County

The easiest way to get from Napa to Sonoma Valley and vice versa is to head to the Carneros District, which serves as the southern end of both valleys, and cross over along the Sonoma Highway (Calif. 12/121). To get from Napa to Sonoma takes about 20 minutes when there's no traffic. Another option: Take the Oakville Grade (also called Trinity Rd.) over the Mayacamas Range, which links Napa's Oakville to Sonoma's Glen Ellen. It's a steep and windy road, but it can be a real time-saver if you're headed to the northern end of either valley. Getting to northern Sonoma is a snap from Sonoma Valley. Just follow Highway 12 north to get to Santa Rosa. From there, take U.S. 101 north and exit at the town of your choice. From downtown Napa, take California 12/121 (Sonoma Hwy.) to Highway 16 to Adobe Road (veer right) to U.S. 101 North. The trip is about an hour and 15 minutes. From northern Napa towns like Calistoga or St. Helena, it's easier to follow Highway 29 north past downtown Calistoga when it becomes Highway 128. Follow Highway 128 for a few blocks and turn left onto Petrified Forest Road. Turn right onto Porter Creek Road and follow it; it becomes Mark West Springs Road, which leads you to U.S. 101 North.

Getting Around in San Francisco

Driving in San Francisco can be frustrating. Along with aggressive local drivers, one-way streets, no right/left turns when you really need one, and dead ends, there's a lack of parking, period. Fortunately, it isn't necessary to drive to most places. You can call a cab (Desoto Cab, ☎ 415/970-1300; Luxor Cabs, ☎ 415/282-4141; Pacific Cab, ☎ 415/986-7220; Veteran's Cab, ☎ 415/552-1300; and Yellow Cab, ☎ 415/626-2345; rates are around $3.50 for the first fifth of a mile and $2.25 for each additional mile) or take Muni, a hodgepodge of county-managed transit systems that includes bus, streetcar, cable car, and subway. For detailed route information, call or go online (☎ 415/673-6864; www.sfmuni.com). Most routes run from 6am to midnight and some busy routes have late-night services. Another helpful website is http://transit.511.org, which also lists schedules and route maps for all Bay Area transit systems. Muni Passports can be a bargain for visitors who plan to take buses, streetcars, or cable cars often. BART, an acronym for Bay Area Rapid Transit (☎ 415/989-2278; www.bart.gov), connects San Francisco with the East Bay (Oakland, Berkeley, Richmond, Concord, and Fremont). Fares range from $1.50 to $7.10, depending on how far you go. Machines in the stations dispense tickets, and computerized exits automatically deduct the correct fare. Children 4 and under ride free. Trains run every 15 to 20 minutes, Monday through Friday from 4am to midnight, Saturday from 6am to midnight, and Sunday from 8am to midnight. Seeing the city on foot, however, is a fantastic way to get around—but remember, the hills can kill you.

Fast **Facts**

APARTMENT & VILLA RENTALS For short-term rentals, your best bet is www.craigslist.org. Click on the "apts/housing" link and put "Napa" into the search bar; you'll likely come up with at least 100 current listings. You'll likely negotiate a rental directly from the unit's owner (or the person subletting). Also check **www.sublet.com** or **www.californiarental.com**. To research house exchanges, check out **Homelink International** (www.homelink.org), which has more than 14,000 listings in several countries, and **Homebase Holidays** (www.homebase-hols.com).

AREA CODE Napa and Sonoma counties both use the **707** area code.

ATMS/CASHPOINTS There are ATMs throughout both valleys, though not as many as you'd find in a big city. Unless you go to your bank's ATM, you'll be charged a fee of $1.50 to $3. The **Cirrus** (☎ 800/424-7787; www.mastercard.com) and **PLUS** (☎ 800/843-7587; www.visa.com) networks span the globe; look at the back of your bank card to see which network you're on, then call or check online for ATM locations in wine country. Find out your daily withdrawal limit before you depart.

BABYSITTING Most hotel concierges will simply provide referrals to a babysitting service, which guests must then call on their own. Local companies supplying short-term sitters are **Nannies of the Valley** (☎ 707/251-8035), **Take A Break** (☎ 707/226-9188), and, a bit farther south, **Bay Area 2nd Mom, Inc.** (☎ 888/926-3666).

BANKS Most banks are open Monday through Friday from 9am to 5pm. Some are also open until midday Saturday. Many banks also have ATMs for 24-hour banking. **Bank of America** has several branches throughout the area, including one at 1001 Adams St. in St. Helena (☎ 707/963-4433). You'll also find **Wells Fargo** throughout the region, including a branch in Napa at 217 Soscol Ave., inside Raley's supermarket (☎ 707/254-8690). The Sonoma Wells Fargo is at 480 W. Napa St. (☎ 707/996-2360). For a complete listing of Wells Fargo branches, call ☎ 800/869-3557.

B&BS Reputable booking services include **Bed & Breakfast Inns Online** (☎ 615/868-1946; www.bbonline.com), **Pamela Lanier's Bed & Breakfasts** (www.lanierbb.com), **BedAndBreakfast.com** (www.bedandbreakfast.com), **Stay Sonoma** (www.staysonoma.com; under "Lodging Type," choose "Bed & Breakfast"), and **NapaValley.com** (www.napavalley.com; click on "Lodging," then "Inns and Bed & Breakfasts"). To read the opinions of those who've already stayed at a place you're considering, enter its name into the search bar at TripAdvisor (www.tripadvisor.com).

BIKE RENTALS One of the best companies is **Napa Valley Bike Tours** (☎ 800/707-BIKE [2453] or 707/251-8687; www.napavalleybiketours.com). Daily rentals range from $30 to $55, depending on the type of bike. Kids' bikes are $25 for the day, and tandems (synchronized fun) are $70. Napa Valley Bike Tours also provides excellent guided tours, ranging from $45 to $149, depending on what's included—but if you go this route, choose a package that includes lunch; the company's gourmet picnics are fantastic. Other area companies providing bike rentals include **Getaway Adventures** (Sonoma and Napa; ☎ 800/499-2453; www.getawayadventures.com) and **Wine Country Bike Rentals** (Sonoma; ☎ 866/922-4537 or 707/473-0610; www.winecountrybikes.com). Also remember that sometimes B&Bs and even hotels will lend out bikes for free; ask if that's the case at your accommodations before renting.

CAR RENTALS See "Getting Around," p 198.

CLIMATE See "The Weather," p 194.

CONSULATES & EMBASSIES All embassies are located in the nation's capital, Washington, D.C. For a directory of embassies in Washington, D.C., call ☎ 202/555-1212 or go to www.embassy.org/embassies. Napa's nearest major city is San Francisco; the following are consulate addresses in San Francisco for a selection of countries: The **consulate of Australia** is at 625 Market St., Suite 200, San Francisco (☎ 415/536-1970). There is no Canadian consulate in San Francisco. The **embassy of Canada** is at 501 Pennsylvania Ave. NW, Washington, DC 20001 (☎ 202/682-1740; www.canadianembassy.org). The **consulate of Ireland** is at 100 Pine St., San Francisco (☎ 415/392-4214). The **consulate of New Zealand** is at One Maritime Plaza, Ste. 700, San Francisco (☎ 415/399-1255). The **consulate of the U.K.** is at One Sansome St., Ste. 850, San Francisco (☎ 415/617-1300).

CREDIT CARDS Credit cards are a safe way to "carry" money, and you can also withdraw cash advances from ATMs using your PIN. Let your credit card company know of your travel plans, so they don't "freeze" your account when you make your big wine purchases.

CUSTOMS Visitors arriving by air, no matter what the port of entry, should cultivate patience and resignation before setting foot on U.S. soil. Getting through immigration can sometimes take a very long time, especially on summer weekends. People traveling by air from Canada and certain Caribbean countries can sometimes clear Customs and Immigration at the point of departure, which is much quicker.

DENTISTS If you have dental problems, a nationwide referral service known as **1-800-DENTIST** (☎ 800/336-8478) will provide the name of a nearby dentist or clinic.

DINING Dining in wine country, as in most of California, is generally casual and a jacket is rarely required, except at Napa or Sonoma's most upscale restaurants. **Reservations:** Call the restaurant directly or try www.opentable.com, a free online reservations site.

DOCTORS See "Emergencies," below.

ELECTRICITY Like Canada, the United States uses 110 to120 volts AC (60 cycles), compared to 220 to 240 volts AC (50 cycles) in most of Europe, Australia, and New Zealand. If your small appliances use 220 to 240 volts, you'll need a 110-volt transformer and a plug adapter with two flat parallel pins to operate them here. Downward converters that change 220 to 240 volts to 110 to 120 volts are difficult to find in the U.S., so bring one with you.

EMERGENCIES Dial ☎ **911** for fire, police, and ambulance. No coins are needed from a working public phone. The **Poison Control Center** can be reached at ☎ 800/222-1222 toll-free from any phone. If you encounter serious problems, contact **Traveler's Aid International**

(☎ 202/546-1127; www.traveler said.org).

FAMILY TRAVEL See www.gocity kids.com, www.familyfun.com, or www.sfvisitor.org for good ideas.

GAY & LESBIAN TRAVELERS See www.sfvisitor.org or www.gay wired.com/travel for good ideas.

HOLIDAYS Banks, government offices, post offices, and many stores, restaurants, and museums are closed on the following legal national holidays: January 1 (New Year's Day), the third Monday in January (Martin Luther King, Jr. Day), the third Monday in February (Presidents Day), the last Monday in May (Memorial Day), July 4 (Independence Day), the first Monday in September (Labor Day), the second Monday in October (Columbus Day), November 11 (Veterans Day), the fourth Thursday in November (Thanksgiving), and December 25 (Christmas). Also, the Tuesday following the first Monday in November is Election Day and is a federal government holiday in presidential-election years held every 4 years (next in 2012).

INSURANCE **For Domestic Visitors:** Trip-cancellation insurance helps you get your money back if you have to back out of a trip or go home early, or if your travel supplier goes bankrupt. Allowed reasons for cancellation can range from sickness to natural disasters to the State Department declaring your destination unsafe for travel. (Insurers usually won't cover vague fears, though, as many travelers discovered when they tried to cancel their Oct. 2001 trips after the September 11, 2001, terrorist attacks.) Trip-cancellation insurance might be a good buy if you're getting tickets well in advance—who knows what the state of the world, or of your airline, will be in 9 months. Insurance policy details vary, so read the fine print—and make sure that your provider is on the list of carriers covered in case of bankruptcy. For information, contact one of the following insurers: **Access America** (☎ 866/807-3982; www.accessamerica.com), **Travel Guard International** (☎ 800/826-4919; www.travel guard.com), **Travel Insured International** (☎ 800/243-3174; www.travelinsured.com), or **Travelex Insurance Services** (☎ 888/457-4602; www.travelex-insurance.com).

Medical Insurance: Insurance policies can cover everything from the loss or theft of your baggage to trip cancellation to the guarantee of bail in case you're arrested. Good policies will also cover the costs of an accident, repatriation, or death. Packages such as Europ Assistance's Worldwide Healthcare Plan are sold by European automobile clubs and travel agencies at attractive rates. **Worldwide Assistance Services, Inc.** (☎ 800/821-2828; www.worldwideassistance.com) is the agent for Europ Assistance in the U.S. Although it's not required of travelers, health insurance is highly recommended. Unlike many European countries, the U.S. does not usually offer free or low-cost medical care to its citizens or visitors. Doctors and hospitals are expensive, and in most cases will require advance payment or proof of coverage before they render their services. Though lack of health insurance may prevent you from being admitted to a hospital in nonemergencies, don't worry about being left injured or ill; the American way is to fix you now and bill you later. **For British Travelers:** Most big travel agents offer their own insurance and will probably try to sell you their package when you book a holiday. Think before you sign. The Consumers' Association recommends that you insist on seeing the policy and reading the fine print before buying travel insurance. **The Association of British Insurers** (☎ 020/7600-3333; www.abi.org.uk) gives advice by phone and publishes *Holiday Insurance*, a free guide to policy provisions and prices. You might also shop around for better deals. **For Canadian Travelers:** Canadians should check with their provincial health plan offices or call Health Canada (☎ 613/957-2991; www.hc-sc.gc.ca) to find out the extent of your coverage and what documentation and receipts you must take home in case you are treated in the U.S. **For Australian Travelers:** Online Travel Insurance (☎ 02/6262-8754; www.travelinsuranceaustralia.com.au) offers a variety of policies for U.S. travel.

Lost-Luggage Insurance: On domestic flights, checked baggage is covered up to $2,500 per ticketed passenger. On international flights (including U.S. portions of international trips), baggage is limited to approximately $9 per pound, up to approximately $635 per checked bag. If you plan to check items more valuable than the standard liability, see if your valuables are covered by your homeowner's policy, get baggage insurance as part of your comprehensive travel-insurance package, or buy Travel Guard's "BagTrak" product. Don't buy insurance at the airport, as it's usually overpriced. Be sure to take any valuables or irreplaceable items with you in your carry-on luggage, since many valuables (including books, money, and electronics) aren't covered by airline policies. If your luggage is lost, immediately file a lost-luggage claim at the airport, detailing the luggage contents. For most airlines, you must report delayed, damaged, or lost baggage within 4 hours of arrival. The airlines are required to deliver luggage, once found, directly to your house or destination free of charge.

INTERNET ACCESS Internet cafes aren't too prevalent in wine country. In Napa, try Wi-Fi hotspot Whole Foods (682 Bel Aire Plaza ☎ 707/224-6300; www.wholefoodsmarket.com). In Sonoma, Wi-Fi is available at Sonoma State Historic Park (363 3rd St. W.; ☎ 707/938-9560; www.parks.ca.gov); and at a coffeehouse called Barking Dog Roasters (18133 Sonoma Hwy.; ☎ 707/939-1905). Note that wireless access fees vary; call in advance to verify.

LIMOUSINE SERVICES There are tens of companies chomping at the bit to chauffer your wine tasting in style. Among the best: **Pure Luxury** (4246 Petaluma Blvd., Petaluma; ☎ 800/626-LIMO [5466]; www.pureluxury.com), **Beau Wine Tours and Limousine Service** (21707 8th St. E., Sonoma; ☎ 707/938-8001 or 800/387-2328; www.beauwinetours.com), and Celebrity Limousine (☎ 707/552-7752 or 800/307-7974; www.celeblimo.com). **Vintage Chrome Tours and Adventures** (☎ 707/225-4943; www.vintagechrometours.com) is unique in that its vehicles are antique Cadillacs and Rolls-Royces. Rates for limos hover around $75 per hour.

LIQUOR LAWS Liquor and grocery stores, as well as some drug stores, are permitted to sell packaged alcoholic beverages between 6am and 2am. Most restaurants, nightclubs, and bars are licensed to serve alcoholic beverages during the same hours. The legal age for purchase and consumption is 21; proof of age is required.

MONEY **Traveler's checks:** You can get traveler's checks at almost any bank. American Express offers denominations of $20, $50, $100, $500, and, for cardholders only, $1,000. You'll pay a service charge ranging from 1% to 4%. You can also get American Express traveler's checks by phone (☎ 800/221-7282; ☎ 0870/600-1060 in the U.K.; Amex gold and platinum cardholders who use this phone number are exempt from the 1% fee). Australians can go to www.americanexpress.com.au. American Automobile Association (AAA) members can obtain checks without a fee at most AAA branches. In the U.S., Visa (☎ 800/732-1322) offers traveler's checks at Citibank locations nationwide, as well as at several other banks. The service charge ranges between 1% and 2%; checks come in denominations of $20, $50, $100, $500, and $1,000. MasterCard also offers traveler's checks (☎ 800/223-9920). Outside the U.S., contact your bank, which will be able to advise you on buying U.S. traveler's checks. If you choose to carry traveler's checks, be sure to keep a record of their serial numbers separate from your checks in the event that the checks are stolen or lost. You'll get a refund faster if you know the numbers. **Credit Cards:** See "Credit Cards," p 201.

PASSES **The Wine Country Explorer Pass** (www.explorerpass.com), presented by Smart Destinations (☎ 800/887-9103; www.gocardusa.com), is an excellent deal. For $45, the pass includes 2 days of prepaid admission to Napa and Sonoma wineries and cultural attractions (which would cost $118 if each was purchased separately), plus some shopping savings.

PHARMACIES **Rite Aid,** a drugstore and convenience chain, has stores just about everywhere. Call ☎ 800/748-3243 or go to www.riteaid.com for the address and phone number of the nearest store.

SAFETY Don't walk alone at night, stay in well-lighted areas, and carry a minimum of cash and jewels. Though wine country isn't crime-ridden by any means, it's not a 24-hour region. One of the dangers here is drunk driving; avoid it at all costs and keep watch for other motorists who may have consumed too much wine.

SENIOR TRAVELERS Many wine-country attractions offer admission discounts for those older than 50; ask if you're not sure. **The Council on Aging Services for Sonoma County Seniors** (730 Bennett Valley Rd., Santa Rosa; ☎ 707/525-0143; www.councilonaging.com) offers day services such as entertainment, gentle exercise, arts and crafts, guest speakers, and current event discussions. The council's special events for active seniors include nature walks, enrichment workshops, and an annual art show (usually in May). Members of **AARP** (601 E St. NW, Washington, DC 20049; ☎ 800/424-3410 or 202/434-2277; www.aarp.org) get discounts on hotels, airfares, and car rentals. Seniors looking to travel with a similarly aged group should visit **Elderhostel**'s website, www.elderhostel.com (enter "Napa" or "Sonoma" into the search bar). U.K. seniors can contact **Saga** (☎ 0800/414-525; www.saga.co.uk) for a range of products and services, including holidays and insurance. Australians over 50 should contact the **National Seniors Association** (☎ 1300/76-5050; www.nationalseniors.com.au).

SMOKING California law prohibits smoking in public buildings, restaurants, and bars.

TAXES California sales tax (9.25%) is added to all purchases except snack foods. The hotel tax, known as the transient occupancy tax, is 10% in Sonoma County and 12% in Napa County (at press time). You won't have to pay sales tax if you have your purchases shipped directly out of state.

TAXIS See "Getting Around," earlier in this chapter.

TELEPHONES For directory assistance, dial ☎ **411.** Pay phones (which are becoming difficult to find) cost 35¢ to 50¢ for local calls, more for long-distance. See "Cell (Mobile) Phones" earlier in this chapter.

TIME California is in the Pacific standard time zone: 8 hours behind Greenwich Mean Time (GMT); 3 hours behind Eastern Standard Time (EST).

TIPPING In hotels, tip bellhops at least $1 per bag and the housekeeping staff $2 to $3 per day (more if you've left a mess); the doorman or concierge $1 to $5 only if he or she has provided you with some specific service (for example, calling a cab or obtaining hard-to-get tickets). Tip the valet-parking attendant $1 each time your car is retrieved. In restaurants, bars, and nightclubs, waitstaff expect 15% to 20% of the check, bartenders 10% to 15%, checkroom attendants $1 per garment, and valet-parking attendants $1 per vehicle. Tip cab drivers 15%, skycaps at airports at least $1 per bag, and hairdressers and barbers 15% to 20%.

TOILETS Public toilets can be hard to find in wine country. Hotels and restaurants are probably the best bet for clean facilities and they're usually friendly about letting stoppers-by use them.

TOURIST INFORMATION See "Tourist Offices," p 194.

TRAVELERS WITH DISABILITIES Many travel agencies offer customized tours and itineraries for travelers with disabilities. Two of them are **Flying Wheels Travel** (☎ 507/451-5005; www.flyingwheelstravel.com) and **Accessible Journeys** (☎ 800/846-4537 or 610/521-0339; www.disabilitytravel.com). From the U.K., **Access Travel** (☎ 01942/888844; www.access-travel.co.uk) offers a variety of holidays for persons with disabilities.

Wine Country: **A Brief History**

1542 Wappo Indians inhabit Napa Valley; **Portuguese explorer** Juan Rodriguez Cabrillo sails up the California coast, the first **European** to investigate the region.

1780 Franciscan missionaries, establishing the first of what would become the state's 21 missions, plant California's first vineyard near San Diego.

1821 Mexico wins independence from Spain and annexes California.

1824 The *padres* of the 21st mission, San Francisco Solano, plant vines near present-day Sonoma.

1825 California's first commercial vineyards are established in Los Angeles.

1825 George Calvert Yount establishes Napa's first homestead (now Yountville) and is the first to plant vineyards in Napa.

1840 California missions become secular and Mission San Francisco Solano's vines become the region's first commercial vineyard.

1846 The Bear Flag Revolt: Americans capture **Sonoma,** arresting and imprisoning resident Mexican governor Mariano Guadalupe Vallejo. The Americans then declare an independent **California Republic.**

1846–48 The Mexican-American War rages between the U.S. and Mexico; Mexico loses about half its territory.

1850 Mariano Guadalupe Vallejo is elected to California's first **State Senate.**

1857 "Count" Agoston Haraszthy plants the first major vineyard of European varieties in Sonoma Valley.

1858 Sonoma's first commercial wines are produced when Charles Krug makes a few gallons for Napa pioneer John Patchett.

1861 Charles Krug goes on to establish Napa's first commercial winery.

1861 Schramsberg is founded.

1875 Sonoma supplants Los Angeles as the state's leading wine region (as measured by acreage).

1875 Beringer is founded.

1885 Napa ousts Sonoma as the state's leading wine region (as measured by acreage). Both valleys' wine industries continue to grow and prosper.

1889 Sonoma has 100 wineries; Napa has more than 140.

1890S Napa loses roughly 75% of its acreage to a plant louse *(phylloxera vastatrix)* epidemic that attacks vineyards.

1919 The 18th Amendment is enacted: "the manufacture, sale, or transportation of **intoxicating liquors...** is hereby prohibited." President Woodrow Wilson vetoes the accompanying Volstead Act but the amendment is made anyway.

1920 Prohibition begins and is enforced. Most of California's wineries shut down, though a few keep operating to produce sacramental and medicinal wine.

1933 The 18th Amendment is repealed by the 21st Amendment, making it the Constitution's only provision to be explicitly modified.

1934 Americans pay almost no attention to dry European-style table wines; the bulk of domestically consumed wines are ports and sherries. This lack of interest persists for 35 years.

1937 Napa has only 37 wineries; Sonoma has 91.

1944 Napa Valley Vintners Association is founded with the mission of promoting local wine worldwide.

1960 Napa dwindles to 25 wineries; Sonoma has even fewer (just 9, by one account).

1960 Robert Mondavi leaves Charles Krug winery to found his own. He develops new winemaking techniques and aggressive marketing strategies.

1972 Wineries start burgeoning again in Napa: This year and next, big players appear on the scene, including Chateau Montelena, Stag's Leap Wine Cellars,

Clos du Val, Franciscan, Trefethen, Joseph Phelps, and Domaine Chandon. In Sonoma, Kenwood, Chateau St. Jean, and St. Francis arise.

1976 At a blind tasting in Paris, French wine experts unwittingly award top honors to Chateau Montelena's chardonnay and Stag's Leap Wine Cellars' cabernet, shocking France and waking the world up to California wines.

EARLY 1980S Vintners in both valleys discover *phylloxera vastatrix* again, requiring replanting of most of their acreage. Wine sales level off.

1981 The first annual Auction Napa Valley takes place, starting a tradition that has raised more than $60 million for charity and helped establish Napa as a prestigious region capable of drawing considerable wealth.

1981 Sonoma Valley is designated an American Viticulture Area (AVA).

1982 Napa Valley is designated an AVA. Since then, more than a dozen other AVAs have been defined.

1990 Replanting continues and new labels steadily emerge; restyled red wines become particularly popular.

1992 Sonoma Valley Vintners & Growers Alliance is formed to promote Sonoma wines and grapes.

2009 Napa Valley boasts more than 300 wineries; Sonoma has about 200.

A Quick Guide to **Wine Varietals**

Major Grape Varietals

Below is a list of some of California wine country's most prevalent grape varietals.

Cabernet sauvignon This transplant from Bordeaux has become California's best-known varietal. The small, deep-colored, thick-skinned berry is a complex grape, yielding medium- to full-bodied red wines that are highly tannic when young and usually require a long aging period to achieve their greatest potential. Cabernet is often blended with other related red varietals, such as merlot and cabernet franc (see below), into full-flavored red table wines. These blends, if sanctioned by The Meritage Association, are often called Meritage wines. Cabernet is often matched with red-meat dishes and strong cheeses. If you're looking to invest in several cases of wine, cabernet sauvignon is always a good long-term bet.

Chardonnay The most widely planted grape variety in wine country produces exceptional medium- to full-bodied dry white wines. In fact, it was a California chardonnay that revolutionized the world of wine when it won the legendary 1976 Paris tasting test. You'll find a range of chardonnays in wine country, from delicate, crisp wines that are clear and light in color to buttery, fruity, and oaky (no other wine benefits more from the oak aging process) wines that tend to have deeper golden hues as they increase in richness. This highly complex and aromatic grape is one of the few grapes that doesn't require blending; it's also the principal grape for making sparkling wine. Chardonnay goes well with a variety of dishes, including seafood, poultry, pork, veal, and pastas made with cream or butter.

Merlot Traditionally used as a blending wine to smooth out other grapes' rough edges, merlot has gained popularity in California since the early 1970s—enough so that wineries such as Sonoma's St. Francis are best known for producing masterful merlots. Though it got a bad rap in the 2004 film "Sideways," it's still America's most popular red (at least by sales figures, if not by chicness). The merlot grape is a relative of cabernet sauvignon, but it's fruitier and softer, with a pleasant black-cherry bouquet. Merlots tend to be simpler and less tannic than most cabernets, and they are drinkable at an earlier age, though these wines, too, gain complexity with age. Serve this medium- to full-bodied red with any dish you'd normally pair with a cabernet—it's great with pizza.

Pinot noir It's taken California vintners decades to make relatively few great wines from pinot noir grapes, which are difficult to grow and vinify. Even in their native Burgundy, the wines are excellent only a few years out of every decade, and they are a challenge for winemakers to master. Recent attempts to grow the finicky grape in the Carneros District's cooler climes have had promising results. During banner harvest years, California's pinot grapes produce complex, light- to medium-bodied red wines with such low tannins and silky textures that they're comparable to the world's finest reds. Pinots are fuller and softer than cabernets and can be drinkable at 2 to 5 years of age, though the best improve with additional aging. Pinot noir is versatile at the dinner table, but goes best with lamb, duck, turkey, game birds, semisoft cheeses, even fish.

Riesling Also called Johannisberg Riesling or white Riesling, this is the grape from which most of Germany's great wines are made. It was introduced to California in the mid–19th century by immigrant vintners and is now used mainly to produce floral and fruity white wines of light to medium body, ranging from dry to very sweet. It's also often used to make late-harvest dessert wine. Well-made Rieslings, of which California has produced few, have a vivid fruitiness and lively balancing acidity, as well as a potential to age for many years. Suggested food pairings include crab, pork, sweet-and-sour foods, Asian cuisine, and anything with a strong citrus flavor.

Sauvignon blanc Also labeled as fumé blanc, sauvignon blanc grapes are used to make crisp, dry whites of medium to light body that vary in flavor from slightly grassy to tart or fruity. The grape grows well in Napa and Sonoma and has become increasingly popular due to its distinctive character and pleasant acidity; indeed, it's recently become a contender to the almighty chardonnay. Because of their acidity, sauvignon blancs pair well with shellfish, seafood, and salads.

Zinfandel Often called the "mystery" grape because its origins are uncertain, "Zinfandel" first appeared on California labels in the late 1800s. Hence, it's come to be known as California's grape. In fact, most of the world's zinfandel acreage is in northern California, and some of the best zinfandel grapes grow in cool coastal locations and on century-old vines in California's more eastern Gold Country. Zinfandel is by far wine country's most versatile grape, popular as blush wine (the ever-quaffable white zinfandel: a light, fruity wine, usually served chilled); as dark, spicy, and fruity red wines; even as a port.

Premium zins, like those crafted by Sonoma's Ravenswood winery, are rich and peppery, with a lush texture and nuances of raspberries, licorice, and spice. Food-wise, it's a free-for-all, though premium zins go well with beef, lamb, hearty pastas, pizza, and stews.

Lesser-Known Grape Varietals

Cabernet franc A French black grape that's often blended with and overshadowed by the more widely planted cabernet sauvignon, cabernet franc was recently discovered to be one of the grape species that gave rise to cabernet sauvignon. The grape grows best in cool, damp conditions and tends to be lighter in color and tannins than cabernet sauvignon; therefore, it matures earlier in the bottle. These wines have a deep purple color with an herbaceous aroma.

Chenin blanc Planted mainly in France, chenin blanc runs the gamut from cheap, dry whites with little discernible character to some of the world's most subtle, fragrant, and complex wines. In wine country, the grape is mostly used to create fruity, light- to medium-bodied and slightly sweet wines. Chenin blanc lags far behind chardonnay and sauvignon blanc in popularity, though in good years it's known for developing a lovely and complex bouquet, particularly when aged in oak. It's often served with pork and poultry, Asian dishes with soy-based sauces, mild cheeses, and vegetable and fruit salads.

Gewürztraminer The gewürztraminer grape produces whites with strong floral aroma and litchi-nut-like flavor. Slightly sweet yet spicy, it's somewhat similar in style to Johannisberg Riesling and is occasionally used to make late-harvest, dessert-style wine. The grape grows well in California's cooler coastal regions, particularly Mendocino County. The varietal is particularly appreciated for its ability to complement Asian foods; its sweet character stands up to flavors that would diminish a drier wine's flavors and make it seem more tart.

Petite sirah Widely grown throughout warmer regions of California, petite sirah's origins are a mystery. The grape, which produces rich, high-tannin reds, serves mainly as the backbone for Central Valley "jug" wines. Very old vines still exist in cooler northern regions, where grapes are often made into robust and well-balanced reds of considerable popularity.

Pinot blanc A mutation of pinot gris, the pinot blanc grape is prevalent in France's Alsace region, where it's used to make dry, crisp white wines. In California, pinot blanc produces a fruity wine similar to chardonnay's simpler versions. It's also blended with champagne-style sparkling wines, thanks to its acid content and clean flavor.

Sangiovese This is Italy's favorite grape; it makes everything from chianti and Brunello di Montalcino to "Super Tuscan" blends. Now it's also making a name for itself in California. Its style varies depending on where it's grown, but it's commonly described as anything from "fruity," "smooth," "spicy," "good acidity," and "medium-bodied" to "structured" and "full-bodied."

Syrah This red varietal is best known for producing France's noble and age-worthy Rhône Valley reds such as côte-rôtie and hermitage. Syrah vines produce dark, blackish berries with thick skins, resulting in typically dark, rich, dense, medium- to full-bodied wines with distinctive pepper, spice, and fruit flavors (particularly cherry, blackcurrant, and blackberry).

Index

See also Accommodations, Restaurant and Winery indexes, below.

A

B

C

D

E

I

J

K

L

M

N

O

P

Q

R

T

U

V

W

Y

Z

Accommodations

Restaurants

Wineries

Photo **Credits**

p i, left: © John Elk III/Lonely Planet Images; p i, center: © Charles O'Rear/Corbis; p i, right: © Walter Bibikow/AGE Fotostock; p ii, top: © Jerry Alexander/Lonely Planet Images; p ii, second from top: © Mike Dobel/Alamy Images; p ii, middle: © Michael Orton/Getty Images; p ii, second from bottom: © Lisa Romerein/Jupiterimages; p ii, bottom: © Brent Miller/WineCountry.com; p iii, top: © Morton Beebe/Corbis p iii, second from top: Courtesy Gaige House Inn; p iii, middle: © Cephas Picture Library/Alamy Images; p iii, second from bottom: © Mitchell Funk/Getty Images; p iii, bottom: © Judy Bellah/Lonely Planet Images; p viii: © Jerry Alexander/Lonely Planet Images; p 3, top: © Jerry Alexander/Lonely Planet Images; p 3, bottom: © Garry Gay/Alamy; p 4, top: © Judy Bellah/Lonely Planet Images; p 4, bottom: © Rick Samuels/Charles M. Schulz Museum and Research Center; p 5: © Mike Dobel/Alamy; p 7: © MedioImages/Getty Images; p 8, top: © Roger Ressmeyer/Corbis; p 8, bottom: © MedioImages/Alamy; p 9: © Michael Orton/ Getty Images; p 11: © Richard Gross/Corbis; p 12: © Tim Andrews; p 13, top: © Pierre Vauthey/Corbis Sygma; p 13, bottom: © Ed Kashi/Corbis; p 15: © Roland & Karen Muschenetz/Cephas Picture Library/ Alamy; p 16: Courtesy Gloria Ferrer Champagne Caves/Freixenet USA; p 17: © Phil Schermeister/Corbis; p 19: © Mick Rock/Cephas Picture Libray/Alamy; p 21: © Morton Beebe/Corbis; p 23: © Michael Schaer; p 24: © Paul A. Souders/Corbis; p 25, bottom: © Robert Holmes/Alamy; p 25, top: © Laura Norcia Vitale; p 27, top: © Robert Holmes/AGStockUSA, Inc./Alamy; p 27, bottom: © Dave G. Houser/Post-Houserstock/ Corbis; p 28: © Stephen Saks Photography/Alamy; p 29: © Gary Crabbe/Alamy; p 30: Courtesy Ferrari-Carano Vineyards & Winery; p 31: © Lisa Romerein/Jupiterimages; p 33, bottom: © C/B Productions/Corbis; p 33, top: © Malcolm Sewell/Alamy; p 34: Courtesy Round Pond; p 35: © Jim White (napaman.com)/ Courtesy Oxbow Public Market; p 37: © Rick Samuels/Charles M. Schulz Museum and Research Center; p 38: © Morton Beebe/Corbis; p 39: Courtesy Benziger Family Winery; p 41: © Aerial Archives/Alamy; p 42, top: © Apply Pictures/Alamy; p 42, bottom: Courtesy The French Laundry; p 43: © Uripos/eStock Photo; p 45, top: © Tim Andrews; p 45, bottom: © Jerry Alexander/Lonely Planet Images; p 47: © Elmtree Images/Alamy; p 48: Courtesy the girl & the fig; p 51: © Robert Holmes/Corbis; p 52: © Dave G. Houser/ Post-Houserstock/Corbis; p 53: © Thomas Hallstein/Alamy; p 55: © Tim Andrews; p 56, top: Courtesy Mumm Napa; p 56, bottom: Courtesy The Hess Collection; p 57: Courtesy Imagery Estate Winery; p 59: Courtesy www.osmosis.com; p 61: © Kim Karpeles/Alamy; p 62: © Matthew X. Kiernan/Strata Art; p 63: © Robert Holmes/Alamy; p 65, top: © John Elk III/Lonely Planet Images; p 65, bottom: © Lee Foster/Lonely Planet Images; p 66: Courtesy Far Niente; p 67, top: Courtesy Napa Valley Wine Train; p 67, bottom: © Nik Wheeler/Corbis; p 69: © Loren Irving/AGE Fotostock; p 70: Courtesy Cline Cellars; p 71: © Brent Miller/ WineCountry.com; p 73: © Bill Bachmann/Alamy; p 74: Courtesy Napa Valley Opera House; p 75: © Danita Delimont/Alamy; p 76: © Stephen Saks Photography/Alamy; p 77: © Melissa Werner/CCS Architecture; p 79: © Rich Bolen Photography; p 80, top: © Stephen Saks Photography/Alamy; p 80, bottom: © Robert Holmes/Alamy; p 83, bottom: © Brent Miller/WineCountry.com; p 83, top: © Chuck Place/Alamy; p 84: © Chuck Place/Alamy; p 85: © Chuck Place/Alamy; p 87: © Robert Holmes/Corbis; p 89: © Clay McLachlan/Cephas Picture Library/Alamy; p 90: Courtesy Cyrus Restaurant; p 93: © Bob Croxford/Atmosphere Picture Library/Alamy; p 95: © Robert Holmes/Corbis; p 96: © Danita Delimont/Alamy; p 97: © Danita Delimont/Alamy; p 99, top: © Peter Horree/Alamy; p 99, bottom: © Roland & Karen Muschenetz/Cephas Picture Library/Alamy; p 101, top: Courtesy the girl & the fig; p 101, bottom: © Roland & Karen Muschenetz/ Cephas Picture Library/Alamy; p 103, top: © Catherine Karnow/Corbis; p 103, bottom: © Danita Delimont/ Alamy; p 104: © Stephen Saks Photography/Alamy; p 105: © Blinkstock/Alamy; p 106: © Scott Nugent; p 107: © Morton Beebe/Corbis; p 109: © Jerry Alexander/Cephas Picture Library/Alamy; p 111: © Bob Croxford/Atmosphere Picture Library/Alamy; p 113, top: © Gary Crabbe/Alamy; p 113, bottom: © image100/ Alamy; p 114: © David Sanger Photorgaphy/Alamy; p 115: Courtesy Gaige House Inn; p 118: Courtesy Auberge du Soleil; p 119: Courtesy Calistoga Ranch; p 121: Courtesy Meadowood Napa Valley; p 123: Courtesy Napa River Inn; p 124: Courtesy Villagio Inn & Spa; p 126: Courtesy The Fairmont Sonoma Mission Inn & Resort; p 128: Courtesy Les Mars Hotel; p 129: © Cephas Picture Library/Alamy; p 133: Courtesy Alexander Valley Vineyards; p 134: Courtesy Artesa Winery; p 135: © Danita Delimont/Alamy; p 136, top: © Cephas Picture Library/Alamy; p 136, bottom: © Bruce Fleming/Cephas Picture Library/Alamy; p 137: © Danita Delimont/Alamy; p 138: © Vladpans/eStock Photo; p 139: © Nathan Benn/Corbis; p 140: Courtesy Chateau Montelena Winery; p 141: © Cephas Picture Library/Alamy; p 142: © Ted Stefanski/Cephas Picture Library/Alamy; p 143, top: © Cephas Picture Library/Alamy; p 143, bottom: © Vladpans/eStock Photo; p 144: © Jerry Alexander/Getty Images; p 145: © Cephas Picture Library/Alamy; p 146: © Ben Margor/SuperStock; p 147: © Swerve/Alamy; p 148: Courtesy Gloria Ferrer Champagne Caves/Freixenet USA; p 149: © Phil Schermeister/Corbis; p 150: © Clay McLachlan/Cephas Picture Library/Alamy; p 151: Courtesy Kendall-Jackson Wines; p 152: © Danita Delimont/Alamy; p 153: Courtesy Ledson Winery & Vineyard; p 154: © Robert Holmes/Alamy; p 155: Courtesy Provenance Vineyards; p 156, top: Courtesy Robert Mondavi Winery; p 156, bottom: © Roland & Karen Muschenetz/Cephas Picture Library/Alamy; p 158: © Robert Holmes/Corbis; p 159, top: © Charles O'Rear/Corbis; p 159, bottom: © Cephas Picture Library/Alamy; p 160: © Brad Perks Lightscapes/Alamy; p 161: © Mitchell Funk/Getty Images; p 163: © Phil Schermeister/ Corbis; p 165, top: © Mark Newman/Index Stock; p 165, bottom: © Allenn Russell/Index Stock Imagery; p 167: Courtesy San Francisco CVB; p 168: © Ed Young/AGStockUSA, Inc./Alamy; p 169, bottom: © Thomas Winz/Index Stock Imagery; p 169, top: illustration by Mary J. Gillot; p 171: © David Wasserman/Index Stock Imagery; p 172: Courtesy The Palace Hotel; p 173: © Walter Bibikow/Index Stock Imagery; p 176: Courtesy Clift Hotel; p 177, top: Courtesy Hotel Triton; p 177, bottom: © Mark Gibson/Index Stock Imagery; p 179: © David Liittschwager; p 180, top: Courtesy Cliff House; p 180, bottom: Courtesy Foreign Cinema; p 181: Courtesy Gary Danko; p 183, top: Courtesy Mitchell's Ice Cream; p 183, bottom: Courtesy The Slanted Door; p 186: © Thomas Winz/Index Stock Imagery; p 187: © Garry Gay/Alamy; p 188, top: © Reid Neubert/ Index Stock Imagery; p 188, bottom: © E. Smith/Alamy; p 189, top: © S.T. Yiap/Alamy; p 189, middle: Courtesy The Boom Boom Room; p 190: Courtesy Clift Hotel; p 191, top: © Anthony Pidgeon/Lonely Planet Images; p 191, bottom: © Morton Beebe/Corbis; p 192, top: © Julie Lenberger/Corbis; p 192, bottom: © Lee Foster/Lonely Planet Images; p 193: © Judy Bellah/Lonely Planet Images